A PRAYER BOOK FOR THE 21st CENTURY

LITURGICAL STUDIES, THREE

Ruth A. Meyers, Editor,
for the Standing Liturgical Commission

The Church Hymnal Corporation, New York

Contents

Contributors

The Rev. William Seth Adams is J. Milton Richardson Professor of Liturgics and Anglican Studies, The Episcopal Theological Seminary of the Southwest, Austin, Texas.

The Rev. J. Neil Alexander is Trinity Church Professor: Liturgics and Preaching, The General Theological Seminary, New York, New York.

The Rev. Paul F. Bradshaw is Professor of Liturgy, University of Notre Dame, Notre Dame, Indiana.

The Rev. Jean Campbell, OSH, is Sister-in-Charge of the Convent of St. Helena in Vails Gate, New York.

The Rev. Gregory M. Howe is Rector of Christ Church, Dover, Delaware.

The Rev. Steve Kelsey is Missioner, Middlesex Cluster, Diocese of Connecticut.

The Rev. Richard G. Leggett is Assistant Professor of Liturgics, Vancouver School of Theology, Vancouver, British Columbia.

The Rev. Ruth A. Meyers is Assistant Professor of Liturgics, Seabury-Western Theological Seminary, Evanston, Illinois.

The Rev. Leonel L. Mitchell is a member of the Standing Liturgical Commission. He recently retired as Professor of Liturgics, Seabury-Western Theological Seminary, Evanston, Illinois.

The Rev. Clayton L. Morris is the Liturgical Officer for the Episcopal Church, New York, New York.

The Rev. Juan M. C. Oliver is Canon Missioner, Diocese of New Jersey.

The Rev. Jennifer M. Phillips is Rector of Trinity Church, St. Louis, Missouri.

The Rev. Joseph P. Russell is a member of the Standing Liturgical Commission. He recently retired as Canon for Education, Diocese of Ohio, and now serves as a consultant in Christian education and liturgy, Cleveland Heights, Ohio.

The Rev. Daniel B. Stevick is Professor Emeritus of Liturgics and Homiletics, Episcopal Divinity School, Cambridge, Massachusetts.

The Rev. Thomas J. Talley is Professor Emeritus, The General Theological Seminary, New York, New York.

The Rev. Louis Weil is Professor of Liturgics, Church Divinity School of the Pacific, Berkeley, California.

The Rev. Ellen K. Wondra is Assistant Professor of Theological Studies at Colgate-Rochester Divinity School/Bexley Hall/Crozer Theological Seminary, Rochester, New York.

Preface

L*iturgical Studies* are collections of essays issued from time to time under the direction of the Standing Liturgical Commission. They reflect the fact that our liturgical prayer, while formally set forth in The Book of Common Prayer and other authorized books and collections of texts, is also continually developing and unfolding as it becomes the experience of Christians continuing week by week "in the apostles' teaching and fellowship, in the breaking of bread, and in the prayers."

To encounter the risen Christ in common prayer is often to find ourselves confronted by questions and new perceptions which arise out of the very act of worship itself. It is these questions and new perceptions which are the subject matter of *Liturgical Studies*.

These essays are offered as a stimulus to thought, reflection and further discussion. It is the hope of the Standing Liturgical Commission that they will be seen as a contribution to an ongoing conversation born out of our experience of worship in the Anglican tradition. The essays do not necessarily reflect the views of the Standing Liturgical Commission, and in some cases a particular essay may be at variance with another essay in the same collection.

We welcome your responses to these essays and see them as a way of expanding the conversation as well as helping the Commission to carry out its canonical mandate "to collect and collate material bearing upon further revisions of The Book of Common Prayer."

The Rt. Rev. Frank T. Griswold
Chair, Standing Liturgical Commission

Introduction:
A Pastorally Sensitive Plan

Leonel L. Mitchell

> *Resolved,* the House of Deputies concurring, That this 71st General Convention direct the Standing Liturgical Commission to prepare a rationale and a pastorally sensitive plan for the next revision of the Book of Common Prayer, and report to the 72nd General Convention.[1]

This is the charge given by the 1994 General Convention to the Standing Liturgical Commission. When the commission was set up by the 1928 General Convention it was charged to continue the work of liturgical revision, which they understood to be ongoing. Just as they realized that the 1928 prayer book was not to be a permanent and unchanging liturgy for the Episcopal Church, so we realize that neither is The Book of Common Prayer 1979 perfect and unchangeable. The work of liturgical revision remains ongoing. There are many reasons why this is so.

The first is that, although the Gospel does not change, the world in which we live does. What communicates well in one time and place does not necessarily do so at all times and in all places. Language changes. Culture changes. Our worship is conditioned by both and must change in order to remain the same. Christian worship is deeply rooted in the past, in the saving events of the life, death, and resurrection of Jesus Christ, and looks eagerly into the future, to the *eschaton* or *parousia*; yet it is always celebrated in the present, and if it is not available and accessible to those who live in the present, then they are denied participation in both the Christian past and the Christian future.

A second reason for liturgical change is that the Church's understanding of itself and its worship is constantly growing and unfolding. In the last twenty-five years, for example, we have grown into a new understanding of the centrality of baptism in Christian life and ministry, and this has led to suggestions for changes in the way we do ordinations and confirmation, as well as baptisms. A new awareness of the place of women in the Church and of the patriarchal bias of much that has become customary in the Church's life and worship has led to a call for other changes, including changes in the language of our worship.

A third reason for liturgical change is to take advantage of the work that has been done by others since 1976. Not only have most of the other churches of the Anglican Communion produced new service books which contain much worthwhile material, such as *A New Zealand Prayer Book* (1989) and the Canadian *Book of Alternative Services* (1985), but other churches have issued significant new service books, of which the *Lutheran Book of Worship* (1978), the Presbyterian *Book of Common Worship* (1993), and the new translation of the Roman *Sacramentary* now in progress are examples.

It is important to recognize that in a real sense it is the success of what has already been done that produces the demand for more change. It is the changes already made in the 1979 prayer book which have brought about the recognition of the centrality of baptism and eucharist in the life of the Christian community, not merely as theological abstractions but as living realities. It is the emphasis which the 1979 prayer book places on the prayers of the people and the importance of offering the actual concerns of the worshiping congregation at the eucharist which causes us to criticize the formality and hierarchical bias of the forms of those prayers we most often use. It is the insistence of the catechism of the 1979 book that "[t]he ministers of the Church are *lay persons,* bishops, priests and deacons"[2] which has sparked the emphasis on total ministry.

In fact, there is little interest in abandoning The Book of Common Prayer 1979 for some new and different liturgy. The interest is in continuing and perfecting the work begun in 1928, continued in 1979 and still ongoing. This is work which by its very nature can never be completed before the *parousia*. Each generation comes to the work of liturgical revision and renewal with the recognition that there is much that remains to be done. Unfortunately, having completed a major revision, it often feels that it has accomplished all that needs to be done and that the "new liturgy," in our case the 1979 prayer book, should outlast the ages—or at least our own lives—and consequently it remains deaf to the cries for change which it once led.

It is inevitable, then, that the prayer book be revised. The first pastoral question is when this should be done. Prayer book revision in the Episcopal Church is a complicated process requiring the action of two General Conventions, entailing the affirmative vote of the bishops and of the clerical and lay deputies voting "by orders" both times.[3] The process is deliberately conservative, designed to put the burden on those desiring change. The process is also democratic and political. Liturgical experts do not have the authority to change the liturgy of the Episcopal Church. This is done by the bishops and elected deputies to General Convention. The process necessarily involves compromise and give-and-take. Rarely does any individual or group get exactly what they would like. By authorizing materials for "trial use" prior to their adoption, it is possible to increase the involvement of the ordinary worshiper in the process and insure that what is adopted at least attempts to meet the needs of actual worshiping congregations.

The result of all this realistically is that a minimum of nine years is required from the beginning of the process to completion. If the 1997 General Convention were to ask to have texts ready for trial use in 2000 and those texts were actually adopted in 2003, then revision of the prayer book could become final in 2006. It is unlikely that this schedule could be met, especially with no one employed full-time on the project. Even if General Convention considered this to be its highest priority and were prepared to commit substantial money and personnel to it, the schedule would be difficult to maintain.

What this means practically is that to decide to begin the process is not to suggest that we stop printing 1979 prayer books. It is to decide to look realistically and systematically at ways to improve The Book of Common Prayer for the Church of the twenty-first century.

As a first step in this process, the Standing Liturgical Commission has invited a number of liturgists, both academic and parochial, to suggest in a series of essays what they see as the issues in prayer book revision. I would tend to group these issues this way:

> *(1) Things in the present prayer book which need to be changed.* This is, of course, the area in which the demand for immediate revision is greatest. Most people agree that these areas exist, but there is no universal list. For some the removal of the *filioque* clause ("and the Son") from the Nicene Creed to correspond to the ecumenical text is crucial. For others the elimination of masculine pronouns to refer to those who are not male has the highest priority. Still others, as many of the essays in this collection bear witness, find problems in the rubrics or texts of various services which are either unclear, misleading or theologically suspect. The requirement that candidates for the priesthood affirm that they believe they are "truly called by God and his Church to the life and work of a deacon" (BCP, p. 543) would be an example.
>
> *(2) Things we would like to see changed in the prayer book.* This list includes all of the items on the first

list for those people who do not feel that strongly about them, and a great many others: rubrics which are unclear or difficult to follow, things that do not work well in practice, little improvements we have all thought of since we began using the rites.

(3) Things we would like to see in the prayer book. These may include additional eucharistic prayers, canticles, prayers of the people, services from other prayer books, etc. In most cases this would simply be a convenience. The material either is or can be authorized for immediate use in other ways.

(4) Things about which decisions need to be made. Should we adopt the *Revised Common Lectionary?* Are there services in The Book of Common Prayer which should be in *The Book of Occasional Services,* and vice versa? Should we use the ELLC (English Language Liturgical Consultation) translations of prayers and canticles? Is ordaining candidates individually in parish churches a good idea, or should priests and deacons be ordained in diocesan services at the cathedral? Most of us do not wish to revise the prayer book to do these things but feel that when the prayer book is revised is the time to decide about them.

There is no doubt that there is a great deal of work that can be done. The question is when we wish to begin. That question must be answered by the General Convention. Revising the prayer book is a great practical nuisance. It involves a considerable expenditure of time and money. It is as unsettling as painting and modernizing your kitchen. It is not reasonable to revise it every General Convention, as we do *The Book of Occasional Services* and *Lesser Feasts and Fasts,* but neither is it reasonable to allow it to become so dated as to be a hindrance to evangelism and to worship.

Bearing in mind that the process will take nine to twelve years, the General Convention will need to weigh the difficulties and the benefits and consider the mind of the Church. In many ways 2000 seems a good year to begin, insuring the present book at least another ten years of life. We cannot decide not to revise The Book of Common Prayer, but only when to do it.

Notes

1. Resolution A051a, *Journal of the 71st General Convention,* 1994, p. 758.
2. BCP, p. 855, emphasis added.
3. Article X, Constitution [of the Episcopal Church].

Acknowledgments

Steve Kelsey's essay, "Celebrating the Ministry of All the Baptized..." originally appeared as "Celebrating Baptismal Ministry at the Welcoming of New Ministers," in *Baptism and Ministry*, Liturgical Studies 1 (Church Hymnal Corporation, 1994), and is printed here in a slightly revised form.

Ellen Wondra's essay, "'O for a Thousand Tongues to Sing...'" originally appeared in *How Shall We Pray? Expanding Our Language about God*, Liturgical Studies 2 (Church Hymnal Corporation, 1994).

I wish to express my appreciation to the Anglican members of the North American Academy of Liturgy who contributed to this collection and encouraged the development of this project, and especially to Jean Campbell, OSH, for her collaboration in gathering these essays.

Ruth A. Meyers, Editor

THE DAILY OFFICE

The Daily Prayer of the Church

Jean Campbell, OSH

A hallmark of the Anglican tradition is the prayer of the daily office. The genius of Thomas Cranmer was the simplification of the medieval office, which had grown to be a very complex and confusing round of daily prayer largely the prerogative of monks and clergy. Cranmer's solution was to create an office accessible to the people of God and for their edification.[1] Daily Morning and Evening Prayer are centered upon the offering of the prayer of the psalter, canticles, the reading of scripture and the prayers. The office gave rise to Anglican chant and shaped the spirituality of Anglicanism for generations. Except for linguistic changes and the addition of prayers, the structure and texts of Morning and Evening Prayer have remained constant in every Book of Common Prayer since 1549.

The 1979 revision of The Book of Common Prayer made some changes in the traditional patterns of the office. New to the 1979 prayer book were the offices of "Noonday Prayer" and "Compline." The "Order of Worship for the Evening" provided a new structure with more variation and additional ceremonial, namely, the lighting of candles or lamps to mark the coming of evening. A shorter pattern of daily prayer was included in "Daily Devotions for Individuals and Families."

The pattern of praying the psalms once a month beginning with Psalm 1 and continuing in sequence through the whole psalter was retained in the body of the psalter,[2] but an alternative seven-week cycle was included in the Daily Office Lectionary. "While this provides a semi-sequential recitation of the entire psalter, care has been taken to assign appropriate psalms not only to morning and evening, but also to Fridays (penitential and passion psalms), to Wednesdays (sections of Psalm 119 at one of the offices), and Saturdays and Sundays (psalms of creation and of paschal deliverance)."[3] Some of the imprecatory psalms were omitted from the seven-week cycle. Canticles and collects were added to Morning and Evening Prayer as well as a more flexible provision for intercessory prayer.

Although the content and structure of Morning and Evening Prayer have remained the same, major transitions in the practice of praying the office have occurred. What was intended to be daily parochial prayer became for many people a private daily devotion. At first, the public corporate worship of the office became in most instances a weekly rather than a daily liturgy, but gradually even the weekly corporate celebration of the office disappeared in most congregations. Choral Sunday Evensong was a major service in many congregations until the Second World War. Today, choral Evensong is celebrated on a regular basis in some cathedrals and large churches, while some congregations have a celebration of choral Evensong occasionally or on a seasonal basis, for instance, on the first Sunday of Advent or Lent. Until the period of the revision of the prayer book in the 1970s, choral Morning Prayer was regularly celebrated on Sunday morning. While there are exceptions, today the practice of choral Morning Prayer as the principal Sunday service is rare. Many regret this loss, but the office was never intended to be the principal Sunday worship of the people of God. The Holy Eucharist is the principal act of the baptismal community on the day of resurrection (BCP, p. 13). Except for seminaries, religious orders and some parish churches and cathedrals, the office as the daily corporate worship of the Church has been drastically diminished. Prayers which had once been familiar and formative for the faith of the community are no longer prayed in the life of the Church.

A major task for the next revision of The Book of Common Prayer is the recovery of the richness of the Anglican tradition in the prayer of the daily office. This task demands a recovery of the pattern of daily prayer for the life of the baptismal community. In the words of George Guiver, the discipline of daily prayer needs a "rediscovery of *motives*, and the discovering of *vocation*. In particular, the demands which we allow prayer to make on us will correspond to the extent that we (a) allow God to be at the very center, and (b) believe that direct access to God through prayer is important and possible."[4] To recover this pattern of prayer the Church needs to discover anew the theology of the daily office and to explore a pattern of prayer which is appropriate for the Church today.

The Church's School for Prayer

The Baptismal Covenant asks: "Will you continue in the apostles' teaching and fellowship, in the breaking of bread, and in the prayers?" (BCP, p. 304). Prayer is not a Sunday-only activity. Rather, as those faithful to the Baptismal Covenant, we are both invited and compelled to be in communion with God every day of our lives. This is both our joy and our task. Daily prayer is not an optional discipline, reserved for a few, but rather the vocation of every Christian. The turning of heart, mind and soul to God "from the rising of the sun to its going down" (Psalm 113:3) is the normative pattern of baptismal life.

Rooted in Jewish daily prayer, Christians developed daily prayer centered in the praise and thanksgiving, the lament and petition, of the psalter. Throughout the history of the development of the daily office, several elements have remained constant. The office is the prayer of the Church and as such is a corporate act of prayer. It is the prayer of Christians gathered in, with and through Christ, for "where two or three are gathered in my name, I am there among them" (Matthew 18:20). The individual who is unable to be present with others is united with the prayer of the whole Church in the prayer of the office.

The act of praying the office is a participation in the very life of the triune God. Gathered in and with Christ, prayer is offered with Christ in the power of the Holy Spirit to the one, holy and living God. At the beginning and the end of the day, the whole of life is placed in the presence of God as Christians participate in the eternal offering of praise at the throne of God. In, with and through Christ, by intercessory prayer we participate in bearing the pain and suffering of the world to the divine activity of grace.

The office is primarily the Church's mode of praying scripture. While the psalms have formed the core of the office, canticles and most especially the Lord's Prayer have also been essential elements of the Church's office. The richness of the canticles and the prayer of the psalms offered in the opening acclamations, "Lord, open our lips" or "O God, make speed to save us," and in the suffrages allow the words of scripture to become our prayer.

The biblical content of the office provides fertile ground for remembering who God is and who we are united with God in Christ Jesus. Praying the office calls God to mind, as we remember who God has promised to be for us and we for God: "when we pray with the Scriptures, we appeal to creation and covenant, we call God to mind (and here is a new kind of wonderful Hebraic twist), *we remind God to be God!* What God has done, what God used to mean for us in the past, is a promise of who God will be for us in the future."[5] To offer the words of the Venite—"Come, let us sing to the Lord; ...we are the people of his pasture and the sheep of his hand/ Oh, that today you would hearken to his voice" (BCP, p. 82)—speaks the words of the writer of Psalm 95, the voice of the people of Israel, the voice of generations of the Church and our voice this day, through which we are invited to attune our mind, heart and soul to the living God.

Not only is it the Church's way of praying scripture, the office is also shaped by the rhythms of times and seasons encompassing the fullness of the paschal mystery. For at the heart of the office is the Church's proclamation and participation in the mystery of our life in Christ.

Robert Taft identifies the office as a "school of prayer" because it is traditional, biblical and objective.[6] The prayer of the office is objective in that it provides a "framework that molds and feeds and moderates our private prayer, and which our private prayer in turn makes more interior and personal and intense." Taft continues,

> When we rise in the morning and come together to sing the praises of God at the dawn of a new day, when we celebrate at the coming of darkness our faith in the true light of the world at evensong, when we keep vigil with the angels and the heavenly bodies of the firmament while the world sleeps, we are doing, in obedience to the command to pray always, what men and women have done since the time of Jesus. In every time, in every land and from every race...someone raises his or her voice in the prayer of the Church, to join with the heavenly and earthly choirs down through the ages in the glorification of almighty God. In our age of narcissistic individualism one often hears people say they "don't get anything out of going to Church." What one "gets out of it" is the inestimable privilege of glorifying almighty God."[7]

The daily office is the Church's process of formation in the traditions of Christian prayer.

Shape and Content of the Daily Office

Numerous scholars have distinguished two strands in the development of the daily office.[8] These have been identified as "cathedral" and "monastic" offices.

The "cathedral" office is the term used to identify the office of the secular church. It was the daily prayer of the whole Church, laity, deacons, presbyters and bishops. The prayer of the "cathedral" office centered upon praise and intercession. The content of the office was appropriate to the time of day and the seasons of the church year. Psalms were chosen because of their content, and only a small number of psalms were used. The office was simple and repetitive with the use of congregational refrains on psalms so that all could participate easily. Symbols such as the lighting of lamps in the evening and ceremonial such as processions and incense were included. A reading from scripture was not necessarily a part of the "cathedral" office. The purpose of the office was to offer the corporate praise and intercessory prayer of the body of Christ.

The "monastic" office was primarily a liturgy of the Word. It was centered around offering the prayer of the entire psalter and reading scripture. The primary mode of praying scripture and the psalms was *lectio continua*, that is, continuous reading from the beginning to the end with little or no attention to the content in relation to the time of day or the seasons. Its purpose was to provide an avenue for personal meditative or contemplative prayer. In contrast to the "cathedral" office, anyone could lead the prayer, and there was very little in the way of symbol or ceremony.

It is important to note that these two strands of the tradition are intertwined, especially in Anglican experience. On the one hand there is a strong tradition of the office being prayed daily in parish communities as the prayer of the whole Church, with stately and sometimes lavish ceremony. Many participants knew the responses and canticles by heart. But on the other hand there is also a strong element of the "monastic" in the Anglican offices. Prayer books have traditionally appointed psalms using *lectio continua*. Even in the seven-week cycle of the 1979 prayer book, all the psalms are used except for the imprecatory psalms, and while the cycle is attentive to the content of psalms with reference to specific times of day, this selectivity can be lost when the option is exercised to use a psalm appointed for Morning Prayer in the evening, or vice versa.[9]

The Daily Office Lectionary follows basically a *lectio continua* reading of scripture on a two-year basis. Again, this is a "monastic" strand, reading the entire New Testament and Old Testament in the course of praying the offices. Its primary purpose is as a method of instruction or edification.

The 1979 Book of Common Prayer incorporated some strands

of the "cathedral" office. The designation of "O Gracious Light" as a set text for the opening hymn of praise of Evening Prayer (BCP, pp. 64, 118) parallels the Venite, Jubilate, and "Christ our Passover" of Morning Prayer (BCP, pp. 44-6, 82-3). In both Morning and Evening Prayer, additional intercessions were introduced which extended the intercessory content of the versicles and responses. The inclusion of a collect for mission also served to emphasize the intercessory content of the office.

The introduction of "An Order of Worship for the Evening" into the 1979 prayer book was an attempt to provide a "cathedral" type of office. There is provision for heightened ceremonial and use of the symbol of light as well as the use of selective readings of scripture and psalms appropriate for the evening. Too often, however, the normative patterns of Evening Prayer tend to overshadow what can be a very simple and highly participatory form of evening worship.

The service of Compline has probably gained more popularity as an evening office than "An Order of Worship for the Evening." Although this office originated in the monastic tradition, it follows the pattern of a "cathedral" office. There are four psalms appointed (Psalms 4, 31, 91 and 134), each appropriate for the close of the day, in addition to four short lessons, consisting of one or two verses each, and a simple invitation for intercessions and thanksgiving for the day that is past.

Future Revisions of the Daily Office

Merely revising the texts of The Book of Common Prayer will not renew or revitalize the office in the life of the Church. Renewing the prayer of the office will be a complex task, encompassing the nature and experience of corporate and individual prayer, the structure of the rite, language, music and the realities of daily life in our congregations.

Paul Bradshaw, in *Two Ways of Praying*, has added considerable depth to the historical discussions of "cathedral" and "monastic" offices by identifying two very different spiritualities or modes of praying inherent in the form and content of these two strands of the tradition. In contrasting the "cathedral" and "monastic" modes of prayer, he makes three very important distinctions. The first is that the "cathedral" way of praying is primarily a corporate act of prayer. The whole Church is gathered and prays in and with and through Christ: "We pray both through Christ and with Christ and in Christ, and Christ prays for us and with us and in us, so that, through the work of the Holy Spirit, our prayer becomes Christ's prayer and his prayer becomes our prayer."[10] It is the participation of the people of God in the priestly ministry of Christ, offering praise and thanksgiving and interceding for the life of the world. The "monastic" tradition is primarily an interior or individual mode of praying, with the content of the office acting as a springboard for meditative or contemplative prayer.

The second important distinction is the use of the psalter: "[O]nly a few psalms were incorporated into the 'cathedral' office, and most of these were repeated every single day.... They were...chosen...because of their suitability as Christian hymns and prayers."[11] The practice of having a cantor chant the verses while the congregation sang a refrain was common in the "cathedral" office. In this manner, there was a dialectic of the Word of God being spoken and the people of God responding.

A third distinction is the use of scripture in the office. In "monastic" prayer, scripture was read so "that those who heard might become acquainted with the contents of the biblical books, or deepen their existing knowledge of them, so as to enrich their understanding and shape their lives in the light of them.... [It is] a didactic ministry of the Word."[12] In contrast, the purpose of scripture in the "cathedral" office was "to provide the biblical warrant and foundation for the liturgical rite being celebrated.... The readings may, or may not, be followed by a homily or other explanation; but both they and the homily, where there is one, will always be closely related to the rest of the liturgical rite with regard to their themes and content, because they serve as a commentary on it and as a stimulus or springboard for the response of praise and prayer."[13]

Any future revision of the office must take seriously the distinctions that Bradshaw has identified. The mode of prayer we are intending as a Church will shape the form and content of the daily office. The major questions to be addressed are: 1) Are the daily offices the corporate prayer of the Church or the basis for private devotion? 2) Are the offices intended to be a context for the exposition of scripture or a service of praise and thanksgiving to God?

If the offices are the corporate liturgy of the Church's praise and thanksgiving, then there must be changes in the use of scripture and the psalter as well as a clarification in the structure of the rite. A revised structure might include:

> Opening sentences
> Psalm or hymn of praise, i.e., Venite or "O Gracious Light"
> Psalm for the morning or evening
> Psalm(s) appointed for the day
> Scripture reading or "short" lesson
> Canticle
> Prayers:
>> Lord's Prayer
>> Intercession
>> Concluding Collect
> Dismissal

The Daily Office Lectionary needs either to be completely revised or to have an alternative set of lections that would provide biblical readings related to the times or seasons and thus could be used for what Bradshaw describes as an "anamnetic" ministry of the Word, in which the readings selected are "intimately related to the meaning of what is being celebrated, interpreting and stimulating the liturgical action itself."[14] *Weekday Readings: A Daily Eucharistic Lectionary for the Weekdays following the first Sunday after Epiphany and the Feast of Pentecost,*[15] authorized by the 1994 General Convention for experimental use, provides a six-week set of readings, each of which is complete in itself. This model might be expanded and the lessons used for celebrations of either the eucharist or the office. Latitude must be given in order to provide offices which can stand independently as services of praise and prayer.

The use of psalms in the office needs to be rethought. *Supplemental Liturgical Materials* introduced the use of morning and evening psalms preceding those appointed for Morning and Evening Prayer.[16] Following this pattern, a more selective use of psalms should be set forth for the morning and evening offices.[17]

An obvious element in the future revision of the prayer book is the need for a new translation of the psalter. *A New Zealand Prayer Book* (1989) includes a translation of the psalms which provides a cadence of language similar to that of the 1979 prayer book. Gail Ramshaw and Gordon Lathrop have published a version of the 1979 psalter, *Psalter for the Christian People,*[18] which alters the language so that it is inclusive both with regard to humanity and in reference to God. The International Commission on English in the Liturgy (ICEL) has completed *The Psalter,*[19] a very modern translation of the psalms, for use in the Roman Catholic Church in the United States.

The current experience of what might be termed "nonsacramental" worship needs to be considered in the process of discerning the future of the daily office. Two experiences are of particular significance. First is the growing popularity of "Taizé liturgy." The community of Taizé, a monastic community in the Reformed tradition of Europe, is an ecumenical community which has made major contributions to the renewal of the daily office. In recent years, the presence of the community of Taizé in the United States and the experience of large numbers of people who gather at the community in France have spread the influence of the prayer patterns of this community.

"Taizé liturgies" consist of gathering, singing psalms and canticles or verses of scripture, and intercessory prayer. The liturgies are marked by repetitive psalm refrains or Bible verses sung to music which brings congregations into a corporate mode of prayer. The pattern of worship is simple, yet there is a high degree of ceremony with a lavish use of candles and icons and often the placement of a cross of candles at which persons are invited to offer prayer.

There is a corpus of Taizé music which consists of verses of psalms or biblical texts repeated over and over, again making it highly accessible to participants. A simple congregational refrain is often embellished by settings done as a canon or with intricate harmonies which enhance the melodic line. Often the full text of a psalm is sung by a cantor or choir while the congregation repeats the refrain. It is singable music and highly adaptable to the musical abilities of any community.

Another experience of nonsacramental worship in the Episcopal Church is the "prayer and praise" liturgies of the various renewal movements. Many of these liturgies have elements of an office liturgy: songs and prayers of praise, reading of scripture, and prayer. The music is usually simple and easy to enter into. Movement and gesture are incorporated and in some cases highly stylized with the lifting up of hands and the laying on of hands with prayer. The texts used are not necessarily those of scripture; many of the popular songs of the "prayer and praise" genre have tended to diminish the depth of prayer found in scriptural texts.[20]

Neither the "Taizé" nor the "prayer and praise" liturgies look or feel like the traditional Anglican Morning or Evening Prayer, yet there are some lessons to be learned which may help to shape what we do with the daily office in the future. In each case, the liturgies are simple, highly repetitive and singable and incorporate gesture, sign and symbol. For significant numbers of people, these liturgies offer a profound sense of prayer in the context of corporate worship.

The lifestyles of most American Episcopalians are such that the possibility of attending Morning or Evening Prayer on a daily basis is unrealistic. However, the popularity of both Taizé liturgy and prayer and praise gatherings indicates that there is a place and a need for regular celebrations of a choral morning or evening office. The rise of services on Saturday evening might provide a time for an evening office which could take the form of a "vigil" of the resurrection rather than, or including, the eucharist.

Essential to the recovery of the daily office will be the accessibility of music, especially for the psalms and canticles. Simple musical settings of the psalms using an antiphon or refrain are needed. Some musical resources already exist, but they are difficult to find and use. The Meacham simplified Anglican chant[21] has gained such popularity over the past twenty years that almost any group gathered in the Episcopal Church can sing a psalm (or any other text) to this tune. The fact that it is easily learned, needs no accompaniment, and can be sung without any pointing (markings of the text), attests to the reality that music rooted in the tradition can be an effective means of praying by small groups of the gathered faithful. These simplified chants need to be in the pew hymnal and their use broadened. *A Year of Grace,* by Carl Daw,[22] is one example of how canticles can be recast, in this case into metrical form, and sung to familiar hymn tunes. The reality is that materials need to be put together in a usable form for congregations.

Conclusion

We are heirs of a rich tradition of the daily office and as Anglicans have carried that tradition in a unique way over the past four hundred years. Nearly half of The Book of Common Prayer is devoted to the liturgy of the daily office. Any future revision of the prayer book must assess seriously the place of the office in the baptismal life of the Church and develop structures and texts with music for the daily offering of the prayer of the Church.

One of the most powerful tools of evangelism is the experience of the Church at prayer. The liturgy of the office, unlike the eucharist, requires no catechesis, nor does it require the commitment of baptism. The office is the prayer of the Church most accessible to the unbaptized. The question for the twenty-first century will be whether we will take up the task of being the body of Christ, faithful to the prayers of the apostles.

> From the rising of the sun to its going down,
>   let the Name of the Lord be praised. (Psalm 113:3)

Notes

1. "Preface: The First Book of Common Prayer (1549)," BCP, 1979, p. 866.
2. See, for example, the rubrics "First Day: Morning Prayer" and "First Day: Evening Prayer," BCP, 1979, pp. 585, 589.
3. Byron David Stuhlman, *Redeeming the Time: An Historical and Theological Study of the Church's Rule of Prayer and the Regular Services of the Church* (New York: Church Hymnal Corporation, 1992), p. 48.
4. George Guiver, *Company of Voices: Daily Prayer and the People of God* (New York: Pueblo, 1988), p. 198; emphasis in original.
5. Don E. Saliers, *Worship as Theology: Foretaste of Glory Divine* (Nashville, TN: Abingdon, 1994), p. 35; emphasis in original.
6. Robert Taft, *The Liturgy of the Hours in East and West: The Origins of the Divine Office and Its Meaning for Today* (Collegeville, MN: Liturgical Press, 1986), p. 367.
7. Ibid., pp. 370-1.
8. See especially Paul Bradshaw, *Daily Prayer in the Early Church: A Study of the Origin and Early Development of the Divine Office* (New York: Oxford University Press, 1982), and Taft, *Liturgy of the Hours.*
9. "At the discretion of the officiant, however, any of the Psalms appointed for a given day may be used in the morning or in the evening" (BCP, p. 934).
10. Paul F. Bradshaw, *Two Ways of Praying* (Nashville, TN: Abingdon, 1995), p. 64.

11. Ibid., p. 77.
12. Ibid., p. 90.
13. Ibid., pp. 94-5.
14. Ibid., p. 96; cf. Stuhlman, p. 53.
15. Joseph P. Russell, ed. (New York: Church Hymnal Corporation, 1995). See below, pp. 213-14.
16. *Supplemental Liturgical Materials*, expanded edition (New York: Church Hymnal Corporation, 1991, 1996), pp. 20-2.
17. See Bradshaw, *Two Ways of Praying*, pp. 122-6.
18. Collegeville, MN: Liturgical Press, 1993.
19. Chicago: Liturgy Training Publications, 1994.
20. A caveat from the history of the office: when hymnody replaced the psalms and canticles of the traditional prayer of the Church, it all too often ventured into dangerous theological territory.
21. S415, *The Hymnal 1982: Service Music* (New York: Church Hymnal Corporation, 1985).
22. Carol Stream, IL: Hope Publishing, 1990.

HOLY BAPTISM

Christian Initiation: Ritual Patterns and the Future Shape of Revision

J.Neil Alexander

When the history of the twentieth-century reform of the western liturgy is written by those who come after us, it is very likely that the major story will be the recovery of the fullness of Christian initiation as a lifelong process of growing ever deeper into the paschal life of Jesus Christ. The reform of the liturgy of the eucharist and the significant progress made in our time toward the restoration of an integrated liturgy of Word and Sacrament on every Lord's Day will also be a major story, as will the reorientation of our ecclesiology expressed by the reform of the ordination rites. Our experimentation with liturgical language will also be a major theme in the history we are presently creating. Nonetheless, it is the boldness of our reform of Christian initiation and our insistence that the rituals which stand at the beginning of Christian life are only that, a beginning, that will surely be the major contribution of our age to the history of the liturgy. We have rediscovered that becoming a Christian is less something one does than it is something one survives and reckons with on a daily basis throughout life.

There are many factors that have influenced the reforms of initiation rites in the second half of our century, but two of particular importance stand out. First, the liturgical scholarship of the last hundred years or so has forced us to re-evaluate many of our inherited and long-cherished notions of baptism, confirmation and first communion. Although every question cannot be answered definitively, we possess a clearer and more comprehensive view of the sources and pastoral practice of these rites through Christian history than ever before. This is not to say, surely, that earlier sources and older practices are always to be preferred. Many changes in the customs and practices of initiation were no doubt made for honorable pastoral (or political) reasons in response to realities we only dimly understand. We need not impugn the judgments of those who undoubtedly understood the needs of their own time better than we ever shall. Ours is the responsibility, and the joy, of looking back through the Church's history and observing, with a precision not afforded those who have gone before us, the paths along which the initiatory tradition has developed.

A second factor that has influenced recent liturgical reforms is that we have come to recognize that the world is quite a different place than it was just a couple of generations ago. A multitude of assumptions—political, cultural, religious—that our grandparents would have taken for granted are simply no longer valid. Not so many years ago in much of the western world one could assume a rather large set of values, and the structures that supported them, that were widely believed to embody the best of Christianity. (Whether this was actually true is a moot point because the majority believed it was true and did so with fervor.) We were the norm and others were the not always graciously tolerated exceptions. The exigencies of the end of the twentieth century have called us, indeed forced us, to rediscover what it means to be the Church, to offer a living witness to Jesus Christ, and to embrace life in response to the Gospel in a context that is largely hostile to the Gospel's demands for justice and mercy. No longer can we assume that human birth is the first stage of an initiatory process that will be completed in the Church and lead to mature Christian commitment. No longer can we assume that the prevailing culture is sufficiently "Christian" so as to provide adequate substitutes for either catechesis or mystagogy. No longer can we assume that citizenship and discipleship are the same thing.

The Church's initiation rites cannot be expected to bear the full force of the turbulence resulting from this new place of the Church in the world. The importance of these rites, however, can hardly be overestimated. The lifelong formation of persons within ritual communities that order their public life according to the paschal patterns of the life of Jesus is surely among the most effective means through which the Church can renew its witness and play an important role in the lives of the people. This will demand of the Church a willingness to live more deeply into the ritual intensity of the rites and not be content with a hasty recitation of the relevant texts. This will demand a steadfast commitment to prebaptismal catechesis and formation and an equally steadfast commitment to continued mystagogy and formation that is not only postbaptismal but truly lifelong. This will demand of those in holy orders a willingness to lay aside much of the work they presently do and rekindle for themselves and for the Church a rabbinical passion for knowing, loving and living the tradition, not as the depository of our past but as the source of our future.

In recent decades as the Church has embraced the results of modern critical scholarship and made some initial efforts to applying that learning to present pastoral need, a milieu has been created in which reform of the rites is not only possible and desirable but required. This task is a great deal more complicated than simply asking relevant questions about the current realities and trying to find an old rite that, when freshly translated and ritually adapted, appears to do the trick. Furthermore, many have discovered that the wholesale creation of new ritual structures rarely accomplishes what they intend for more than a passing moment. Most such efforts generally yield new rites whose field of vision is limited to a very narrow point in time and place and make it impossible for the rite to possess any enduring character. Put another way, the sort of ritual authority that enables genuine formation of a liturgical community and its members suffers as the result of the pastoral agenda being in control of the rite rather than emerging from it.

The process of liturgical reform in the Episcopal Church that led to the present Book of Common Prayer not only was the result of new scholarship and changing pastoral need, but received additional energy from the efforts toward liturgical renewal present in virtually all western churches since the Second Vatican Council's *Constitution on the Sacred Liturgy*. A large part of this process was devoted to establishing new liturgies that attempted to bridge the inherited rites with models derived from the evidence of earlier ages, most often patristic models from the second to fourth centuries. In this process, a new appreciation developed among scholars for "ritual patterns" or "liturgical structures." It became obvious, certainly not for the first time but with renewed conviction, that a liturgical structure is not simply the sum of a group of discrete ritual moments that can be ordered, amplified or abbreviated at will, but that the structure of a rite itself possesses a ritual authority that shapes those who encounter it. It is no longer possible to assume that the meaning of a rite can be controlled solely by painstaking attention to the formulation of the words to be spoken and heard. This is not to say that speech, silence, movement, music, light and color are not extremely important components of any ritual experience, but only to note that the structures that shape our ritual encounters themselves possess a power and authority that is more profound than a mere accumulation of the constitutive parts.

As we begin looking toward the next round of liturgical revision, it is quite probable that this renewed appreciation for the integrity of liturgical structures will play an important role. The need to make a variety of liturgical materials available to an increasingly diverse Church while at the same time fortifying a common sense of shared tradition may well find one of its solutions in a commitment to standardized liturgical structures that attract an almost unlimited number of liturgical formulae adaptable to local pastoral need. This could mean, for example, that a local community would be free to say its prayers in traditional, contemporary, inclusive or expansive language, while continuing to share the substance of the tradition by adhering to a common liturgical structure. In other words, we would find our unity in diversity by faithful adherence to liturgical structures whose ritual authority is strong enough to withstand appropriate local adaptation in response to genuine pastoral need.

If there is anything commendable in the foregoing argument, then it will require that those whose task it is to revise the rites look critically at our present liturgical structures and determine what sort of refinements are needed so that the structures possess the necessary strength to bear the tradition while at the same time being adaptable to local requirements. By way of example, the remainder of this essay will be devoted to an analysis of a portion of the structure of the present baptismal rite and a suggestion for a change in that structure that will yield a ritually stronger and more adaptable rite.

The liturgy for Holy Baptism in The Book of Common Prayer is appropriately set within the larger ritual structure of The Holy Eucharist. The entrance rite follows the normal pattern with the addition of versicles from Ephesians 4. The liturgy of the Word is identical in structure to that of every eucharist. Following the sermon, the structure of the baptismal rite is as follows:

> Presentation of the baptismal candidates
> Threefold renunciation
> Threefold act of adherence
> (Presentation of candidates for confirmation, reception,
>   reaffirmation)
> The Baptismal Covenant
> Prayers for the Candidates
> Thanksgiving over the Water
> (Consecration of the Chrism)
> The baptismal water bath
> Prayer for the gifts of the Spirit
> Consignation, with optional anointing
> Welcome and Peace

The baptism rite continues with the celebration of the eucharist, beginning with the Prayers of the People or the Offertory. The rubrics provide for adjustments in the rite to accommodate candidates for confirmation, reception or reaffirmation.

Although every ritual community is at the mercy of its liturgical space, most parishes have been able to create a sense of movement within this rite. Such movement serves not only to punctuate discrete parts of the rite but also to engage both those receiving sacramental initiation and the congregation in a symbolic journey that ritualizes, often with great solemnity, the momentous redirection of life that baptism requires. The candidates for baptism are presented in full view of the congregation, "down front" as we are apt to say. The candidates (or, in the case of young children, their sponsors and parents) renounce Satan, evil and sin, then promise to adhere to Jesus Christ. Then, any candidates for confirmation, reception and reaffirmation are presented, and they, using a quite brief form, renew their renunciation of evil and their commitment to Jesus Christ. The entire congregation then pledges its support for all the candidates and joins with them in the Baptismal Covenant.

The Prayers for the Candidates follow, during which the clergy, the baptismal candidates and sponsors, and the candidates for episcopal hand-laying move to the place of baptism. Hopefully this journey, led by the paschal candle, is ritually significant. Upon arriving at the place of baptism (not always a font), the water is prepared and blessed with a sense of care and dignity parallel to that of the preparation of the altar and the Great Thanksgiving. The water bath follows immediately unless chrism is to be blessed. The postbaptismal portion of the rite will not concern us here.

Analyzing more carefully the structure of the rite from the Presentation of the Candidates to the water bath, one is immediately struck by the distance (a lapse of both time and space) between the Baptismal Covenant and the water bath. This stands in rather stark contrast to the close ritual relationship between these two components which may be observed in many, though certainly not all, ancient baptismal rites. In *The Apostolic Tradition* of Hippolytus, for example, the candidates are in the water at the time of their profession of faith. The blessing of the water takes place before the renunciation, the profession of faith and the water bath, perhaps at an earlier hour.[1] A similar picture of the relationship between the profession of faith and the water bath may be observed in the third- and fourth-century writers Tertullian, Cyprian, Ambrose, Cyril and Chrysostom, among others. Even so late a document as the Gelasian Sacramentary, reflecting the practice of Rome in the early sixth century, makes visible the close ritual relationship between the profession of faith and the water bath.[2]

The most important text that displays an alternative structure is *The Apostolic Constitutions*, Book 7.[3] This late fourth-century Syrian source is a composite text that represents significant structural development when compared to the prototypes that stand behind it. It is impossible in this brief essay to provide a detailed analysis of the text, but it seems likely that the shift in structure as outlined in the initiatory sections of *Apostolic Constitutions* may result from the compiler's (or compilers') attempt to describe the expansion of the rite in response to the increased demands placed upon it by the requirements of the catechumenal process. If, in the final analysis, this suggestion proves untenable, it nonetheless seems quite probable that the separation of the profession of faith from the water bath does not represent an original structure unique to the Syrian tradition, but is rather the result of editorial work that tries to capture the increasing complexity of the Syrian rite near the end of the fourth century.

This brief exploration of the ancient rites provides a useful starting place, but historic precedent alone, while critically important, is an insufficient basis upon which to critique or construct contemporary rites. At least as important is examining carefully the structure itself and trying to discern if an inherent ritual pattern exists. Compare the following:

Present Prayer Book Structure	*Alternative Structure*
Renunciation/adherence	Renunciation/adherence
The Baptismal Covenant	Prayers for the Candidates
Prayers for the Candidates	Thanksgiving over the Water
Thanksgiving over the Water	(Consecration of the Chrism)
(Consecration of the Chrism)	The Baptismal Covenant
The Baptism (water bath)	The Baptism (water bath)

In the present prayer book structure, the acts of renunciation and adherence (ritual acts of intention) are followed immediately by the profession of faith in the form of the Baptismal Covenant. The relationship between these two components is clear enough, but the ritual momentum they establish is interrupted by the Prayers for the Candidates and the Thanksgiving over the Water. In other words, the strong ritual association between the profession "I believe" and the water bath is lost.

One suspects that the present structure was designed so that all candidates, whether for baptism itself or for one of the forms of reaffirmation, can share together in the Baptismal Covenant, after which the rite neatly proceeds to the water bath, the postbaptismal rites and, as necessary, confirmation, reception and reaffirmation. The fact that everyone professes the faith together underscores that being "in Christ" means being a member of the community of faith and participating in its common life. But this desire that all candidates establish or renew the Baptismal Covenant with each other and with the whole Church would be ritually strengthened by its occurring at the place of the water bath. To say "I believe," for the first time or the thousandth, at the place of one's birth is a ritual sign that a presentation "down front" can never approximate. Water is the principal sign of sacred birth and new life not only for those who come for the first time but for all of us, everywhere, everyday, every time, every moment.

Turning now to the alternative structure, we shall assume that it is desirable that we retain all the components of the present rite (that is certainly the bias of the writer) and that what is at issue is only their rearrangement in an effort to increase ritual effectiveness. The alternative structure makes only one change—moving the Baptismal Covenant to take place immediately before the water bath—but like moving one part of a mobile, everything else shifts and something different emerges.

Beginning at the same place, the alternative structure provides for the same threefold renunciation and a parallel threefold act of adherence to Jesus Christ. Understanding these to be ritual acts of intention, this rite would move immediately to the Prayers for the Candidates. These prayers, even in their present form, would possess a greater sense of immediacy if they took place *before* the Baptismal Covenant. Although cast in the present tense, the existing form of the prayers does have a "future sense" that "leans" toward the water bath. If the Baptismal Covenant and the water bath were viewed as an indivisible unit, then this future sense growing out of the immediacy of the present moment would be greatly enhanced. Moreover, by placing the Prayers for the Candidates immediately after the acts of renunciation and adherence, singing (or saying) them in procession to the place of baptism strongly ritualizes the movement from intention to commitment.

The Thanksgiving over the Water would then follow using the present form or something similar to it. In one sense this water blessing seems like little more than an act of preparation. Yet it is far more than that, far more than simply a ritual requirement that must be accomplished, and structurally this is the place for it. The candidates for baptism and renewal have been brought to the water by prayers and singing. Now by still more prayer, and one hopes by more singing, thanksgiving is offered for water and for the role it has played in our redemption. The waters of baptism are then stirred up by God's Spirit to receive those who are moved to say, "Yes, I believe!" The Thanksgiving over the Water is in fact a water blessing, but more importantly it is the great prayer at the font in the same way that the eucharistic prayer is the great prayer at the table. Both prayers are consecratory, but to focus on that fact alone is to miss the larger sense of proclamation out of which the thanksgiving emerges. This prayer is not just about making holy water for baptism and asperges. It vividly reminds us that what is happening here is not the application of holy water to an individual for his or her sake alone, but that a person is being inserted into the life of a community whose God has employed water as a sign of redemption at least since the creation of the world. The Thanksgiving over the Water, then, not only proclaims redemption and blesses water, it also possesses an undeniable ritual magnetism that might well animate one's desire to say, "Yes, I believe!"

In a time of emerging ecumenical consensus, especially concerning matters of liturgy and preaching, it is important to note what other churches have done in their revision of this portion of their baptismal rite. It is impossible to review every reform in detail, but it is possible to capture a general sense of how our practice compares to that of other churches. Of particular interest here is not whether the baptismal rites of other churches duplicate exactly, in all details, the structural pattern of the prayer book or of the alternative structure provided above, but how other churches have ordered the relationship between the Thanksgiving over the Water, the Baptismal Covenant and the water bath.

Two recent revisions that seem to follow the same structure as the prayer book are the rites of the United Methodist Church (1992)[4] and the Presbyterian Church (U.S.A.)(1993).[5] In both rites, the Thanksgiving over the Water takes place between the Baptismal Covenant and the water bath. However, Lutherans[6] and Roman Catholics[7] both follow the alternative structure. In each case, the water is blessed first, and the profession of faith leads directly to the water bath. Some variation occurs in these rites with respect to the acts of renunciation and adherence, most notably in the Roman rite, but the order of the three components in question is secure.

Within the Anglican Communion, five rites have been consulted for purposes of comparison. The *Alternative Service Book* (1980) of the Church of England, the *Alternative Prayer Book* (1984) of the Church of Ireland, the *Book of Alternative Services* (1985) of the Anglican Church of Canada, and *An Anglican Prayer Book* (1989) of the Church of the Province of Southern Africa, all follow the pattern of the alternative structure. *A New Zealand Prayer Book* (1989) follows a structural pattern different from either the prayer book or the alternative structure. At first glance its structure may appear closer to that of the prayer book, but the insertion of a new element referred to as "God's Call" and the placing of the Baptismal Covenant at the end of the rite as "The Celebration of Faith" obscure the structure to the point that useful comparisons are impossible.

It is also interesting to note that the Fourth International Anglican Liturgical Consultation, meeting in Toronto in 1991, commended to the churches of the Anglican Communion the following structure:

> Presentation of the candidate(s)
> Renunciation of evil
> Prayer over the water
> Profession of Christian faith
> The administration of water
> Post-baptismal ceremonies[8]

Although using different terminology, this pattern follows exactly what we are referring to here as the alternative structure.

Another factor also commends the use of the alternative structure. The prayer book anticipates that there will be occasions for baptismal renewal at times when there are no candidates for initiation. The use of The Renewal of Baptismal Vows (BCP, p. 292) in place of the Nicene Creed at the eucharist is expressly commended for the baptismal feasts: Easter Vigil, the Day of Pentecost, All Saints' Day or the Sunday after All Saints' Day and the Baptism of Jesus (BCP, p. 312). Although some may find the simple recitation of the Baptismal Covenant a sufficient alternative to the Nicene

Creed, many have desired a fuller rite of renewal than simply the recitation of another text. The present book makes no such provision. It may well have been a wise decision by the framers of the present book not to provide an elaborate rite for baptismal renewal that might compete in popular piety with the baptismal rite itself. It is, however, a law of liturgical development that when richer and more profound ritualizations are needed, if they are not provided then they will be invented. Many communities have found that renewing baptismal vows is nonsensical apart from the baptismal space and some ritual association of water with renewal in Christian life.

One way to address this would be to adopt the alternative structure and provide rubrical amendments necessary for its use on those occasions when there are no candidates for baptism. Such an adaptation of the alternative structure might look like this:

> Address by the presider
> Prayers (in procession to the place of baptism)
> Thanksgiving over the Water
> The Baptismal Covenant
> A prayer over the people

The address would follow the sermon and be similar to that provided by the prayer book for the Easter vigil (BCP, p. 292). A new book might provide such an address for each of the baptismal feasts and one or more general ones for use on other occasions. The prayers might follow a litany form similar to the present Prayers for the Candidates (BCP, p. 305) or provide a means by which the regular prayers might be easily adapted. A litany would make it possible for these prayers to be sung in procession. It seems important that the text of the Thanksgiving over the Water remain stable for all baptismal feasts, but some attention might be given to emending the petition for the sanctifying power of the Holy Spirit for use at times no baptisms will take place. During the interrogation of the Baptismal Covenant, water might be sprinkled on the people or, if the congregation is not too large, the people might be invited to come to the font to touch the water, splash their faces, or simply make the sign of the cross. A prayer over the people, not unlike that provided for the Easter vigil (BCP, p. 294) although perhaps seasonably variable, would conclude the rite.

Not every parish, of course, will desire this level of ritualization for baptismal renewal. There are many, however, that would delight in a baptismal rite that could be adapted in its structural integrity for use on occasions of baptismal renewal. If the keeping of baptismal feasts in the absence of candidates for initiation is a good thing, then surely it is appropriate to provide a liturgical structure that approximates the ritual depth of the event that first established the promises being renewed.

As noted earlier, this essay has been devoted to the analysis of only one section of the baptismal rite. There are certainly a number of other issues that will need to be addressed when the Episcopal Church declares officially that prayer book revision has begun. In the baptismal rite alone, we will need to address again the question of the baptismal formula. Not only will questions of language and the Trinity emerge, but also whether the continued use of the first-person singular pronoun for the presider best reflects our present ecclesiology and understanding of the baptismal community. The current Thanksgiving over the Water is one of the treasures of the 1979 book, but are we now prepared to move even deeper into the water metaphors of the tradition? The giving of a baptismal candle, provided for in the present rite but without an accompanying formula, will need to be rethought. Another structural question concerns the order of the postbaptismal prayer for the Holy Spirit and the consignation. The current book presents one order and rubrically provides for the order to be reversed. Are we still satisfied with that solution, or is it time we decided that it really does make a difference and make a choice? The question of whether the Prayers for the Candidates is a sufficient substitute for the Prayers of the People in the eucharist also needs to be revisited and the rubrics clarified. Questions abound.

The initiatory rites are among the present prayer book's greatest gifts to us. This is true in spite of whatever imperfections in them may have surfaced in two decades of use. As we anticipate the revision of these rites, some structural fine-tuning will be required, and a few enrichments will no doubt be added to respond to the requirements of an increasingly diverse Church in a rapidly changing world. But nothing less than Holy Baptism, together with all that anticipates it and all that overflows from it, has the capacity to hold us together and serve as the locus of our identity. One hopes that our revision of initiatory rites will serve only to move us as a Church more deeply into the paschal life of Jesus Christ.

Notes

1. *Apostolic Tradition* 21, in E. C. Whitaker, *Documents of the Baptismal Liturgy*, second edition (London: S.P.C.K., 1970), pp. 4-6. The text indicates that the water was blessed at cockcrow. The baptisms appear to have taken place somewhat later as indicated by the phrase "and at the time determined for baptizing."

2. Ibid., pp. 7-12, 23-30, 35-41, 127-33, 186-8.

3. Ibid., pp. 31-5.

4. *The United Methodist Book of Worship* (Nashville, TN: United Methodist Publishing House, 1992), pp. 88-91, 95-8.

5. *Book of Common Worship* (Louisville: Westminster/John Knox Press, 1993), pp. 406-13.

6. *Lutheran Book of Worship* (Minneapolis: Augsburg; Philadelphia: Board of Publication, Lutheran Church in America, 1978), pp. 122-3.

7. *The Rites of the Roman Catholic Church as Revised by the Second Vatican Ecumenical Council,* Study Edition (New York: Pueblo, 1976), pp. 143-7.

8. "Walk in Newness of Life: The Findings of the International Anglican Liturgical Consultation, Toronto 1991," in David R. Holeton, ed., *Growing in Newness of Life: Christian Initiation in Anglicanism Today* (Toronto: Anglican Book Centre, 1993), pp. 252-3. An explanatory note concedes the possibility of the prayer book structure, but the alternative structure is preferred.

THE HOLY EUCHARIST

Scope and Focus in Eucharistic Celebration

Louis Weil

In only a quarter-century, the Church's liturgical agenda has changed enormously. Then, we were well settled into the unfolding of the twentieth century. The two world wars had undermined the political and social structures which were taken for granted in the nineteenth century and earlier, and nations were engaging the emerging realities of a very different world. The Church on the whole continued to operate on the foundation of the older paradigm, but it was becoming increasingly obvious that in what came to be called the postmodern world, that foundation was seriously eroded. The implications of the collapse of that model with regard to the Church's traditional structures were profound, and on the whole, the institution tried to avoid them. But something new was (and is) being born.

Now we cannot escape the awareness that we are at the threshold of the twenty-first century and that we are caught up in an enormous shift of perspective at every level of the Church's life. What was long taken for granted can no longer be taken for granted. We are obliged to look beneath the surface of our inherited forms and ask what the essential energies of the Christian tradition are and in what models of faith and practice those energies can take appropriate expression in the complex and pluralistic world in which we live.

In May 1969, Professor Massey Shepherd delivered the John Purser Shortt lecture at Trinity College in Dublin, Ireland, on

"The Dimension of Liturgical Change."[1] At the time that Dr.
Shepherd delivered his lecture, the American Episcopal Church
was caught up in prayer book revision. The final authorization of
the current American Book of Common Prayer was still ten years
in the future. I can remember how the process of prayer book revision dominated the liturgical consciousness of the Episcopal
Church, and, of course, the process of revision was going on at
more or less the same time in other provinces of the Anglican
Communion. For Anglicans, given the close relation of the prayer
book to our own spiritual identity, it was as though the revision of
the texts (the continuing rearrangement of Archbishop Cranmer's
materials and, increasingly, the introduction of new, so-called con-
temporary-language texts) was the entire scope of liturgical reform.
That attitude was indicative of a certain clericalist understanding
of liturgical development which I shall consider later. We could
not yet see beyond the process of prayer book revision to the larger
issues of liturgical reform. We can now see that the prayer books
authorized in our various provinces in recent decades represent the
end of a model of liturgical evolution which had dominated our
understanding of the liturgy since the Reformation—a model, in
fact, of clerical authority over the liturgy which had its origins in
early medieval Christianity, when a hierarchical ecclesiology gradually replaced the earlier baptismal ecclesiology.

In Professor Shepherd's address in 1969, in spite of the intense
revision process which was going on in the Episcopal Church, he
makes it clear that his vision of liturgical change is much larger
than merely the then-current debates about proposed rites. He sees
the Church of the mid-twentieth century as living after the
Constantinian era which had been characterized by an establish-
ment model of relation between Church and State: in our time, he
says, Christianity finds itself disestablished with regard to political
and social privilege. The secular world is autonomous; the Church
can no longer live in terms of a model which has ceased to exist.
Shepherd thus sets a large and challenging context in which he

then places the liturgical agenda. Liturgical revision must be far more radical than heretofore; the modest adjustments of past revisions are not adequate, he says, as a resource for Anglican liturgical prayer in today's world. Our inherited texts, being rooted in a world which has disappeared, often seem "romantic, nostalgic, and on the whole ridiculous." The reform we need does not look to the past for its models but to the life-situation in which we actually live today.[2]

Professor Shepherd's lecture suggests an enormous agenda with regard to the Church's liturgical task. It is an agenda which, in the quarter-century since, we have begun only tentatively to address. This larger vision has direct bearing on future prayer book revision. In this essay, we shall look at the issues from two perspectives: first, "The Scope of Eucharistic Celebration," and second, "The Focus of Eucharistic Ministry."

I. The Scope of Eucharistic Celebration

At a meeting of Anglican liturgists in Boston in 1985, the English bishop Colin Buchanan made a casual remark which struck home very convincingly to me. He said, "The trouble is that when we assemble, we don't meet." Since that time, I have found the phrase emerging in a wide variety of contexts and with some far-reaching implications. This phrase is linked for me to a reclaiming of the larger context of eucharistic celebration, and in that regard I want to consider three matters which have received a great deal of attention in recent decades in theological discussion and formation and in much published material. The three issues are: baptism as it relates to our understanding of the assembly, the nature of the eucharistic prayer, and some factors related to culture. These are all, of course, major subjects about which much has been written. My goal here is simply to look at certain aspects of these three matters as they relate to the larger framework of the eucharist. They are not separate subjects, but rather three complementary perspectives to the primary issue.

1. The nexus between baptism and the assembly

It is evident to all of us that remarkable attention has been given to Christian baptism in this century. We might say that it is a compensating attention, long overdue. The evidence suggests that this is a dramatic shift in the Church's consciousness, a needed attention to the meaning and implications of the foundational outward sign of Christian identity. Both in meaning and in practice, baptism was taken for granted. As recently as the late fifties when I was preparing for ordination, very little attention was given to baptism in theology or liturgy courses; in pastoral theology I remember the professor made sure that at a baptism we knew how to hold the baby! I cannot help but wonder how many of us can recall hearing a sermon in that period on the relation of baptism to the Gospel.

I refer to this neglect of attention to baptism because I think it makes the burst of attention which has characterized recent decades all the more significant. It is closely related to a recovery of what I would call a "baptismal ecclesiology," an understanding of the Church in terms of the identification of all its members with the paschal mystery of Jesus Christ and through that with the common life of the body of Christ. As baptism marks us as members of the universal community of faith, so also it brings us into the local assemblies of Christians as we gather on the day of the resurrection to signify our union with Christ and with each other.[3]

In practice, however, that theology must work its way through a number of inherited filters which reflect a different ecclesiology and which often create a deeply entrenched barrier to experiencing that baptismal ecclesiology in the day-to-day realities of local communities. As the Church truly sees itself shaped by its baptismal identity, there are inevitable consequences with regard to what I am calling the larger scope of eucharistic celebration. If the local assembly constitutes the body of Christ in that place, then, I would suggest, it is the whole action of the members gathered which constitutes the full meaning of eucharistic celebration.

It is the whole Church assembled which celebrates the eucharist, and its full meaning is more than the ritual blessing of bread and wine. I am reminded of a comment made by a friend many years ago: "When we celebrate the eucharist we are only doing a part of what Jesus did with his disciples." This is a simple observation with some far-reaching implications. To say the most obvious, the whole assembly in its whole action is the primary sign of the priesthood of Jesus Christ; the whole baptized assembly is the primary minister of Christ in its place. All particular and specialized ministries are derived from the general ministry of the assembly. The sacraments of the Church are not objects which are provided for the assembly by a special group whom we call clergy. The sacraments are actions which are done—"celebrated"—by the whole assembly and which use the particular charisms of pastoral leadership which become manifest among the wide range of gifts which the Holy Spirit pours out upon the members of the assembly.[4]

This understanding of the integral role of all the people assembled in the celebration of the eucharist influenced the members of the committee which prepared the texts eventually incorporated into the 1979 Book of Common Prayer. We see this not because of any heavy-handed inclusion of theologically loaded phrases. The new eucharistic prayers are, in fact, far less didactic in style than the work of Thomas Cranmer and thus more akin in spirit to the ancient models of eucharistic praise. The fully participatory role of the laity is suggested rather in more subtle ways, such as the rubrical authorization of the option of a standing posture (BCP, pp. 334, 341, 362, 368, 373) by which the people share with the presider a commonly identifying posture for the eucharistic prayer. The problem in the two decades since is that this new ecclesial mentality has had to pass through the heavy mesh of an inherited piety formed by decades of personal experience in a passive mindset. This is a pastoral issue which extends beyond merely the further revision of texts into the more subtle area of a liturgical mentality in which the fuller implications of baptismal identity are claimed.

What I am suggesting is that the social framework, the attention given to shared study (what we might call the catechetical aspect of the community's life), the proclamation of scripture and preaching grounded in it—all of these aspects of the assembly's activity are ways in which the community manifests its baptismal identity; all of these are constitutive of the full meaning of eucharistic celebration as the action of the entire assembly. To suggest this, of course, raises the question of the role of the eucharistic prayer in this larger context.

2. The eucharistic prayer within the whole rite

I would like to begin with a story which dates back to the early sixties, when I was a missionary in Latin America. Visitors from the United States were frequent, and one Sunday, after services at our cathedral, I was taking friends into old San Juan (in Puerto Rico) for lunch. The restaurant was near the Roman Catholic cathedral, which is a wonderful example of colonial Spanish baroque architecture, and I wanted my friends to see it. As we approached the entrance, the tower bell rang, indicating that the priest had reached the words of institution in the eucharistic prayer. A group of men had been talking together near the steps, and when the bell sounded, they put out their cigarettes and walked through the main door with us. As I watched, each man knelt down on one knee, devoutly made the sign of the cross at the elevation of the host and again at the elevation of the chalice. Then they stood up and walked back outside to resume their conversation.

I am not sharing this memory with you to ridicule their piety. In terms of the view shared within their culture, these men had fulfilled their Sunday mass obligation. Admittedly, this was at a very minimal level, but it was an acceptable minimum from their point of view. The story offers a useful point of reference for what I want to say about the role of the eucharistic prayer.

As Anglicans, we would be quick to say that we dealt with this problem of a eucharistic piety entirely focused on the words of institution and the elevations at the time of the Reformation.

Although certainly understanding the words to be our link with the dominical institution and so continuing to serve as the scriptural focus of the eucharistic action, on the whole, at least in my experience, Anglicans representing the whole range of our tradition would want to claim the eucharistic prayer as an integral whole rather than a momentary focus within it. I think this can be asserted, even allowing for the nineteenth-century influence of Roman ritual practice and theology upon the Catholic revival within Anglicanism. Generally, even in the way the prayer book is printed, there is no highlighting or isolation of particular phrases, as was true in medieval missals and continues to be true in modern Roman Catholic altar books in which the words of institution are printed in much larger type. We have as a norm looked at the prayer as a whole.

But I am obviously leading this point further down the road in regard to my concern for the integrity of the whole eucharistic action. We have been the beneficiaries in recent decades of an extraordinary level of study on the structure and theology of the eucharistic prayer. This work has served the Church remarkably in deepening our insight into the eucharistic prayer as not merely a formula of consecration but as a living proclamation of the Church's faith.[5] Yet if we have seen this in theory, have we not stopped short in this recovery and failed to reclaim the role of the prayer within the larger framework of eucharistic celebration? Although we do not hang all meaning on the words of institution as did the men I observed that day in Puerto Rico and our ancestors in the Middle Ages, are we not asking the prayer to carry too great a part of the meaning of the eucharistic action?

It was from a distinguished Anglican liturgist, now departed, that this idea first came to me. In September 1983, Professor Geoffrey Cuming gave a short communication at the Ninth Oxford Patristic Conference which was titled "Four Very Early Anaphoras."[6] Since the text of Professor Cuming's comments has been published, I shall not summarize them here, but only note how they influenced my thinking on our subject. He notes that the four prayers are "characterized by extreme brevity and simplicity." In one prayer of only a few lines, the themes of creation and redemption and a doxology are included. The text reads as follows:

> It is fitting and right that we should adore you and glorify you, for you are truly God, and your only-begotten Son and the Holy Spirit. For you brought us out of non-existence into existence; and when we had fallen, you recalled us, and did not cease to work until you brought us up to heaven, and granted us the kingdom that is to come. For all these things we give thanks to you and to your only-begotten Son and the Holy Spirit.[7]

When we compare to this the prayer of Thomas Cranmer, not to mention the ancient prayers of John Chrysostom and Basil in the East and the Roman Canon in the West, we are struck by how great a verbal (and theological) weight the eucharistic prayer later came to assume.

Even modern prayers in which an attempt at brevity is sometimes made still give a dominance to the role of the presider which implies a primacy that dwarfs the liturgical roles of other ministers and reduces the assembly to little more than observer status. As Professor Cuming says: "We have probably allowed the medieval [manuscripts] of the great liturgies to impress upon us too easily the image of the anaphora as a long, seamless robe." Recent revisers have taken almost exclusively "the fourth-century anaphora as their model."[8] This is, I believe, a good example of a type of filter about which I spoke earlier. We have experienced the celebration of the eucharist for so many centuries in the model of the dominant presider proclaiming a long eucharistic prayer, that the experience has formed a filter which inhibits our imagining that the eucharistic celebration might be structured differently.

Cuming suggests that the constituent parts of the prayer might occur at appropriate places in the whole rite so that their particular theological weight might be more effectively realized and the presider's prayer might no longer be expected to carry the whole meaning. Although Professor Cuming does not explicitly say this, it would seem appropriate that some of these diffused elements might find their place in the liturgical ministries of other ministers within the assembly, with the presider's prayer serving as a focus of thanksgiving within the rite as a whole.[9]

The various forms of the eucharistic prayer in the 1979 prayer book, in spite of their diversity, maintain the "dominant presider" model of the prayer book tradition. Future revision should include, I would suggest, a still wider diversity of forms in which, while not rejecting the heritage, we might find models of eucharistic prayer in which the theological substance of our liturgical thanksgiving might be carried more evidently by the rite as a whole. Even if such forms were viewed as tentative and experimental, they would serve the purpose of expanding our understanding of eucharistic prayer.

I would conclude this second point by repeating that my primary concern is to find appropriate ways to reclaim the eucharistic celebration as an integral whole. Following Professor Cuming's insight, I feel that the patterns of our eucharistic prayer, even those composed in this century, tend to imply that the presider's role is dramatically more significant than the roles of the other members of the assembly and thus tend to erode our experience of the Church at worship as a community defined by its baptismal identity. Future revision must seek to articulate this shared identity upon which the eucharistic action itself is based.

3. The culture of clericalism
The intense study of the eucharistic prayer in recent decades has been matched by work in another field which on the surface seems to involve a very different set of concerns. That field is liturgy and culture. Discussion of the inculturation of the liturgy has been wide-ranging and has produced a substantial literature.[10] The third meeting of the International Anglican Liturgical

Consultation, which took place at York in 1989, gave its attention to this theme and produced the statement entitled "Down to Earth Worship."[11] Grove Books has published several works on this subject in the past decade.[12]

Discussion of the issue of inculturation and the indigenization of the liturgy often begins with the acknowledgment of the monolithic character of our inherited liturgical models. Whether it be the normative influence of Archbishop Cranmer's work upon the later evolution of The Book of Common Prayer or the comparable but even more absolute authority of the missal of Pius V (1570) upon the Roman rite until very recent times, it is generally acknowledged today that the Church's situation in our pluralistic world requires a far deeper and more positive attention to the diverse cultures in which our traditions have taken root. The decontextualized rites of past centuries had remained in their textual and rubrical components virtually untouched by the diverse cultures in which they were celebrated. We have seen the breakup of that rigidity in our own time.

Yet I believe there is an aspect of our past models, an aspect shaped by the societies that produced them, which continues to work as an inhibiting filter of authentic inculturation. This issue is closely related to the matters which were discussed above. Our classical models were not only characterized by a certain fixity of their authorized texts, but also by a clerical control of the development of these rites and certainly of any proposed revision of them. I can look back at the rather recent process in the Episcopal Church which produced our 1979 book, and although laity were drawn into the committee work, the entire process strikes me as having taken place very much within the domain of clerical authority. This did not have entirely negative results; in a real sense, this pattern fit with the common view of the ordained as stewards of the sacraments. Even in the York statement on inculturation, which offers many important perspectives to the imperatives of inculturation, there is no indication of how easily these imperatives can be undermined by the "culture of clericalism," the filter of clerical control which continues, perhaps even at an unconscious level, to interpret this whole area in the Church's life as the domain of the clergy. Paul Gibson raised this issue in an essay published with the Grove edition of the York statement. In suggesting that we must re-examine the *method* which underlies authority in Anglicanism, he points to the matter of liturgical evolution in the various cultures in which Anglicanism has taken root and then offers a passionate *cri de coeur*:

> We cannot go back on developments in our view
> of the world and our responsibility within it; we
> cannot go back to a clerical ecclesiology; we cannot
> go back to the suppression of cultural distinctions;
> we cannot go back to the denial of the over-
> whelming creativity of the ecumenical experience.
> In short, we cannot go back.[13]

From the perspective of a baptismal ecclesiology, another model and a new process will be required from now on. If public worship is rooted in shared baptismal identity, then our rites must emerge not from the rearrangement of hallowed ancient texts but from the faith life of our communities. Revision in the past, what I would call the clerical model of prayer book revision, has been based on the principle that safety is in the past. An ecclesial model of revision would hold that through the grace of the Holy Spirit there is safety in the future, that we may rely upon the Spirit to lead us into forms of worship which carry both the finest elements of our heritage and yet are open to the realities and gifts that characterize each age and culture.

The highly pluralistic world in which we live makes this imperative an awesome task but one that must be undertaken in future prayer book revision. There is no static formula which will enable us to incorporate the diverse gifts of many cultures in an appropriate tension with the universal aspects of the inherited tradition. Experimentation and critical discernment will be needed as new and varied models emerge which manifest a grounding in the common tradition and at the same time an embracing of the best cultural expressions of the local community. For this to be achieved, the authorized forms of future prayer books must be more flexible than ever in the past, and the requirements for liturgical leadership among laity as well as the ordained will go far beyond mere obedience to the rubrics.

II. The Focus of Eucharistic Ministry

It might seem from what I have said in the first part of this address that I would support the idea of authorizing laity to preside at the eucharist. If it is the entire community which acts in the eucharistic celebration, why should not any baptized member of the community be qualified to exercise that representative role?

On the other hand, given my own formation in the Catholic tradition of Anglicanism, it might seem, to the contrary, that I would be opposed to anyone presiding at the eucharist who is not a presbyter (or bishop) ordained for the sacramental ministry of the Church by prayer and the laying on of hands by a bishop in the apostolic succession. In this approach, anyone not so ordained could not preside at the eucharist; the act would not be valid.

Actually, I do not want to approach the question of lay presidency from either of these perspectives. Rather, I would like to look at this issue within a larger pastoral context which would both affirm the normative character of episcopal ordination within our tradition and also link that norm to the New Testament evidence about designated offices in the Church in connection with pastoral oversight and care.

A few months ago I received an item in the mail from a former student. It was the text of a talk which the bishop had asked the priest to prepare as part of a discussion at a clergy conference of the diocese. The subject was whether laity might preside at the eucharist. My former student sent it to me because she knew the subject was related to many of my own concerns, and she wanted my reaction.

My reaction was complex. She described quite vividly how her ordination had produced a feeling of separation from laity, even from members of her own family, which she had not anticipated. It all began with the ordination itself at which, she felt, laity were left merely as an audience to a very clerical event. Then as months passed, she felt pained by the expectation on the part of many laity that, as a priest, she had a special claim on holiness, that somehow, without this being said, clergy were in the first rank, laity in the second.

I suspect that many of us have had experiences which are to some degree related to these. In my own experience, this has operated at the level of a kind of folk theology among the laity, a theology which has little to do with the authentic understanding of holy orders but which certainly shapes the attitudes of many of our people. I remember once standing in line to get on a plane (I was wearing clericals), and a woman behind me turned to her companion and said, "Thank God, there's a priest. We won't crash." These attitudes may be amusing but they are certainly wrong, and they deeply influence how the ordained are perceived.

So I share my former student's agony with all that: it is very uncomfortable to be placed on a pedestal when you know how fallible and vulnerable you are, just like every human being. But then my student and I parted company. On the basis of her experience, she discussed the value of lay presidency as a way to solve the problem of the elevation of the clergy, or the setting of the ordained into a somewhat more than human category. I felt immediately that she had linked two things that do not necessarily go together and which need to be looked at with a penetrating eye, each in its own frame of reference.

The first issue, the setting apart of the ordained into a separate, rather supra-human category, is, I believe, a continuing remnant of what I spoke of earlier as "the culture of clericalism." It is a continuing vestige of a world in which the clergy really were set apart not only through a shift in theological perspective, but also in very real structures imposed by medieval canon law in terms of legal status and made definitive with regard to society in general through the imposition of celibacy for the so-called higher orders. What I am suggesting is that even if the Reformation reopened the matter of clerical marriage, the tenacity of "the culture of clericalism" has maintained something of the aura of the celibate model: clergy are often perceived as apart from ordinary people.

The relation of an ordained presbyter (or bishop) to the ministry of presiding at the eucharist, comes, I believe, from a very different context, a context which still has a convincing theological weight and a very ancient place in the Church's understanding of ordination. Clericalism needs to be addressed forcefully, and I believe theological education and formation is the primary arena in which to recover a more ecclesial understanding of ordination. Lay presidency offers no guarantee for that and might well produce the opposite. A second layer of clericalism which I have observed, at least in America, is found in people we might call "lay popes." Clericalizing laity is not the answer. This is related to my anxiety about ever calling confirmation "the ordination of the laity." We need to see all our *particular* ministries, whether ordained or not, as diverse expressions of our shared baptismal identity: *diverse* because the gifts of the Holy Spirit are diverse and complementary. The building up of the body is accomplished through this rich diversity: the baptismal identity is not manifested through all the members doing the same things.[14]

Then we must ask, from where does the particular association of the ordained presbyter with presiding at the eucharist come? It is here that a threading-out of issues is important. We do need to rid ourselves of a mechanistic and quasi-magical understanding of the role of a presbyter as presider at the eucharist. At its worst, that distorted theology turns the presider into a sacrament machine, a person who by ordination has power to confect the sacrament. It is not a question of power.

Yet I would keep the presbyter (or bishop, of course) as the presider, but on the basis of a very different theology. The larger context is framed by a lively awareness that it is the whole baptized assembly which celebrates the eucharistic rite: it is the action of the whole community of faith. The role of the presider does not derive from some mechanistic power but rather from the charisms given by God for the purposes of pastoral care and oversight. Ordination is the Church's response to the discernment that God has given a person particular gifts of communal and pastoral leadership. The larger issue behind liturgical presiding is the New Testament concept of *episcope*: the community designates through ordination those persons in whom the gifts of pastoral care have been discerned and then nurtured.[15]

There is an ironic aspect to the fact that at least some people who have called for lay presidency have seen it as a death blow to clericalism. With no intention to do so, they fall into the trap of separating the ministry of presiding from its context in pastoral care. The clericalist model requires an ordained person and the right matter and form. It is a minimalist model, with no explicit relation to pastoral care. It in no way requires that the presider be a member of the local faith community nor its pastoral leader. Lay presidency extends the role, presumably, to any baptized person, but in so doing maintains, perhaps even more emphatically, the separation between the liturgical action and its relation to the larger pastoral context. Yet if the gifts for pastoral leadership and care are present, why would this person not be an appropriate candidate to receive the laying on of hands with prayer? If the full meaning of the eucharistic sign is to be claimed, then its relation to pastoral care and oversight is imperative.

The proclamation of the eucharistic prayer is far more than the reciting of a formula to produce a sacrament. It articulates the community's shared, baptismal faith. In that light, the presider is not an autocrat on a pedestal but rather a pastor committed in service to the people who assemble because of that common faith. The eucharistic prayer is the Church's prayer, not an expression of *power over* but of *service to* the people of God. I am convinced that it would ultimately be injurious to the Church's life if future prayer book revision were to erode the established relationships of the ordained ministries to the liturgical and sacramental actions of the Church. At the same time, it is imperative that the formation of persons for these ministries be grounded in a model of pastoral service for the building up of the common life. That imperative, however, cannot be fulfilled through prayer book revision or legislation. It requires a profound change in the Church's self-understanding on the part of all its members through an abiding accountability to the Gospel.

What, then, can be done about an entrenched clericalist point of view? I have suggested that the character of the training of candidates prior to ordination is an important element toward recovering an ecclesial sense of ordained ministry, but in itself it is not enough. If candidates complete their theological training and then go on to minister within the clericalist model, the impact is overwhelming either to give in to it or perhaps to leave the ordained ministry. The other necessary element is a restructuring of how ordained ministry is enacted in our dioceses. To this suggestion there is a tendency to say that nothing can be done, that the pattern is too deeply rooted. But with courage, transformation can take place.

I want to share with you, by way of example only, a program which has been undertaken in one diocese of the Episcopal Church to reshape the model of ordained ministry in relation to the larger ecclesial context. I am not proposing this as a blueprint to be adopted elsewhere. In fact, this is a good example of how local conditions and culture have contributed to a reassessment of the whole pattern of ministry, and so it would be in other parts of the world where the local realities would be a constitutive influence upon the emergence of a new model. The classical model which has shaped our own experience is really *de*-contextualized: the pattern of holy orders was maintained as a kind of supra-cultural tradition, a mark of the timeless character of Christianity. We could claim this rather innocently as long as we overlooked the obvious influence of secular models of leadership upon both the episcopate and the presbyterate of the Church from the fourth century onward.

The example I want to discuss is a model which has been unfolding in recent years in the Diocese of Northern Michigan. It is a model which has been referred to by outside observers as "a quiet revolution." When Thomas Ray became bishop in 1982, he began leading the diocese, with the support of an unusual group of laity and clergy, away from the idea that local ministry is identified wholly with the work of a single ordained (and usually seminary-trained) presbyter. This traditional model had created an enormous burden in an area which is economically very limited: too much of the available resources was required to educate and maintain this model.

I can sum up the effects of the new model by telling about one small church: Trinity Church in Gladstone, Michigan. As recently as 1988, this congregation was struggling to pay their share of the priest's salary (divided between themselves and the church in another town), to pay off the debt on their building, and to pay their diocesan assessment. In other words, virtually all the energy of this small congregation was taken to maintain the classical model. By the mid-nineties the parish had two priests, two deacons, five preachers and several other leaders in the shared ministry of the parish. The church is now economically self-sufficient, pays its share of the diocesan budget, and is deeply involved in outreach with substantial economic commitment, whereas eight years ago they were struggling to pay half of the salary of the parish priest.

More than a third of the congregations in the diocese have adopted this model, what they call "Total Ministry," in which the old educational process is turned upside down. Local candidates who have demonstrated the appropriate charisms for ministerial leadership are trained as a team to work as a team to serve in their communities. The members of a parish define the ministry needed in their area and then seek out from their community the persons with gifts to carry out those forms of service.

Under guidance of the bishop, an intensive educational program is undertaken for the group as a whole for some two years, using seminary-trained clergy (who are regional missioners in the new model) and other educators who share their expertise. At this point in its evolution, the program prepares people in five categories: presbyters, deacons, vestry, educators and administrators. The traditional identification of the presbyters with sacramental ministration is kept, but the isolation of these presbyters into the clericalist model is avoided: ministry as a whole is a shared undertaking, according to differing gifts, from the start.

Obviously, this transformed model requires a new form of liturgical expression. The highly clerical focus of our ordination rites which so pained my former student and led to her reflections on lay presidency, those rites would not fit the emerging model in Northern Michigan. The rite which has been developed is entitled "A Celebration of Baptismal Ministry with the Commissioning of a Ministry Support Team." This reflects Bishop Ray's often expressed concern "that we have exaggerated ordination. We have taken all of the preparation and attention that belonged to baptism and transferred it to ordination." (He also says that this attitude is manifested in our ordination certificates, which are often ten times the size of our baptismal certificates.) In the rite, the entire community renews its baptismal promises to set the context of all that follows. The entire ministry of the Word reflects the baptismal focus. Then the commissioning takes place, first of the entire congregation, then of particular members for particular forms of ministry, next those who will be primarily concerned with preaching and the sacramental ministry, with the support of the members of the congregation in their priestly ministry. Although the rite is a work in process, it makes a powerful statement about the rooting of all forms of ministry within the baptismal identity and also is very clear that ministry is not a solo performance but a common work shared by people with varying gifts.

I have discussed the Northern Michigan model in order to demonstrate how it is possible to maintain the traditional sacramental ministry of the presbyterate and yet reject a clericalism which connects a presbyter to the eucharist in a way more akin to hocus-pocus than to the Gospel. Moreover, I would insist, the integrity of the eucharistic action requires that it be an articulation of the community's common faith within a framework of pastoral care and oversight.

The Northern Michigan model in its details cannot be universally applied. It is a "contextualized" model, just as the classical model was characteristically decontextualized. The example I have given at least shows us that it is possible to look again at the inherited model and to breathe new life into it, or better, to invite the Holy Spirit to breathe new life into it and so to see it transformed as we reclaim a renewed sense of the baptismal character of the Church. The great tradition of the Church tells us that it pertains to those who are called and designated to preside over the building up of the local communities also to preside over the sacramental actions which, in their way, are a fundamental aspect of the building up of our common life of faith. In this sense, the ordained presider serves as the focus of the eucharistic ministry in which all the baptized share.

If public worship is as fundamental to Anglican identity as is generally acknowledged, the work of recovering the theological balance found in the earlier centuries in regard to the relation of the eucharist (and all sacramental acts) to the whole body of the baptized is imperative. For an array of reasons, the classical model of sacraments and ministry which emerged in the context of a Christendom pattern for the Church's life is bankrupt. It is bankrupt not merely because of major shifts in the cultural realities of what we call the secular world, but more significantly because it failed to give adequate weight to the fundamental role of the shared baptismal identity which is the authentic ground plan of the Church's life. The recovery of that role inevitably leads to a new integration of all the parts as we interpret the imperatives of the Gospel in a dazzling new world. If we can undertake those tasks with humility, we shall carry the best aspects of our heritage into the twenty-first century and find our God already there before us.

Notes

1. Published in *Anglican Theological Review* 51 (1969): 241-56.
2. Ibid., p. 249.
3. The published literature on this question is enormous. See especially the papers from the fourth meeting of the International Anglican Liturgical Consultation at Toronto in 1991: David R. Holeton, ed., *Growing in Newness of Life* (Toronto: Anglican Book Centre, 1993). For a survey of the issues and an excellent bibliography, see Daniel B. Stevick, *Baptismal Moments; Baptismal Meanings* (New York: Church Hymnal Corporation, 1987).
4. See the papers presented at the second meeting of the International Anglican Liturgical Consultation at Brixen, Italy, in 1987: Thomas J. Talley, ed., *A Kingdom of Priests: Liturgical Formation of the People of God,* Alcuin/GROW Liturgical Study 5 (Bramcote, Nottingham: Grove Books, 1988). For a useful discussion of the theological context, see Louis-Marie Chauvet, *Symbol and Sacrament* (Collegeville, MN: Liturgical Press, 1995), pp. 180-9.
5. See my article on the eucharistic prayer as creedal proclamation: "Proclamation of Faith in the Eucharist," in J. Neil Alexander, ed., *Time and Community* (Washington, DC: Pastoral Press, 1990), pp. 279-90.
6. Published in *Worship* 58 (1984): 168-72.
7. Ibid., p. 168 (Translation from R. C. D. Jasper and G. J.

Cuming, eds., *Prayers of the Eucharist: Early and Reformed,* third edition [New York: Pueblo, 1987], pp. 124-5).

8. Ibid., p. 171. For recent Anglican discussion of future directions in the reshaping of the eucharistic prayer see Thomas Talley, "Eucharistic Prayers, Past, Present and Future," and Colin Buchanan, "Future Directions for Eucharistic Revisions," in David R. Holeton, ed., *Revising the Eucharist: Groundwork for the Anglican Communion,* Alcuin/GROW Liturgical Study 27 (Bramcote, Nottingham: Grove Books, 1994), pp. 6-27.

9. From this perspective, it might be interesting to reconsider Thomas Cranmer's placement in the 1552 Book of Common Prayer of the Prayer of Oblation after Communion and said by all the people.

10. Particular attention must be given to the work of the Roman Catholic Benedictine scholar Anscar J. Chupungco. See, for example, *Cultural Adaptation of the Liturgy* (New York: Pueblo, 1982); *Liturgies of the Future* (New York: Pueblo, 1989); *Liturgical Inculturation: Sacramentals, Religiosity, and Catechesis* (Collegeville, MN: Liturgical Press, 1992).

11. David R. Holeton, ed., *Liturgical Inculturation in the Anglican Communion,* Alcuin/GROW Liturgical Study 15 (Bramcote, Nottingham: Grove Books, 1990).

12. Phillip Tovey, *Inculturation: The Eucharist in Africa,* Alcuin/GROW Liturgical Study 7 (Bramcote, Nottingham: Grove Books, 1988); Bosco Peters, *The Anglican Eucharist in New Zealand 1814-1989,* Alcuin/GROW Liturgical Study 21 (Bramcote, Nottingham: Grove Books, 1992); David Gitari, ed., *Anglican Liturgical Inculturation in Africa,* Alcuin/GROW Liturgical Study 28 (Bramcote, Nottingham: Grove Books, 1994).

13. Paul Gibson, "What is the future role of liturgy in Anglican unity?", in Holeton, ed., *Liturgical Inculturation in the Anglican Communion,* p. 21.

14. For further reading on the debate over lay presidency in Anglicanism, see Trevor Lloyd, ed., *Lay Presidency at the Eucharist?* Grove Liturgical Study 9 (Bramcote, Nottingham: Grove Books, 1977); Paul Gibson, "Lay Presidency of the Eucharist?" *Open* (Summer 1994), pp. 1-3. See also the article by the American Jesuit John F. Baldovin, "Liturgical Presidency: The Sacramental Question," in *Worship: City, Church and Renewal* (Washington, DC: Pastoral Press, 1991), pp. 115-34.

15. For the historical foundations of this theological claim, see Hervé-Marie Legrand, "The Presidency of the Eucharist According to the Ancient Tradition," in Kevin Seasoltz, ed., *Living Bread, Saving Cup* (Collegeville, MN: Liturgical Press, 1982), pp. 196-221.

"Let Us Pray for the Church and for the World"

Daniel B. Stevick

The Prayers of the People are, generally speaking, a weak point in Episcopalian worship. In some congregations, to be sure, the intercessions are prepared and led responsibly and caringly. Yet in many places they seem dull and habituated—seldom really slap-dash, but evidencing little attention and imagination. In view of the responsibility which the prayer book gives to local leadership and the possibilities it opens, our prayers for the Church and the world seem the greatest undeveloped opportunity in the prayer book.

What the Prayer Book Gives and Requires

The prayer book introduces the Prayers of the People with a general rubric which directs, "Prayer is offered with intercession for...," and continues with a series of subjects that begins with the large units of society and the Church and passes to the specific and close-at-hand and finally to "the departed." This rubric says, in effect, to congregations: "Pray. Take this act in the liturgy into your own hands. Let your prayer grow out of your living and dying. You are the experts—the only experts—on the world in which you live, on the concerns that fill your hearts. When you pray, do not become too parochial. Expand your awareness to include the big world of which you are part and for which God cares. And oh yes, be sure also that you do not get so caught up in that big world that you neglect the things that are close to you. And do not forget the greater part of the Church, which is in the life beyond." Having said this, the prayer book adds, "If it will help you, 'See the forms beginning on pages 383.' These printed forms will model good wordings, economical structure, and ways of bringing in the congregation."

Some congregations catch this intention and prepare their own prayers honestly and competently Sunday after Sunday, exercising freedom while taking some guidance from the prayer book forms. No one who has heard such prayers would willingly settle for anything else.

However, most congregations, faced with this invitation to independence and responsibility, turn at once to the prayer book's forms and choose one of them, which they use, making some rather timid insertions into the printed text. Even though the prayer book does not require it, they confine themselves to these authorized forms. The Church's liturgy trusts them more than they are willing to trust themselves.

A Weakness with a History

Eucharistic intercessions have long been a problem:

* From the sixteenth century, Anglican prayer books restored the people's prayers, which had long dropped out as a clear unit of the mass. In editions from 1549 to 1928 worshipers continued to use what was essentially Cranmer's Prayer for the Whole State of Christ's Church, which by custom was said from the remotest point in the room by the celebrant alone, with his (for they were all "he" at the time) back to the people. The structure and wording of this prayer assumed the social order of Tudor England. It was quite unsuited for a church with representative polity serving in a nation in which Church and state were separate. It described the society and

the Church in terms of the governors and the governed, casting citizens and the laity in passive roles. The only governmental function it mentioned was the punishment of wickedness and vice. It took no account of the Church's mission, and it certainly entertained no possibility that the Church might ever think itself called to be prophetic critic of state policies or actions. Towards the end of the use of the 1928 book, some clergy showed their restlessness by prefacing the Prayer for the Church with biddings or by interpolating within or between its paragraphs specific matters for prayer or by introducing a congregational response after each section. No doubt over the years a great deal more was prayed during this prayer than was said in its actual text, but as a form of regular intercession for a twentieth-century American church, it was quite inadequate.

• The "Prayer of Intercession" in the 1967 *Liturgy of the Lord's Supper*, the first authorized intercessory prayer to break with the sixteenth-century forms, was a notable improvement. It was in litany form, so the voice of the people was heard. It sought to pray for the world in which we actually live, introducing prayer for areas of life that had previously gone unmentioned—those who labor in industry and agriculture, those who are engaged in the arts and sciences, those who teach and study and who train children. It even showed an ecological awareness. Nevertheless, this "Prayer of Intercession" had an air of unreality. It was written during the 1960s when cities were burning, the society was bitterly divided—blacks vs. whites, the young vs. the old, hawks vs. doves—and all authority was in question. Yet this prayer projected a harmonious world in which everyone had a niche in life and filled it conscientiously. If Cranmer's prayer spoke for Tudor Christendom, the 1967 prayer spoke for ruskinian romanticism.

• The six forms of intercession in the 1979 Book of Common Prayer all involve the congregation. (Some of them do so more successfully than others.) They seek to pray for our twentieth-century world with both comprehensiveness and economy. Their wordings, although unexciting, have worn fairly well. It is no doubt better in an official text to underwrite than to overwrite. We may be grateful for these low-key, serviceable forms.

Yet they have grave shortcomings. *With respect to the Church,* the general rubric proposes prayer for "the Universal Church, its members, and its mission," and some of the forms do pray for "God's people throughout the world," or for "your holy Catholic Church." But when the provided forms speak of the Church more specifically, they mention the Presiding Bishop, our own bishop(s) and the local clergy. All these persons should be prayed for, of course, but what has happened to the vision of the *totus Christus* that the general rubric opened? There is no sense of the ecumenical Christian world—the other churches with which we share faith, struggle, vision, disappointments and joys. (With some of them we are engaged in serious dialogue, and some of them may be praying as we are within a block or two of our place of worship). These forms express no whisper of worldwide Anglicanism, and they say nothing of the other people of the Covenant, the Jews. These prayers give a highly parochial reading of the Church. We do not pray so as to teach, yet our prayers, by their terms and structures, teach anyway. Minds are shaped by the way reality is named in the Church's prayers. Regrettably, Forms I-VI in The Book of Common Prayer, by their inclusions and omissions, suggest that a prayer is complete and adequate that defines "the Universal Church" by the Episcopal Church, our diocese, and our own congregation—a terribly truncated ecclesiology.

Rather similarly, when the prayers turn to *the political order,* the general rubric bids prayer for "the Nation and all in authority." Yet while one of the forms speaks of the president and some of them mention the leaders of the nations, there is no mention of legislatures or of courts and no inclusion of state or local authorities. The prayer book seems to need an elementary civics lesson. Moreover, there is no recognition of instrumentalities that unite nations in common effort for peace, human rights, environmental responsibility, or the relief of refugees or the poor and the hungry. Virtually no attention is given to the powerful non-governmental forces such as education, the arts, communication or finance that shape the common life—and shape it badly as often as they shape it well.

With regard to prayer for "the local community" and for "those who suffer and those in any trouble," one could ask concerning the prayer book forms: "Do our eucharistic intercessions give voice to the misery (often the hidden misery) that pastors know to exist in our towns or cities or the quiet desperation that pervades our congregations?"

One can easily make a list of urgent concerns too large to be mentioned on any Sunday—or on a year of Sundays. But the priestly task of the Church asks us to articulate a human reality that bursts beyond the pallid phrases of our prayer book forms. Some time ago, Krister Stendahl counseled preachers before they planned a sermon to ask first not what they want to preach about but what they might suppose to be "God's agenda." The advice applies to the preparation of intercessions. Before we pray, we seek to look at ourselves and our world in the mind of Christ, a standard more just and more merciful than we can imagine. We ask "What really matters?" When we have asked that question, and not before, we are ready to "pray for the Church and for the world." In view of the large and urgent needs of the Church and the world, Forms I-VI, used as they stand, seem woefully confining.

With such dissatisfactions in mind, and thinking towards liturgical revision, *what shall be done?*

(1) Provide better forms and more resources: This critique of the forms in the 1979 prayer book would suggest that our intercessions need more comprehensive and specific content and a more

urgent, even passionate tone. Yet any new prayers should hold to about the length of the present forms, for they are only one part of a complex liturgical event. The Standing Liturgical Commission could ask a committee to consider appreciatively and critically the forms for the Prayers of the People in the 1979 prayer book (which are probably better than we had any reason to expect) and to seek to enlarge and enrich them—providing stronger wordings, more choices, more back-up resources and more guidance for congregations in using this material.

(Persons using enriched official prayers could be encouraged to make use of the work of the writers and anthologists who have offered models for good corporate intercessions. A few such resources are mentioned at the end of this essay.)

But are better texts what we really need? No doubt leaders will often find an idea, a phrase, or even an entire prayer in a published text to be of real value. But model prayers, prepared long in advance—whether by a single author or by an official group—inevitably have a considerable measure of sameness; they lack the closeness to event and circumstance and the engagement with current social and political crisis that the people's prayers should express. Moreover, if one is urging congregations to handle the people's prayers more independently and to draw on their current experience, will not the availability of printed texts tend to shut off creativity? For the Episcopal Church or for private publishers to provide larger texts with more choices for the people's prayers would very likely heighten rather than reduce the Church's dependence on the printed page.

The Church is too varied and history moves too rapidly for anyone to be able to draft prayers that speak circumstantially of the Church and the world and that can be found fully applicable throughout a large diversified Church over a span of years. The "Prayers of the People" should have a particularity, a here-ness and now-ness that no wording prepared outside the congregation can really provide. While it is desirable that many parts of the liturgy have an objective, traditioned and universal character, is not an authorized printed text really incompatible with the function of the people's prayers?

(2) Provide no developed form of intercession: A radically different direction might be taken. Rather than offering better authorized forms of intercession, might this be the time for the Episcopal Church to break with its past and, in any revised prayer book, include no printed text nor even a choice of texts for "The Prayers of the People"? (No doubt "The Great Litany," "The Litany for Ordinations," and other prayers for special functions should continue to be used in full text. They are carefully worded, participatory and suit their purposes admirably.)

This is the direction that has been taken in the revised service books of the Roman Catholics and the Lutherans (our nearest relatives in matters of worship), neither of which prints a text for the prayers of the people:

- The Roman *Sacramentary*, in a General Instruction, gives a sequence of intentions and a few minimal directions but no prayer text. The practice in Roman congregations varies from free intercessions by members of the congregation to fully prepared biddings and prayers by a leader. A variety of printed helps are used, some of them considerably better than others.

- The *Lutheran Book of Worship* provides no prayer text. It does give some rubrical directions about "The Prayers," and the *Manual on the Liturgy* gives generous and helpful counsel on the function, character and style of the prayers. This *Manual* says:

  > Since the formulation of the prayers is not specified, they must be prepared for each service. Persons involved in the local situation are best able to balance properly the universal scope proper to Christian concerns with the specific petitions of a given congregation. The preparation of the prayers

> is no less important than the preparation of the ser-
> mon.
>
> (This last comment seems particularly striking coming from a
> Lutheran source.)

Clearly, in the matter of liturgical intercession, the Episcopal Church is now more prescriptive than either of these traditions, neither of which provides eleven pages of forms for intercession followed by two pages of concluding collects. Episcopalians are indisputably a "people of the book."

Yet before we decide to drop an authorized text for the intercessions we should note that the experience of both the Roman Catholics and the Lutherans is quite mixed. Clearly, both of these churches felt that authority for the people's prayers should be locally exercised, and in some congregations intercessions are in fact shaped and led expertly week after week. The people's prayers may be quite informal in some congregations or fairly controlled in others, and in either style they can be done well. However, in many congregations of both these churches intercessors look somewhat desperately for printed texts, often accepting those from a church publisher, which they read rather perfunctorily. Such intercessory prayers speak neither in the voice of the general Church nor in the voice of the local community, but in the voice of a staff writer in an editorial office. Both Lutherans and Roman Catholics express considerable dissatisfaction with their present practice, and in both there is hunger for reliable printed texts that intercessors can pick up and use. Some members of those churches look enviously at the prayer book's six forms and their steady competence.

While there is a great deal to be said for dropping an authorized text for the Prayers of the People, the proposal should be met with caution. Such an act might do little more than exchange one set of problems for another.

(3) Education for intercessors: Perhaps the choice should not be presented as one between a fuller and better text or no printed text. Episcopalians characteristically fasten on what should or should

not be in the prayer book. But intercessions can be either good or bad whether they come from an authorized text or are freely prepared. The crucial factor may not be the liturgical text but the competence and discrimination of the intercessors.

It would be a fair guess that most intercessors have taken on their task with little prior understanding of it and little coaching once they had begun. Many of them must feel that they were coaxed into a public role in which there was little modeling and for which they had no special qualifications. Yet persons in this "minor order" have done the best they can with the job as they understand it. The official text in the prayer book has given them their legitimation and their protection. Any change in the provisions of the liturgy would change the task of the intercessors, requiring them to learn new habits and to acquire internalized criteria so that on their own they can avoid ill-composed or preachy prayers.

Whatever is done about the prayer book text, responsibility for the people's prayers must be locally exercised. Dedicated people in each congregation must be prepared to carry out an important, complex, but rewarding liturgical task. Although general guidance or modeling can be offered, each prayer of intercession arises from a particular people in a place and time, expressing the uniqueness of its life, its configuration of experience, its insights and limitations, its passions, discoveries and disappointments, its commitments and its betrayal of its commitments. Each prayer seeks to give voice to a moment, to an angle of vision and at times to a cry. Each prayer will necessarily have an element of venture and incompleteness.

The Church cannot, in fairness, redefine the intercessor's task without taking account of the inward reorientation that such change would require. If intercessors are to be confident in a freer, more responsible role, they must be supported. *The purpose of this paper is to propose that a church-wide program of training be undertaken for leaders of intercession* (perhaps somewhat like the programs that some dioceses have developed for lay readers). If this were done, publications (by authors who have not yet been identified) would have to be issued. Regional and local workshops would have to be organized and staffed to guide intercessors into a more confident discharge of their role. (Leaders of these workshops might be lay persons as well as clergy. Few clergy have had much experience or guidance in framing eucharistic intercessions. Is any other task of comparable importance given so little attention in clergy training?) Since what is sought is change in understanding and behavior, modeling and coaching may be more important than printed material. It would be more a task of education and formation (which we may not be very good at) than a task of revising printed texts (which we seem to do pretty well).

Five Emphases

I envision a program of education for intercessors with five emphases, which are separable for analysis, but are interrelated.

(a) The intercessors themselves: The task of the intercessor, before it is a practical assignment, is a spiritual, pastoral task. The leader of the people's prayers is asked to articulate the common life wisely and sensitively and hold it before God. Here is where the challenge of the task is greatest and where intercessors' misgivings about themselves may be most acute and help most needed. Distributive responsibility for the Church's intercessions implies finding in each congregation persons with the gift for shaping corporate intercessory prayer. This gift is doubtless more widespread in the community of faith than previous experience would have given anyone any way of knowing. Many persons who could do this task very well do not know that they could do it.

But giftedness is only a starting place. While some people may carry out this task well from the start, most will welcome some guidance as to what is intended, some opportunity to gain confidence, some criteria, some room in which to make early mistakes and some encouragement and friendly criticism. Experience indicates that some parts of the intercessor's task can be done collaboratively. The task is modest—not one for virtuosos, but for persons who can be self-critical and can submit their work to the judgment of others. Lacking structures of support, to launch a large number of people in this new or redefined ministry would be like expecting persons to preach well Sunday by Sunday with no prior training, no modeling and nothing to interpret for them what it is they are doing.

(b) The theology of intercession: An educational effort should provide intercessors with an understanding of the ministry of prayer in which they are engaging—an understanding rooted in the Gospel and the Church.

Why we pray and why we pray for others is wrapped in the mystery of the bonds that link us with God and with one another. Intercessory prayer has deep roots. The Jewish scriptures depict passionate intercessors (Abraham, Genesis 18:16-33, 19:29; Moses, Exodus 32:11-14). We have the model of the synagogue benedictions, the example and teaching both of Jesus (Luke 6:28, 22:32, 23:34) and of Paul and his tradition (Romans 15:30; Ephesians 6:18; Philippians 1:4,19; 2 Thessalonians 3:1), and the practice of the early Christians (1 Timothy 2:1f; 1 Clement, 59-61, and Justin Martyr, *Apology,* 65 and 76). Prayer gives expression to the bonds that link Christians to one another in Christ. But more fundamentally, Christian intercession rests on the conviction expressed in the New Testament that the living Christ intercedes for the Church (Romans 8:34; 1 John 2:1). The book of Hebrews sets Christ's work as heavenly high priest in the context of the Day of Atonement, finding it significant that the high priest entered the Holy Place bearing the names of all the tribes of Israel (Exodus 28:1-4, 9-10, 29f). The high priest was a representative, an intercessor, carrying the people before God. Intercession is our responsible and joyful participation in a ministry that belongs first of all to the living Christ, but is shared by him with his priestly people.

Any prayer that we speak with urgency arises from a persuasion that God, as made known in Jesus Christ, is not indifferent. When we pray for strength and wisdom, for peace and not conflict, for justice and not oppression, health instead of sickness, or life where there is death or the threat of death, our prayer accords with the will of God. Yet in prayer we must be honest, not facile. Our peace, justice, health and life come out of struggle; they are scarred, fragile and impermanent. Our prayer is authenticated by our commitments; indeed, our prayer is itself a part of our continual sharing in the struggle. When peace, health, justice, strength and life are granted, we give thanks; when they are not granted or are granted only partially, we register our pain and bafflement, asking God to teach us to utilize our pain and confusion for redemptive purposes. And then we go on praying, convinced that with all of our ability to get things wrong, we care, and in praying we give words to our care. Greatly daring, we are persuaded that our caring is no more than a faint echo of God's caring.

(c) The agenda for intercession: Intercessory prayer arises from two sources: (i) the scriptures and the liturgy, and (ii) the current life of the praying community. Leaders should be helped to draw on both.

(i) In the unfolding order of the eucharist, our prayer for the Church and the world follows our fresh encounter with the Gospel in scripture and preaching. In the days before the liturgical event, the intercessor, like the preacher, lives with the appointed scriptures, seeking first not to relate them to known needs but to hear them on their own. We do not rightly identify our profoundest needs until we encounter the biblical message. But soon one who is thinking about public prayer will ask what these scriptures say to us and our situation. The intercessor seeks to turn the biblical material into petition and thanksgiving so that the Word of God informs our response to the Word of God. Just how and how much the biblical material will influence any prayer of intercession will vary. Sometimes it will energize the intercessor's imagination and provide an organizing theme for the people's prayers, while at other times it may give only an introductory line or an image. Didacticism is to be avoided; the intercessions are not to be a reprise of the readings and the sermon.

(ii) The intercessions also take their material from world events and from local circumstance—asking where God may be acting in all of this bewildering mix and not always having good answers. Intercessors gather their material from the soul of a community of Christians—listening to it, observing it, being part of its inner life and struggle, seeking to discover and speak the secrets of the hearts of their fellow believers. People's lives are shaped and their inner resources are sorely tested by our confused and fragmented world. Prayer which seeks to bring our life before God will, if it is honest, carry marks of the drabness, the horror and trauma of the twentieth century, even as it claims roots in a Good News that is greater than that trauma.

The people's prayers grow from a trust in God who is before all things, in all things and beyond all things. Yet at the same time these prayers express the inner and outer life of this people in this time and this place. Hence, one Sunday's intercessions should no more be like the previous Sunday's than this week's sermon should be a repetition of last week's. We name our names and cite our circumstances.

(Congregations which hold a daily eucharist will very likely fall, in intercessions as in much else, into quite a lot of routinization. One cannot be original and creative every day. A more or less patterned prayer would suit each day's intercessions well. However, the Sunday eucharist which gathers up the week's experience of a heterogeneous congregation requires something more considered.)

The intercessor must not impose his or her own agenda. Many persons who accept this liturgical task will be people of conviction who will know, at least in a general way, that political, social and ecological issues are at root theological issues with moral implications.

Yet as intercessors they do not take sides on matters in which conscientious, informed Christians differ, nor do they adopt a moralistic stance—especially avoiding any stance that would cast the congregation in the wrong. An intercessor who promotes favored interests subverts the role, which requires a representative voice—not informing either God or one's fellow Christians, nor exhorting, nor riding hobbies.

Yet our prayers can legitimately be ahead of us. Prayers that take account of the ecumenical world, of social justice or of mission ordinarily arise from a congregation that is committed to ecumenicity, social justice and mission. Yet since our prayers grow from the Gospel, they can call us from complacency. They should be like us; yet at the same time they may be better than we are, asking us to become like our prayers.

An attentive intercessor knows that needs fill the church every Sunday. Each week brings impacting events—some of them distant but known and felt, and some close at hand and occasionally virtually traumatic. However, the pressing matters may not be so much specific events as the pervasive anxiety, indeed the near-despair of our time. The room which holds the congregation can seem thick with the burdenedness of the people. Any intercessory prayer that does not, in a way appropriate to itself, bring that weight of current experience to articulateness before God fails the community of faith.

(d) Diction, writing, and style: The preparation of the Prayers of the People is a verbal—usually a writing—task, asking intercessors to acquire some rhetorical skills.

There is a basic question of form. Does the intercessor, in the name of the people, address God? Or does the intercessor bid the prayer of the congregation? The latter is generally preferred. It has a deep history, it keeps the prayer clearly the people's act, and it is the style of most of the forms in the prayer book.

The day's scriptures and this week's events must be woven into a well-formed intercession—a task requiring focus, structure and sequence. At times the lessons and the occasion will virtually hand the intercessor a unifying theme which then needs to be opened into a series of related petitions. On other occasions one may begin with a handful of separate ideas which need to be grouped, put in intelligible sequence, and given unity.

Some things that take place in a congregation can be spoken of publicly in the prayer of the faithful, but some represent confidences that if they are mentioned must be mentioned indirectly. Intercessors must be sensitive to their public role. Even when a written or printed text is used, the liturgical intercessions are an act of oral communication. Even though the leader may commonly hold a prepared prompt-sheet, the prayer is *spoken* and *heard*. The leader is seeking to bring the voice of the congregation before God—a role that both enables and restrains the speaker. It should be simple to set down one's own thoughts on a page and speak them. But most of us do not fully know what we think, and when we try to put our thoughts in words, we become artificial and affected. Moreover, we do not write as we speak. Can we listen to our words as we write? Can we let our phrases breathe and fall naturally? There seem to be no rules in this matter. Speech patterns are quite individual. What is authentic in tone and clear in wording when one persons speaks it can sound contrived and awkward when another person says much the same thing.

As to involving the congregation, when a printed text is in everyone's hand, the people can follow the leader's lines and know when to enter and what to say; their response can change throughout the prayer, advancing the thought of each petition or marking the changing character of sections of a long intercession. But in a prayer that is not printed and held by everyone, the congregation must *hear* its cues, and its response must be announced in advance, be easily remembered and remain constant throughout the prayer.

Intercessions should be terse. Things should be named, not explained. The prayer should exhibit economy, taking its proportionate place in the total liturgical event. Many things that might fittingly be prayed for must be left out. It is better to be restrained, and perhaps a little dull, than to risk overstatement, sentimentality or false dramatics by saying too much. Our spoken intercessions must select and focus, trusting that through the suggestion of our words people pray more than we say.

Our prayer will implicitly interpret our shared experience, and experience is interpreted by general terms, perhaps somewhat abstract. Yet we live in a world of particulars. In naming our experience before God can we be specific without being too graphic or giving lists? And can we order our experience into significant aggregates without seeming to philosophize or moralize?

(e) Practical considerations: In order to lead the people's prayers in a relaxed and confident way, one must be secure about such practical matters as: Where should the leader stand in order to symbolize her/his role and to be heard? Should (must) he/she use a microphone? What about pace? Most of us speak too rapidly, especially in public. How can one coach people in their use of silences after petitions? Is it practicable in this space to invite free petitions from the congregation? How can an intercessor be informed about current pastoral needs in the congregation?

One should not wait until all of these skills and understandings are acquired before one begins to lead intercessions. None of them is ever in hand to one's satisfaction. One begins as an intercessor because one finds the task to be a call to which one brings some gifts. Then having begun, one goes on learning.

Conclusion

A program of education and formation such as has been sketched here is not itself a proposal for prayer book change—although it might correlate with a determination either to improve or to delete a printed text of the Prayers of the People. Yet the presence in the

Church of a group of competent intercessors is something on which the vitality and believability of one act of the prayer book liturgy depends.

For the Episcopal Church (led by the Standing Liturgical Commission) to initiate such a program would no doubt be complex, demanding and perhaps expensive. Yet it might be thought a piece of unfinished business, inasmuch as it would be addressing one of the most obvious deficiencies in the program of education and publication which in the 1960s and 1970s gave the Episcopal Church its present prayer book. And one may ask: should the Church give to anything higher priority than it gives to its prayers?

For Reading

The amount of published material on liturgical intercessions is not large. Has any other feature of the prayer book of comparable importance been given less attention by liturgists and had less written about it? But some resources are in hand, and to a great extent they agree as to what is desirable and where the problems lie.

Discussions of the intercessions:

Robert Hovda, "The Amen Corner: Real and Worshipful General Intercession," *Worship* 60 (1986): 527-34. Critical and constructive ideas.

_____, "The Prayer of General Intercession," *Worship* 44 (1970): 497-502. A short, wise pioneering article.

Walter C. Huffman, *Prayer of the Faithful: Understanding and Creatively Leading Corporate Intercessory Prayer*, revised ed., Minneapolis: Augsburg Fortress, 1992. About two-thirds of this small book from the Lutheran tradition is a thoughtful explanation of liturgical intercession, and one-third contains suggested texts.

David E. Johnson, *The Prayers of the People: Ways to Make Them*

Your Own, Forward Movement, 1988. A small book about intercessions and the prayer book forms and ways of adapting them; it contains some model texts.

John Melloh, "The General Intercession Revisited," *Worship* 61 (1987): 152-62. A basic article which contains analysis and theoretical and practical counsel. Roman Catholic, but ecumenically accessible.

Kenneth Stevenson, "'Ye shall pray for...': The Intercession," in Kenneth Stevenson, ed., *Liturgy Reshaped* (London: S.P.C.K., 1982), pp. 32-47. A good general chapter.

Daniel B. Stevick, *The Crafting of Liturgy* (New York: Church Hymnal Corporation, 1990), chapter 3, "The Prayers of the People," pp. 119-57. Thirty-five pages introducing the ministry of intercession, giving some historical material, and offering comment on the prayer book forms and on style and techniques for framing and wording corporate intercession.

Michael Vasey, *Intercessions in Worship*, Bramcote, Nottingham: Grove Books, 1981. A wise, informative booklet from England, keyed to the *Alternative Service Book* but generally helpful in the U. S.

E. C. Whitaker, "The Intercessions," in R. C. D. Jasper, ed., *The Eucharist Today* (London: S.P.C.K., 1974), pp. 54-65. An informed English essay, giving special attention to the place that the intercessions take in the eucharistic action.

E. C. Whitaker, *The Intercessions of the Prayer Book*, London: S.P.C.K., 1956. An English booklet, predating the *Alternative Service Book*; deals with the prayers in the Daily Office, the Litany and the Prayer for the Whole State of Christ's Church.

Joyce A. Zimmerman, "The General Intercessions: Yet Another Visit," *Worship* 65 (1991): 306-19. An article giving informed counsel on the sort of language and the level of specificity suitable for public intercessions.

Compilations of prayers:

John Carden, ed., *With All God's People*, World Council of
Churches, 1990. A 52-week ecumenical prayer cycle.

Jay Cormier, *Lord, Hear Our Prayer: Prayer of the Faithful for
Sundays, Holy Days, and Ritual Masses*, Collegeville, MN:
Liturgical Press, 1995. A sizable, attractively-printed work
which follows the three-year cycle of the Roman lectionary
(similar to but not identical with the prayer book Sunday lectionary); each Sunday's prayer echoes phrases and ideas in the
lectionary readings; each contains a place for introducing local
concerns, an opening for silent prayer, and a concluding
prayer. The tone and content of the prayers is quite pastoral.

Ormonde Plater, *Intercession: A Theological and Practical Guide*,
Cambridge, MA: Cowley Publications, 1995. This book introduces the ministry of intercession and gives some historical
information. It is one of the best books in a somewhat limited
literature, and congregations should find it a useful resource.
Yet it seems to me to have real limitations. Its many model
prayers for liturgical and pastoral occasions are heavily drawn
from early Christian sources. Even though such material gives
a sense of tradition, it seems rather remote. The pages on
process and language, toward the end of the book, do not, in
my opinion, give the help they might. The model texts that are
provided strike me as too churchy, showing little concern for
social justice, little sense of a world in crisis, and even too little
room in which to develop the needs of the close-at-hand community.

Prayers of the Faithful, Collegeville, MN: Pueblo, 1977. Prayers by
several contemporary writers, suggested by the three-year lectionary readings and suited to twentieth-century life. The
readings may not always be those in the BCP. Although this
collection is now a little old, its prayers seem to find the right
tone, conciseness, specificity and verbal energy; they provide
suggestions and idea-starters.

Gail Ramshaw, ed., *Intercessions for the Christian People*, Collegeville, MN: Pueblo, 1988. This collection, successor to the above work, contains prayers at a generally high level, by an ecumenical group of authors, for the Sundays and major feasts, turning the three-year cycle of liturgical readings into prayer. An admirable work.

Jeffrey W. Rowthorn, ed., *The Wideness of God's Mercy: Litanies to Enlarge Our Prayer*, Harrisburg, PA, Morehouse, 1995. A generous gathering of prayers from many sources which attend to a large agenda; all are adapted for congregational use.

The Structure of the Eucharistic Prayer

Thomas J. Talley

O ver the past decade and a half we have learned again, as we did in the years following 1928, that the revision of The Book of Common Prayer amounts to little less than a serious trauma at the very heart of the Church's life. Liturgical revision is a grave matter, deeply disturbing to the praying assembly's sense of continuity, and a thing to be undertaken only in fear and trembling, and only when it is clear that the forces that demand it are truly irresistible. Nonetheless, we have now had sufficient experience of the 1979 book to begin to recognize its brilliant successes and to take note of some matters that might be open to improvement if the coming century should see the need for a further revision. It will be the concern of this present chapter to examine those matters in the limited area of the structure of the eucharistic prayer, that which in this prayer book has recovered the designation, "The Great Thanksgiving." Until the present Book of Common Prayer, most Episcopalians and other Anglicans had been accustomed to but one, relatively invariable text of the eucharistic prayer or, as we more commonly referred to it, "the Prayer of Consecration," although that text might vary considerably from one national church to another.

Variation and Continuity in the Eucharistic Prayer

Surely, one of the major departures of the 1979 prayer book from its predecessors is that to the eucharistic prayer we have had since

1789 have been added five other complete prayers and two forms that allow the insertion of extempore passages. Such proliferation of eucharistic prayers, of course, has not been a peculiarity of the new Book of Common Prayer. In Roman Catholic discussions following the Second Vatican Council it became clear rather early that no single revision of the old Roman Canon would meet the varied demands for reform. In 1966, following a meeting of Cardinal Lercaro with Pope Paul VI in late June, work began that would issue in the inclusion of three new eucharistic prayers in the Roman *Sacramentary*, in addition to the Roman Canon, retained as Eucharistic Prayer I. That seemed to open the floodgates, and the years since have seen in most western churches a proliferation of new eucharistic prayers unparalleled since the fifth century. A critical appreciation of the new eucharistic prayers requires careful study of that earlier period of development, and consideration of the factors that produced the classical prayers that have remained in use (albeit with some further development) to our own day, although joined by alternatives in this recent round of new compositions.

Although the use of multiple eucharistic prayers had been a phenomenon that we in the West associated especially with eastern churches or the vanished liturgies of Gaul,[1] it was a somewhat reduced understanding of the eucharistic prayer's shape that closed our eyes to the fact that we had always had a variable thanksgiving. This was called the "preface," and it was common to think of that as a sort of prelude or foreword to the actual "prayer of consecration" that followed the *sanctus*. That more fixed prayer, which Roman Catholics and many Anglicans referred to as the *canon*, began in the Latin rite with the words *Te igitur*, and the medieval custom of illuminating capital letters often treated the "T" of the opening word as the basis for an image of the crucifixion. This image grew until it occupied the entire left-hand page of the altar book, the text continuing only on the facing page. This had the effect of interposing a barrier between the *sanctus* and the prayer, with the result that the seasonally variable preface seemed oriented only to the *sanctus*, not an integral part of the prayer. Still in the prayer book of 1928, it is after the *sanctus* that we read the rubric: "When the Priest, standing before the Holy Table, hath so ordered the Bread and Wine, that he may with the more readiness and decency break the Bread before the People, and take the Cup into his hands, he shall say the Prayer of Consecration, as followeth" (BCP, 1928, p. 80). This misunderstanding was encouraged by the fact that since the sixteenth century and until fairly recent times there had not been many of those "proper prefaces." There are a great many more of them now, and very early on in Latin liturgy there was such a variable thanksgiving at every eucharist.

That is the case in what is called the *Veronese Sacramentary* (once known as "the Leonine Sacramentary"). This seventh-century manuscript in the Chapter Library at Verona is the earliest extant collection of western prayers for use at the eucharistic liturgy and presents a series of variable prayers in groups, each group providing all the variable prayers for one service. One of those prayers in each group always begins with the words *Vere dignum*, "truly worthy." This is the proper preface, and there is one for each celebration. What is surprising is that most of them show no sign whatsoever of leading into the *sanctus*. The *sanctus* was added to the Latin rite only at some point in the fifth century, and many of the sets of prayers for the eucharist in this archival collection are older than that.

What this shows is that the preface and what came to be called the canon are both integral to the eucharistic prayer. By the late fourth century there was a fixed text of the prayer that began with intercession, proceeded to pray for the acceptance of our offering, and then passed into the account of our Lord's institution of the eucharist and a memorial oblation (the offering of our gifts as memorial of his sacrifice), further prayer for the acceptance of our offering, and a final doxology. All of this was supplicatory, that is, it was a request for God to act on our behalf. In that fixed prayer there was not a word of thanksgiving for what God has already done for us. That thanksgiving, the real meaning of *eucharist* and the heart of eucharistic prayer, preceded the fixed prayer and was still variable, continuing the tradition of extempore prayer by the bishop (although, in fact, these thanksgivings were usually written down by the late fourth century). These thanksgiving prefaces are almost always concerned with one or another aspect of what God has done for the people through the mediatory actions of Christ, and these along with the supplicatory prayers of the canon made up what we know as the eucharistic prayer. How the thanksgiving and supplication were connected can be seen in an orthodox preface cited in defense of his own theological expressions by an unknown Arian writer in northern Italy at the end of the fourth century:

> It is fitting and right, it is just and right, that we should give you thanks for all things, O Lord, holy Father, almighty eternal God, for you deigned in the incomparable splendor of your goodness that light should shine in darkness, by sending us Jesus Christ as savior of our souls. For our salvation he humbled himself and subjected himself even unto death that, when we had been restored to that immortality which Adam lost, he might make us heirs and sons to himself.
>
> Neither can we be sufficient to give thanks to you for your great generosity for this lovingkindness with any praises; but we ask (you) of your great and merciful goodness to hold accepted this sacrifice which we offer to you, standing before the face of your divine goodness, through Jesus Christ our Lord and God, through whom we pray and beseech...[2]

Several scholars, seeking to reconstruct the eucharistic prayer of that time, have supposed that this transition to supplication flowed directly into some such fixed supplicatory prayer as that quoted by Ambrose of Milan in the late fourth-century:

> Make for us this offering approved, reasonable, acceptable, because it is the figure of the body and blood of our Lord Jesus Christ; who, the day before he suffered, took bread in his holy hands, looked up to heaven to you, holy Father, almighty, eternal God, gave thanks, blessed, and handed it to his apostles and disciples, saying, "Take and eat from this, all of you; for this is my body, which will be broken for many."[3]

Since this narrative describes the institution of the eucharist by Christ, it seems curious to find it included within this fixed supplication to the Father, rather than in the opening thanksgiving that proclaims our Lord's acts for our salvation. That thanksgiving, however, was still variable and composed for each occasion by the bishop. Evidently, once it was determined that this charter narrative should have a place in the eucharistic prayer, it was deemed insufficient to leave it subject to the variable composition of the thanksgiving by the bishop, and it was set instead within the fixed supplicatory prayer that followed.

Eucharist without the Narrative?

That last statement can sound shocking, implying as it does that there was once a eucharistic prayer that did not include the narrative of the institution of the eucharist. Such, nonetheless, seems to be the case, however contrary to our expectations. A fragmentary Greek papyrus at Strasbourg was taken, in its original publication,[4] to be an early (300-500 A.D.) fragment of the Alexandrian Anaphora of St. Mark, previously known only through medieval manuscripts. Further study of this text over the past two decades, however, has yielded broad agreement that, in view of an evidently final doxology, this is in fact the text of a complete eucharistic prayer.[5] The Anaphora (i.e., eucharistic prayer) of St. Mark had long been recognized to have an unusual structure. A long invariable preface opened with praise of the Creator and oblation of the sacrifice of thanksgiving, then turned to extended intercessory supplication, all before reaching the introduction to the *sanctus*. In the Strasbourg papyrus there is a final doxology instead of the introduction to the *sanctus*, and it now appears that that introduction, *sanctus* itself, and all that follows, including the institution narrative, is a later appendage to the original nucleus. Further, the eucharistic prayer described by Cyril of Jerusalem in the fifth of his *Mystagogical Catecheses* makes no mention of the institution narrative, and recent studies have argued convincingly that, indeed, the narrative was not part of the eucharistic prayer at Jerusalem at the time Cyril delivered those lectures to the newly baptized in the late fourth century.[6]

That these do not represent the excision of the institution narrative from a prayer that had once included it,[7] but are indeed conservative of an older tradition, is suggested by chapter IX of *Didache*, a catechetical and liturgical manual now commonly dated to the closing years of the first century. There, short thanksgivings over the cup and the broken bread lead into a supplication for the gathering of the Church. That structure of thanksgiving and supplication, familiar to us in the broad tradition of eucharistic prayer, replicates a similar pattern in prayers after communion in chapter X. These three short prayers, in turn, seem to many to represent a revision of a common Jewish grace after meals.

We really have little precise knowledge of Jewish prayer in the first century of our era, because for early Judaism prayer was an oral tradition, not committed to writing; but that such a meal grace was current then is secured by the fact that a version of it was placed on the lips of Abraham by the author of *Jubilees* (xxii:5-9). *Jubilees* is a retelling of Genesis written late in the second century B.C., but the prayer put on the lips of Abraham there shows the same pattern as the Grace after Meals (*Birkat Ha-Mazon*) as we encounter it in the earliest full Jewish prayer book preserved to us,

Seder Rab Amram Gaon, compiled in the ninth century of our era, about a millennium later. That pattern consists of three paragraphs: first, a benediction of God as creator and provider of food for all humanity; second, a thanksgiving for God's saving intervention on behalf of the covenant people; third, a supplication for the future of Israel.

Such a grace after eating may well have been prayed by Christians at ordinary meals, but we could not recover the text if that were the case. What we encounter in *Didache*, in any case, is not an ordinary meal, but eucharist, and there food and drink themselves have become a part of the economy of salvation, like the covenant and the law that are mentioned in the thanksgiving in later texts of the Jewish prayers. The initial benediction of God as provider of food to all is omitted, and the prayers after communion begin with a thanksgiving "for your holy Name which you have enshrined in our hearts, and for the knowledge and faith and immortality which you made known to us through your child Jesus." A second paragraph of thanksgiving says:

> You, almighty Master, created all things for the sake of your Name, and gave food and drink to mankind [sic] for their enjoyment, that they might give you thanks; but to us you have granted spiritual food and drink and eternal life through your child Jesus. Above all we give you thanks because you are mighty.[8]

This is followed by a supplication for the gathering of the Church, like the final section of chapter IX.

In none of what is said of the eucharist in chapters IX and X is there any reference to its institution by Jesus. The earliest account of the institution remains that of St. Paul in 1 Corinthians 11, written from Ephesus around 55 A.D. There, too, nonetheless, Paul recounts that our Lord broke the bread "when he had given thanks." The accounts of the last supper in Mark and Matthew say, instead, that he "blessed" before breaking the bread. This is but a beginning of the continuing variation in the text of this narrative, which suggests that it continued to be treated as oral tradition not only before it was incorporated into written Gospels, but even later as it began to find its way into eucharistic prayers. It has been suggested that before its inclusion in the eucharistic prayer, the narrative was recited just prior to the distribution of communion, and that would be consistent with descriptions of the supper in the Gospels. There is nothing in *Didache* IX and X to suggest that, however, and we probably should not discount the possibility that the narrative was sometimes transmitted before the table rite, as an interpretative word of Christ in a germinal liturgy of the Word.

The Evolution of the Eucharistic Prayer in Greek Tradition

The earliest textual evidence for a eucharistic prayer that includes the institution narrative is found in a work known as *Apostolic Tradition*, generally dated in the second decade of the third century. Although commonly ascribed to the Roman theologian Hippolytus, both authorship and title remain disputed, as does the local church (if any is intended) whose liturgy it describes. Originally written in Greek, this reconstructed church order is known now chiefly from a Latin translation whose occasional lacunae are most commonly supplied from versions in Ethiopic or the Sahidic dialect of Coptic. Little of the original Greek can be recovered securely.

There, nonetheless, in the context of the rite for the ordination of a bishop,[9] we are given the text used by the new bishop at the following celebration of eucharist. At a later point, *Apostolic Tradition* notes that the texts of such prayers are given as models only, and it is not expected that they will be committed to memory. No thought was given, evidently, to reading them from a book or other prepared text, but that passage shows that the composition of such prayers by the bishop was still active.

The pattern commended by *Apostolic Tradition* begins with the familiar dialogue: the salutation, *sursum corda* ("lift up your hearts") and response, and the invitation to give thanks, with the response, "It is right and just." The prayer then begins with a thanksgiving for the coming of Christ, the Word through whom all was created, into the womb of the virgin, and continues through references to his voluntary suffering, "that he might release from suffering those who have believed in you." This leads into the account of his institution of the eucharist, the text not taken strictly from any New Testament source, but basically conflating the accounts of Paul and Matthew. In this context, it is clear that this is the climax of a recitation of the history of our Lord's saving work. Thanks is offered for what he did, and only then does the prayer turn to the present act of worship in the Church. In response to the command to "make my remembrance," the bishop prays: "Remembering therefore his death and resurrection, we offer to you the bread and the cup, giving you thanks because you have held us worthy to stand before you and minister to you." Such a sentence, combining the themes of remembering, offering and thanksgiving, appears attached to the institution narrative in all the classic liturgies before the Reformation (although the Roman omits thanksgiving, for reasons we shall examine shortly). This sentence, the carrying out of the command to repeat, is often referred to as the *anamnesis*, the Greek word we render "remembrance." Louis Ligier has argued that the institution narrative and this *anamnesis* or memorial oblation entered the tradition of the eucharistic prayer as a unit. Given the unanimity of the evidence, that seems likely. We find no instance of the institution narrative without the immediately connected memorial oblation until we get to the sixteenth-century reforms.

It is this memorial oblation, in any case, that brings to a conclusion the thanksgiving in the prayer of *Apostolic Tradition*, and the prayer then turns to supplication. We noted above that the supplication that followed the thanksgiving in the Jewish grace after meals prayed for the future of Israel, and that the supplications following the thanksgivings in *Didache* IX and X prayed for the gathering of the Church. The concern of the supplication here is again focused on the gathering of the Church, but by the time of *Apostolic Tradition* theological development had more firmly associated the Holy Spirit with the doctrine of the Church. It is not surprising, then, that this supplication for the Church includes an invocation of the Holy Spirit:

> And we ask that you would send your Holy Spirit upon the offering of your holy Church; that, gathering her into one, you would grant to all who receive the holy things (to receive) for the fullness of the Holy Spirit for the strengthening of faith in truth; that we may praise and glorify you through your child Jesus Christ....[10]

As the parenthesis demonstrates, this invocation has proved highly resistant to intelligible translation, and it remains unclear on whom or what the Spirit is invoked. That ambiguity, however, is probably fed by later theological development, posing questions that were not under consideration at the time the prayer was written. What does seem clear is that this invocation does not have in very focused view the transformation of the bread and wine into the body and blood of the Lord, as would be the case two centuries later when we find a prayer that follows the structure of that in *Apostolic Tradition* precisely, but in which this invocation of the Spirit is explicitly consecratory. By the time of that prayer, attributed to Epiphanius, Bishop of Salamis,[11] the consecration of the eucharistic gifts was a prominent theological issue, and the invocation or *epiclesis* (to use the Greek equivalent) prays that the bread may become the body of Christ and the contents of the cup the blood of Christ. It is important, however, that we not suppose that the *epiclesis* emerges as an independent element of eucharistic prayer structure. In its beginnings, it is simply the significantly older supplication for the community, which begins to reflect the theology of the Holy Spirit as does the doctrine of the Church. It cannot be dissociated from that supplicatory environment.

Like the prayer in *Apostolic Tradition*, this prayer of Epiphanius begins immediately with a thanksgiving for the coming of Christ and his saving work, including the institution of the eucharist. Other prayers in Greek, however, begin (after the initial dialogue) with a long praise of the Father as Creator which ends with the *sanctus*, before turning to this thanksgiving for Christ and the supplication for the Spirit. One of these, commonly taken to be of Cappadocian origin and perhaps as old as the end of the third century, came to be associated with the name of Basil, eventually Bishop of Caesarea in Cappadocia.[12] Through him (before he became a bishop) or some other source, this prayer found a new home in Egypt, eventually displacing the old Anaphora of St. Mark, and it remains today the normal liturgy of the Coptic Church. Basil himself would, as Bishop of Caesarea, rework this shorter version to produce the much longer Anaphora of St. Basil still celebrated in Lent in the Orthodox churches. It is the shorter "Egyptian" text, however, that formed the basis for the text drafted by an ecumenical committee, *A Common Eucharistic Prayer*, which forms Prayer D in Rite II of our prayer book.

This would be the structure—dialogue, praise of the Creator and *sanctus*, thanksgiving for redemption (with institution narrative and memorial oblation), and invocation of the Holy Spirit upon the gifts and on the community—that would spread to virtually all the churches of the eastern empire. Often known as "Antiochene," and perhaps native to that ancient see, it became the pattern of eucharistic prayer throughout Greek-speaking Christianity, was found also in Syriac and Armenian prayers, and passed with the Byzantine liturgy into Georgian and Slavonic and the other languages that adopted the liturgical tradition of Constantinople. Whether by design or through more unconscious liturgical evolution, the concern of its major sections with the Creator, the Redeemer and the Sanctifier makes this eucharistic prayer structure a reflection of the same concerns in baptismal creeds. Much modern commentary has focused on the role of the eucharistic prayer as proclamation of the faith before there was any text of the creed in the eucharistic liturgy. That would seem to encourage our retention, where possible, of a creedal pattern.

In the fully developed Greek eucharistic prayers of the fourth and fifth centuries this proclamation both praises the Creator and gives thanks for the redemptive work of Christ before turning to supplication for the outpouring of the Spirit. That turning point, the transition from proclamation to supplication, comes after the institution narrative and *anamnesis* (memorial oblation). It is the following supplication that includes the invocation (*epiclesis*) of the Holy Spirit for the consecration of the gifts. In other words, the remembrance of Christ's unique sacrifice and the offering of the gifts of bread and wine in thanksgiving for that sacrifice *leads into* the prayer for their consecration as his body and blood. Because this brings to present fulfillment what he instituted on the night of his betrayal, both that narrative of institution and the invocation of the Spirit for its realization have been treated by such Greek theologians as St. John Chrysostom as critical points in the eucharistic prayer.[13] Nonetheless, in the "syntax" of the prayer, if we may call it that, it is offering that leads to consecration and on to communion.

The Eucharistic Prayer in Latin Tradition

Both the eucharistic prayer and the theology that grew out of it developed differently in Latin tradition. While Roman liturgy was still in Greek, Latin tradition developed first in Africa and took root as well in northern Italy. Unfortunately, the literary remains of African liturgy and theology have left us no text of the eucharistic prayer. We have noticed earlier, however, two important items from northern Italy, an orthodox preface cited by an anonymous Arian (one of two fragments presented in a collection of texts by Cardinal Mai) and a short passage from *De Sacramentis* by Ambrose, Bishop of Milan. That this latter document comes from

Ambrose was once a matter of some doubt, but it is now generally recognized that it represents a transcript by a *notarius* of a series of instructions delivered by Ambrose to the newly baptized during Easter week, intended to lead the neophytes through the rites of initiation (which had not been explained to them before they experienced them) and to unfold their meaning.

It is in that connection, primarily in Book 4, speaking of their first communion, that Ambrose discusses the eucharist and quotes the eucharistic prayer. There he addresses the possibility that some will say that what they receive is but common bread, to which he replies:

> But that bread is bread before the words of the sacraments; when consecration has been applied, from (being) bread it becomes the flesh of Christ. So let us explain how that which is bread can be the body of Christ. And by what words and by whose sayings does consecration take place? The Lord Jesus'. For all the other things which are said in the earlier parts are said by the bishop: praise is offered to God; prayer is made for the people, for kings, for others; when the time comes for the venerated sacrament to be accomplished, the bishop no longer uses his own words, but uses the words of Christ. So the word of Christ accomplishes this sacrament.[14]

These foregoing words of the bishop evidently refer to those matters in which the text was not fixed. "Praise is offered to God" would refer to the variable thanksgiving preface, discussed earlier, while the prayers made for the people, for kings and for others could well correspond to the intercessions that are later encountered in the paragraph beginning *Te igitur* at the beginning of the canon, intercessions that would also vary from one liturgy to another. By contrast to these variable expressions by the bishop, Ambrose says, "when the time comes for the venerated sacrament to be accomplished, the bishop no longer uses his own words, but uses the words of Christ."

We noted above that St. John Chrysostom, Ambrose's contemporary, also laid great emphasis on the words of Christ in the institution narrative as determinative of our understanding of the eucharist, but he laid equally strong emphasis on the invocation of the Holy Spirit as effecting consecration. In the prayer quoted by Ambrose, however, there is no invocation of the Holy Spirit, and even the institution narrative appears as a relative clause explicating the statement that the offering is "the figure [*figura*] of the body and blood of our Lord Jesus Christ." It is difficult not to suspect that Ambrose's eucharistic theology, fully current with theological development in his time, is poorly supported by the older traditional liturgy of Milan. That suspicion is confirmed when we next encounter the text, considerably developed, as the *canon actionis* in the sixth century.[15] There, the supplication for the acceptance of the offering that precedes the institution narrative does not characterize the gifts as "the figure of the body and blood," but rather prays: "that they may become for us the body and blood of our Lord Jesus Christ." Because either form would set the following narrative and *anamnesis* in a supplicatory context, the memorial oblation, by contrast to Greek prayers, makes no mention of thanksgiving.

If the old prayer for the acceptance of the offering thus became a supplication for the consecration of the bread and wine, western theological development would nonetheless cling firmly to the view that it was the words of Christ in the following institution narrative that effected that consecration. That identification of the consecratory words would, for some, raise a question about what was offered to the Father in the following memorial oblation. We noted above that in Greek tradition it is that oblation that leads into the supplication for consecration (through invocation of the Spirit). Here, in the Latin prayer, the assignment of the consecration to the institution narrative would mean that the consecration leads into the oblation. Although there has been much concern about precisely when the consecration occurs, that is not the question we pose here. The question is whether the association of consecration with the institution narrative led to an interpretation of the following *anamnesis* as offering the body and blood of Christ to the Father. Nothing in the words of the *anamnesis* (i.e., the memorial oblation) suggests that what is offered is identified as the body and blood of Christ. The prayer speaks of the oblations as "a pure victim, a holy victim, an unspotted victim, the holy bread of eternal life and the cup of everlasting salvation." The earlier text cited from Ambrose in *De Sacramentis* spoke of "this spotless victim, reasonable victim, bloodless victim, this holy bread and this cup of eternal life."

The greatest of medieval western theologians, St. Thomas Aquinas, while not questioning the prevailing view that it is the words of Christ that effect consecration, still reiterated the view that oblation leads to consecration, not vice versa. After discussing the opening rites and the liturgy of the word, he wrote:

> So then, after the people have been prepared and instructed, the next step is to proceed to the celebration of the mystery, which is both offered as a sacrifice, and consecrated and received as a sacrament: since first we have the oblation; then the consecration of the matter offered; and thirdly its reception.[16]

By the oblation, in which the eucharist is "offered as a sacrifice," he means the chant sung as the elements are brought to the altar and the variable prayer recited over them prior to the beginning of the eucharistic prayer. Of the memorial oblation following the narrative, he says only that the priest "makes excuse for his presumption in obeying Christ's command," and ignores that prayer's explicit verb "we offer," *offerimus*.

His view may not have been held generally in his own time, but two centuries later, at least, it had been decisively eclipsed by the view that the words of Christ in the institution narrative have made his body and blood really present on the altar, and, therefore, it is Christ himself, present under the species of bread and wine, that is offered to the Father in the following memorial oblation. In that view, stated by such theologians as Gabriel Biel, the first professor of theology at the University of Tübingen,[17] the consecration is oriented toward that sacrificial act, not primarily toward communion. It was this sort of theology against which the Reformers revolted, unaware that it was a too exclusive emphasis on the effect of the words of institution that lay at the heart of the matter. Clinging to that same emphasis, Luther discarded the entire canon and included the institution narrative within a preface, concluded with the *sanctus*.[18]

That the Reformers did not misunderstand the eucharistic theology predicated upon the structure of the canon of the mass has become clear in our own day in Prayer IV of the new Roman missal. There what appears to be closely related to the Greek eucharistic prayers in fact distorts that structure by placing an invocation of the Holy Spirit for the consecration of the gifts *prior to* the institution narrative, and the memorial oblation that follows the narrative, in an expression that for the first time in liturgical history makes explicit the later medieval theology, prays: "Father, we now celebrate this memorial of our redemption. We recall Christ's death, his descent among the dead, his resurrection, and his ascension to your right hand; and, looking forward to his coming in glory, *we offer you his Body and Blood,* the acceptable sacrifice which brings salvation to the whole world" (emphasis added). If that expression is novel in liturgical prayer, it nonetheless reflects the theology of the fifteenth century that was rejected by the Reformers. What they did not reject, however, was the late medieval conviction that it is the words of institution that consecrate the sacrament.

Anglican Eucharistic Prayers

In the first (1549) Book of Common Prayer, Cranmer, probably influenced by Calvin, enriched the supplication for consecration before the institution narrative with an invocation of "thy Holy Spirit and word," and after the narrative he carefully removed from the *anamnesis* any reference to the offering of "these thy holy gifts." It is now widely recognized, however, that this was never intended to be more than a transitional rite, and in 1552 the prayer before the narrative was reoriented toward reception of communion rather than consecration, and the act of communion itself, coming immediately after the narrative, replaced the *anamnesis*. That novel stroke lost its point when Elizabeth I, in the prayer book of 1559, inserted an "Amen" at the conclusion of the institution narrative. With that, the act of communion was no longer integrated into the eucharistic prayer but followed it, as had been the tradition, although the eucharistic prayer it followed was a radically truncated one. Nonetheless, in spite of some changes in the Restoration prayer book of 1662, the structure of the prayer preceding communion in the English Book of Common Prayer remains virtually that given to it by Cranmer in 1552. Although it comes to an abrupt stop at the end of the institution narrative, that structure is still, to that point, basically the same structure as the Roman Canon: dialogue, preface, *sanctus*, supplication for consecration (or a receptionist equivalent) and the institution narrative.

In the eighteenth century, however, patristic studies began to give attention once again to the Greek tradition in eucharistic theology and liturgy. One of the more important of these voices within the Church of England was John Johnson, and his views were espoused by some of the Nonjurors, shorn of their appointments in the established church because of their inability in conscience to foreswear their oath to James II when William and Mary of Orange acceded to the throne. Some of them began to set forth experimental liturgies, and in Scotland these patristic studies eventually resulted in what was called "the Scottish Liturgy," given official recognition by the Episcopal Church of Scotland in 1764. That liturgy was brought back by Samuel Seabury after his consecration as Bishop of Connecticut at the hands of Scottish bishops and was reissued for the church in Connecticut.

Under the influence of Seabury and other American clergy of Scottish background, a modified version of the Scottish eucharistic prayer was adopted in the first American Book of Common Prayer in 1789 and appears still as Prayer I of the present prayer book. Like the Greek prayers whose study gave rise to it, this prayer remains a proclamation of praise and thanksgiving down to and including the institution narrative and its attached memorial oblation. Only then does it turn to supplication, with an invocation of Word and Spirit upon the gifts just offered. Here, as in the Greek eucharistic prayers of the third and fourth centuries, oblation of the gifts is the thankful response to our Lord's command that we "Do this," and that oblation leads into the prayer for the consecration of the gifts that we have offered. Oblation is oriented toward consecration.

Implications for Future Prayer Book Revision

In light of that, it must be considered something of an anomaly that the institution narrative, clearly a historical account and, as such, part of our thanksgiving for the work of Christ, should be accompanied, in every prayer in the present prayer book, by rubrics that seem to be meaningless unless the words they accompany are seen as consecratory. These rubrics might be interpreted as merely mimetic, the imitation by the priest of the actions of Christ while reciting the words of Christ. That would not account, however, for the requirement that the priest "hold or place a hand upon the cup *and any other vessel containing wine to be consecrated*" (BCP, pp. 334, 342, 362, 368, 371, 374, 403, 405; emphasis added). Such a direction seems totally at variance with the clear meaning of the text.

The implication that the manual acts of the celebrant are related to consecration appears first in the prayer book approved for the Church of Scotland in 1637. There, a rubric on the words "took the cup" says "he is to take the chalice in his hand, and lay his hand upon so much, be it in chalice or flagons, as he intends to consecrate." In the English revision of 1662, partly in response to Puritan objections to the absence of any such directions, the 1637 rubrics (slightly rephrased) were adopted and, since in that book (like its predecessors since 1552) communion was distributed immediately after the institution narrative, a further rubric directed the breaking of the bread at the words "he brake it." It is important, nonetheless, to note that in both of those books the supplication for the consecration of the gifts *precedes* the institution narrative, as had been the case in Latin tradition.

However, in the eighteenth century the Scottish text underwent significant further evolution, and by the time of the adoption of the Scottish liturgy of 1764, that invocation of the Word and Spirit upon the gifts came *after* the narrative and memorial oblation, a shift influenced by studies in the Greek tradition of eucharistic prayer.[19] In other words, in the Scottish liturgy and the American prayer books, as in the Greek anaphoras discussed earlier, the institution narrative is the climax of the thanksgiving and leads into the memorial oblation. That seal of our thanksgiving, in turn, leads into the supplication for consecration (the invocation, *epiclesis*). Given that structure, any suggestion that the words of our Lord in the institution narrative should be treated as the point of consecration seems inappropriate, to say the least. That would not preclude mimetic actions, such as those prescribed in the first Book of Common Prayer in 1549, where the priest takes the paten in his hands while reciting our Lord's words regarding the bread and takes the cup in his hands during the words regarding the cup. If, however, it is thought necessary to indicate by gesture the elements to which the invocation for consecration refers, those gestures should accompany the invocation. The retention of those

1637 rubrics can only be regarded as a sort of inertia in the making of liturgical books, and its reconsideration in light of the altered structure of the prayer is long overdue.

While our own tradition has shown a strong preference for the structure found in Greek anaphoras, recent Roman Catholic reforms, clinging to the view that it is the words of Christ (*verba Christi*) that effect consecration, have enriched the supplication before the narrative with an invocation of the Holy Spirit, and we noted above the novel impact this had upon the memorial oblation in Eucharistic Prayer IV. The English *Alternative Service Book* (*ASB*) has also strengthened the supplication before the narrative to be a "consecratory invocation" and, in consequence, confronts again the English Reformers' fear of the oblation. When the structure of the prayer makes consecration lead into oblation, there is a justifiable fear that what is offered is just what that new Roman Catholic Eucharistic Prayer IV declares, "his Body and Blood." To avoid that notion, the English prayers avoid explicit offering of the gifts in the memorial following the narrative, though one of them (the Third Eucharistic Prayer of Rite A) does allow itself an expression that may be said to be a translation of *offerimus*, "we bring before you this bread and this cup" (*ASB*, p. 138).

That same expression *precedes* the invocation in the only full eucharistic prayer in our prayer book that places the invocation before the narrative, Eucharistic Prayer C of Rite II. There, following the *sanctus*, the celebrant prays, "And so, Father, we who have been redeemed by him, and made a new people by water and the Spirit, now bring before you these gifts. Sanctify them by your Holy Spirit to be the Body and Blood of Jesus Christ our Lord" (BCP, p. 371). The institution narrative follows, and there is no specific reference to the gifts in the memorial oblation. This ingenious arrangement does retain the order that makes oblation lead into consecration, while still doing all that before the institution narrative. It remains true that in such a structure the narrative of the institution of the eucharist finds no place in our thanksgiving for the work of Christ, but is locked into a supplicatory context that is hard put to honor the narrative's historical reference.

Another development that tends to isolate the narrative from its classical relation to the rest of the prayer is the popular acclamation inserted between the narrative and the memorial oblation. The purpose of that memorial oblation is to relate what Christ did historically to what the Church is doing in this liturgy, and therefore its connection to the institution narrative is critically significant. It is not the notion of a popular acclamation as such that is the problem, but its location between the narrative and *anamnesis*. The desire to increase congregational participation is both understandable and laudable, and such a popular acclamation in Prayer D wonderfully illuminates the structure of the prayer, marking the turning point between the memorial oblation, the end of the thanksgiving, and the supplication which invokes the Holy Spirit. Much less happy, I am sure, are the acclamations in Prayers A and B that insert a wedge between the narrative and the memorial oblation, which (as we noted above) seem to have entered the tradition as a unit.

It is often said that these popular acclamations derive from eastern church practice. It is certainly true that the Byzantine liturgy marks the shift from thanksgiving to supplication with the acclamation that we find in Prayer D, broadly based on the Liturgy of St. Basil. Some pre-Chalcedonian liturgies have an acclamation of the paschal mystery between the narrative and *anamnesis*, not *instead of* that between the thanksgiving and supplication (i.e., between *anamnesis* and *epiclesis*), but in addition to it. This is also the case in the liturgy of the Church of South India, which exercised strong influence on western liturgical reformers in this century. It is not, however, in eastern anaphoras, but only in modern western liturgies that the sole popular acclamation after the *sanctus* falls between the institution narrative and the memorial oblation. It seems likely that the second of South India's two acclamations, marking the turn from thanksgiving to supplication, was abandoned in the West where the transition to supplication had already occurred much earlier, prior to the institution narrative. Experience has shown that this sole remaining acclamation functions as a punctuation point, marking a division in the prayer precisely where one is neither desired nor appropriate. For that reason, later Roman Catholic eucharistic prayers for services with children have placed the popular acclamation after the memorial oblation, preserving its original continuity with the institution narrative.

In addition to the disruption of the close connection between narrative and memorial oblation, the popular acclamation in Prayer B constitutes the memorial itself, and the continuation of the prayer by the celebrant supplies the oblation. However, as happened with the *sanctus*, these popular acclamations are being set to music and often to music that neither the congregation nor the celebrant can or is intended to sing. This really sunders the two aspects of the *anamnesis*, memorial and oblation, that must be seen in clear relation to one another. The eucharist, we must be clear, is not some other sacrifice than that of Christ, but it is the memorial of that unique sacrifice. That is why the memorial oblation is one of the more sensitive sentences in any eucharistic prayer. When the memorial is given a choral setting, it can seem as dissociated from the textual continuity of the prayer as does the *sanctus*. In such a case, the oblation expressed by the celebrant is effectively dissociated from the memorial, the sacrifice of praise and thanksgiving no longer clearly related to the one sacrifice of Christ, an effect never intended and not evident in the text itself.

For these reasons, it seems appropriate to hope that any future revision will follow the example of those who drafted the Eucharistic Prayers for Masses with Children in the Roman Catholic Church and will place any popular acclamation in Prayers A and B following the memorial oblation. There, as can be seen in the case of Prayer D, it significantly marks the transition from the thanksgiving to the supplication (the invocation of the Spirit). Further, it would no longer interrupt the continuity between the institution narrative and the memorial oblation which relates that institution to the present act of worship of the Church.

Prayer D, again, calls our attention to another difference of its Greek tradition from the Latin tradition that looms so large in our background. This prayer's extended praise of God as Creator speaks powerfully to the concerns of our generation and is so fundamental a theological theme that one may well wonder how we lived so many centuries with so little reference to creation in this central prayer of our liturgy. The reason, of course, was that we had treated it as a prayer of consecration and not as a primary proclamation of our faith. Today, however, the significant role of the eucharistic prayer in the proclamation of faith has been reasserted, and with that have come renewed calls for the expansion of the prayer's treatment of creation.

In such a Greek tradition as is represented by Prayer D, the initial praise of the Creator, leading into the *sanctus*, is followed by the thanksgiving for the work of Christ, ending in the memorial oblation. Then a further popular response makes the transition to the supplication, with its invocation of the Holy Spirit. This pattern replicates the three paragraphs of the baptismal creeds and seems an ideal pattern for the proclamatory function of the eucharistic prayer. However, we cannot shrug off centuries of association with Latin tradition and, perhaps, its most telling feature for us, the variable thanksgiving that we noted as characteristic of Latin tradition already in the fourth century. These seasonal prefaces follow, for the most part, a liturgical year whose pattern is primarily christological, but newer prefaces for ordinary Sundays have afforded opportunity for texts based on the theology of creation. Worthy of consideration, beyond that, is the common preface of the Book of Common Order of the Church of Scotland. That fixed preface gives full attention to the theology of creation, but then provides as well the opportunity to insert proper prefaces. Such a solution seems preferable to the insertion of reference to creation in the fixed body of the eucharistic prayer after the *sanctus,* in a context that is primarily soteriological.

This matter of the treatment of creation is symptomatic of the peculiar character of the structure of eucharistic prayer in our tradition, viz., that our tradition blends into one the very different structures of Greek and Latin eucharistic prayers. Like the Greek prayers, ours (apart from Prayer C, an exception from many standpoints) treat the institution narrative as part of our thanksgiving for the work of Christ, a treatment that makes it inappropriate to force onto that narrative the role of "words of consecration." Again like Greek prayers, we pray for the consecration of the gifts by the invocation of the Holy Spirit in the supplication that follows the narrative and memorial oblation. On the other hand, like the Latin tradition, most of our prayers begin with a variable preface, itself derived from the early Latin christological thanksgivings, and this has in the past allowed for scant reference to creation. This hybridization of eastern and western traditions is not general in Anglican history, being primarily a feature of Scottish and North American liturgical histories, but it has commended itself to many other Anglican provinces. We should engage the questions posed by our eucharistic prayer structure not as a conflict between two eucharistic traditions but as an opportunity to give further expression to our owning of the whole of Christian tradition, acknowledging our debt to both Greek and Latin traditions while doing violence to neither.

Most important of all, we must begin to recognize the text of the eucharistic prayer as an intelligible literary construction. The prayer means what it says. Its recounting of past historical events in thanksgiving is just that, not a mystical formula. Its supplication for the present action of God is just that, not an appreciative nod toward a foreign and exotic tradition. We must find the courage to read the eucharistic prayer without interjecting extraneous presuppositions. If we do that, just that, we may find questions to be addressed, but we will surely find as well the lucid clarity appropriate to our worship of the One who is the source of light.

Notes

1. The Orthodox use the anaphora (eucharistic prayer) of Chrysostom most of the time, the anaphora of Basil in Lent and a few other occasions, and the anaphora of James on his feast in some jurisdictions; other oriental churches may acknowledge several eucharistic prayers but tend to use only one on ordinary occasions. The Gallican church, before its adoption of the Roman rite, built variable elements around the two fixed texts of *sanctus* and the institution narrative.

2. Cited here from R. C. D. Jasper and G. C. Cuming, *Prayers of the Eucharist: Early and Reformed*, third edition (New York: Pueblo, 1987), pp. 156-7 [Cited hereafter as *PEER*]. The division into two paragraphs is an initiative of the translator. For the Latin text, see L. C. Mohlberg, ed., *Sacramentarium Veronense, Rerum ecclesiasticarum documenta*, series major 1 (Rome, 1956), p. 202.

3. Cited from Ambrose, *De Sacramentis* [addresses to the newly baptized], in *PEER*, p. 145.

4. M. Andrieu and P. Collomp, "Fragments sur papyrus de l'anaphore de saint Marc," *Revue des Sciences Religieuses* 8 (1928): 489-515.

5. G. J. Cuming, "The Anaphora of St. Mark: A Study in Development," *Le Muséon* 95 (1982): 115-29; H. A. J. Wegman, "Une anaphore incomplète," in R. van den Broek and M. J. Vermaseren, eds., *Studies in Gnosticism and Hellenistic Religions* (Leiden: E. J. Brill, 1981). The demurrer of B. D. Spinks, "A Complete Anaphora? A Note on Strasbourg Gr. 254," *The Heythrop Journal* 25 (1984): 51-5, has evidently been satisfied by E. Mazza, "Una Anafora Incompleta?" *Ephemerides Liturgicae* 99 (1985): 425-36.

6. E. Cutrone, "Cyril's Mystagogical Catecheses and the Evolution of the Jerusalem Anaphora," *Orientalia Christiana Periodica* 44 (1978): 52-64; John R. K. Fenwick, *The Anaphoras of St Basil and St James, Orientalia Christiana*

Analecta 240 (Rome: Pontificium Institutum Orientale, 1992).

7. As some now believe to have been the case with the Liturgy of Addai and Mari, once considered a peculiar example of a eucharistic prayer without the narrative.

8. *PEER*, pp. 23-4.

9. The prayer for his consecration is the source of that in our present prayer book (BCP, pp. 520-1).

10. *PEER*, p. 35.

11. *PEER*, p. 141. Almost surely composed in Greek, this fragmentary text has been recovered from an Armenian translation. Epiphanius died in 403, but this prayer includes language about Christ that suggests a date after the Council of Chalcedon (451). This language may well be a later addition to a significantly earlier prayer, as its simple structure suggests.

12. *PEER*, pp. 67-73.

13. See Chrysostom, *De resurrect. mortuorum* 8; *De proditione Judae* 1,6.

14. *PEER*, pp. 144-5.

15. This is in what is called the "Gelasian Sacramentary." Although the manuscript that presents the canon is of the eighth century, it represents a Gallican copy (with further development) of a Roman text of the sixth century.

16. *Summa Theologica* III, Q.83.a.4. resp.

17. Gabriel Biel, *Canonis missae expositio*, Heiko A. Oberman and William J. Courtney, eds. (Wiesbaden, 1965), Part 2, lect. 54 [Vol. I, pp. 335-44, especially 340-2].

18. Such is the arrangement in his *Formula Missae et Communionis*, *PEER*, pp. 192-3.

19. Although there were earlier similar experiments by English Nonjurors, the Scottish development was stimulated especially by the publication (in 1744) of a translation of the Liturgy of St. James by Thomas Rattray, entitled *The Ancient Liturgy of the Church of Jerusalem*.

PASTORAL OFFICES

What Shall We Do about Confirmation?

Leonel L. Mitchell

Confirmation is one of the problems left unresolved in The Book of Common Prayer 1979. What appears in the book is a compromise between the position originally set forth by the Drafting Committee on Christian Initiation in Prayer Book Studies 18[1] and those who wish to maintain the position that confirmation is a necessary component of Christian initiation. The same division was manifested in the change in the title of Prayer Book Studies 26 made by the General Convention of 1973. As presented to General Convention the full title was *Holy Baptism together with A Form for the Affirmation of Baptismal Vows with the Laying-On of Hands by the Bishop also called Confirmation.*[2] What emerged was *Holy Baptism together with A Form of Confirmation or the Laying-On of Hands by the Bishop with the Affirmation of Baptismal Vows as authorized by the General Convention of 1973.*[3] Similarly, the text of *The Draft Proposed Book of Common Prayer* presented to the General Convention in 1976 did not contain the second rubric now included in "Concerning the Service," prefatory to the confirmation service: "Those baptized as adults, unless baptized with the laying on of hands by a bishop, are also expected to make a public affirmation of their faith and commitment to the responsibilities of their Baptism in the presence of a bishop and to receive the laying on of hands" (BCP, p. 412). This was drafted on the floor of the House of Bishops and added to the proposal.

In his recent article "To Confirm or To Receive?"[4] Daniel Stevick bears witness to the continuing division among the bishops as manifested in their practice in receiving into the Episcopal Church members of those churches which do not practice episcopal confirmation. Stevick questions the basis on which the common practice of receiving Catholics and confirming Protestants rests. "The sum of this argument," he concludes, "is that no distinction should be made between baptized Christians of mature faith who come to the Episcopal Church from other communions. Such persons are all fully initiate sacramentally, and they are all on this occasion doing the same thing, viz., promising to carry out the obligations of their baptism in the...Episcopalian community of faith."[5] Stevick goes on to ask:

> Have dioceses which now receive persons from all Christian communions and dioceses which continue the old distinctions both thought the matter through and come out at different places? Or are some dioceses continuing past practice unexamined? Must this issue be addressed by each diocese independently?[6]

Charles Price, in an Occasional Paper of the Standing Liturgical Commission,[7] lays out the situation well, attributing the ambiguity of the rite of the 1979 prayer book chiefly to the use of the title *Confirmation* to describe it. Price makes a distinction between what he calls Confirmation A and Confirmation B. Confirmation A is that part of the older Anglican confirmation service now restored to the baptismal liturgy: the laying on of hands with the prayer for the sevenfold gift of the Spirit. Confirmation B is the service called Confirmation in The Book of Common Prayer 1979: a service of mature commitment to baptismal promises. Price concludes that the result is that the rites of the present Book of Common Prayer are capable of at least two interpretations:

> (a) Many Episcopalians, including a number of bishops, recognize no substantial change in the initiatory rites.... Those who interpret the provisions of BCP 1979 in this way will expect confirmation to be administered *not only to "those baptized at an*

early age," but also to those baptized in other denominations who have not received episcopal laying on of hands, as well as those baptized in this church as adults by presbyters....

(b) Those who accept the intention of the revisers acknowledge that this liturgy for Holy Baptism 1979 has restored the primitive unity of baptism, confirmation, and first communion.[8]

Those who follow interpretation (b), according to Price, will wish only those baptized as infants to be confirmed so that they may make a mature commitment to their baptismal faith. Those baptized as adults should not be confirmed, since they have already made such an affirmation. Those baptized in other churches who have already made such a commitment should be received by the bishop with the laying on of hands.

I discussed many of the same points in an article in *Anglican Theological Review* in 1973.[9] I concluded:

We find, therefore, at least two ideas concerning confirmation in the [1928] Prayer Book. First, we find the traditional Catholic teaching that confirmation is the bestowal of the sevenfold gift of the Holy Spirit, symbolized by the imposition of hands (or anointing). Second, we find the Reformed concept of confirmation as the act of the candidate, confirming and ratifying his baptismal allegiance to Christ. Third, we find traces of the medieval idea that confirmation provides the strengthening gifts of the Spirit appropriate to adolescence. I believe that a great deal of the present controversy and confusion concerning confirmation comes from a failure to distinguish among these views about the nature of confirmation.... It would probably be best if we avoided official use of the word [confirmation] altogether, since its meaning today

is almost always ambiguous.[10]
This brings us to the present and the practical question of how we proceed from here. The pattern set forth in the 1979 prayer book for the initiation of children seems clear. It needs to be more fully implemented. In this pattern confirmation has a reasonable place as the rite in which those baptized as infants have the opportunity to own the faith in which they have been brought up and to affirm (or confirm) the baptismal covenant by personal affirmation of faith. This is essentially an adult act. It is not appropriate for pre-adolescents, but neither is it possible or desirable to set an age at which this should take place. People mature spiritually at different rates. Some high school students are clearly ready and able to do this, and some working young adults clearly are not. Personally I feel we should be ready to present people for confirmation when they "are ready and have been duly prepared to make a mature public affirmation of their faith and commitment," as the rubric says (BCP, p. 412), and do it without coercion or peer pressure, recognizing that some baptized communicants may never be ready. This stance should be supported by canonical revision to remove canonical requirements that people be confirmed in order to do certain things in the church, such as be members of the vestry, eucharistic ministers or candidates for ordination.

In the case of adults coming to baptism, I believe we should make it clear that those who personally make their own profession of faith at their baptism do not need to be confirmed. They have made their "mature public affirmation." This would eliminate the theological nonsense of initiating an adult catechumen at the Easter vigil after an extensive period of preparation involving the whole congregation, and then "expecting" that this adult communicant will make a further profession of faith before a bishop three weeks later when the episcopal visitation occurs.

Finally, we need to resolve the confirm-receive dilemma. It would seem reasonable to require that reception and affirmation as well as confirmation have as their ritual action the laying on of hands. This is extremely traditional. The traditional reason for receiving those baptized outside the Church, such as Arians, was not to confirm them, but because they were baptized without the bishop's oversight, and this was supplied by a formal rite of reception in which the bishop imposed hands on the convert. In modern terms, it would seem most appropriate for the bishop to receive, with the laying on of hands, those who come into his or her jurisdiction from another Christian church in which they have been communicant members. This should be seen as a formal sacramental act, not simply a nice thing to do. The bishop recognizes the person as a member of the one Church of Jesus Christ and receives him or her into the Episcopal Church and the Anglican Communion with an episcopal blessing and prayer, of which the imposition of hands is the traditional outward sign. This joined with the exchange of the peace and the reception of communion at the bishop's hands should be a sufficient rite for accepting baptized Christians into our fellowship.

At the Toronto International Anglican Consultation, one of the formal recommendations was that presbyters be permitted to substitute for the bishop at confirmation.[11] I do not think that we should simply follow the Lutheran model and permit parish pastors to confirm, but there is good reason to permit the bishop to license priests to confirm, especially in remote places. It is certainly appropriate to license presbyters to "receive" and "affirm," since otherwise these actions might have to be unduly postponed.

Notes

1. *Holy Baptism with the Laying-on of Hands, Prayer Book Studies 18, On Baptism and Confirmation* (New York: Church Pension Fund, 1970).
2. New York: Church Hymnal Corporation, 1973.
3. New York: Church Hymnal Corporation, 1973.
4. In Ruth A. Meyers, ed., *Baptism and Ministry,* Liturgical

Studies 1 (New York: Church Hymnal Corporation, 1994), pp. 55-85.

5. Ibid., pp. 78-9.

6. Ibid., pp. 82-3.

7. "Rites of Initiation," Occasional Paper 4, 1984, reprinted in Meyers, ed., *Baptism and Ministry*, pp. 86-102.

8. Ibid., pp. 93-4; emphasis in original.

9. "What Is Confirmation?" *Anglican Theological Review* 55 (1973): 201-12.

10. Ibid., pp. 209, 211.

11. "The pastoral rite of confirmation may be delegated by the bishop to a presbyter": "Recommendations of the Fourth International Anglican Liturgical Consultation at Toronto 1991 on Principles of Christian Initiation," in David R. Holeton, ed., *Growing in Newness of Life* (Toronto: Anglican Book Centre, 1993), p. 229.

A Critique of the Rite of
The Celebration and Blessing of a
Christian Marriage

Jennifer M. Phillips

Some Historical Background

Although there were Jewish traditions of marriage involving betrothal, procession to the bride's home, vows, a written covenant, a blessing of a cup of wine in the presence of at least ten witnesses, and a feast, there is no indication in Christian scriptures of a specifically Christian rite of marriage. In Roman practice in the first century there was also a betrothal and contract, sealed with a kiss, the giving of a ring, and the joining of hands, along with a sacrifice to the gods. The earliest Christians probably celebrated similar rites, although apparently a bishop gave consent and attended some marriage ceremonies. Some of the earliest Christian writers saw marriage as a concession to cupidity and an inferior state to celibacy but better than unchastity.

In the middle ages, marriage was largely a civil affair and tended to be an upper class event, with the poor simply living together and being considered married once children appeared. The Church desired to take some authority over marriages (and perhaps also over the property transactions that accompanied the conveyance of a woman from the possession of her father to the possession of her husband). Thus civil marriages began to be celebrated in the church porch, followed by a liturgical ceremony and the giving of blessed bread and wine inside the church.

Luther identified marriage as a vocation proper to Christians and developed a shorter rite concluding with the words "what God has joined together, let no man [sic] put asunder," and followed by prayers and scripture readings. Reformed tradition allowed an exchange of rings, but without blessing them, and solemnized marriages within the Sunday service.

Marion Hatchett notes that the 1549 Book of Common Prayer derived its marriage rite from the Sarum and York traditions, the *Consultation* of Hermann and other Teutonic sources.[1] The three purposes of marriage were identified as:

> the procreacion of children, to be brought up in the feare and nurture of the Lord, and prayse of God. Secondly it was ordeined for a remedie agaynst sinne, and to auoide fornicacion.... Thirdelye for the mutuall societie, helpe, and coumfort, that one oughte to haue of thother, both in prospcritie and aduersitie.[2]

In the second (1552) prayer book, marriage was seen as a second-best state for those persons "as haue not the gyfte of continencie,"[3] an addition to the previous book. Minor revisions followed in each edition of the prayer book, including a compromise with the Puritans in 1662 that made the eucharist optional at the marriage.

The American prayer book of 1789 did not list the causes for matrimony, deleted the words "with my body I thee worship" that accompanied the giving of the ring, and shortened the ceremonial to resemble the earlier civil marriage form. Various scriptural images came and went in the course of prayer book revision in the United States from 1892 to 1928. The 1928 prayer book removed the unilateral promise of the woman to obey and the necessity of endowing one another with one's worldly goods.

In the 1979 book, options for readings from scripture were broadened, the congregational pledge and prayers for children added, the giving of the bride made optional, and marriage placed within the liturgy of word and sacrament. The amen following the pronouncement of marriage was to be said by the congregation, not just the presider. An informal "Order for Marriage" was added along with a separate "Blessing of a Civil Marriage."

The trajectory of revision, then, was toward increasing recognition of the eucharistic context of marriage, acknowledgment of changing roles of the family, and emphasis on the role and presence of the community as part of the covenant process. All these elements continue in force as we approach another time of prayer book revision.

Assumptions of the Rite

In our contemporary Book of Common Prayer, marriage is described as "a solemn and public covenant between a man and a woman in the presence of God" (p. 422). The language of *sacrament*, from the Latin *sacramentum* ("oath"), is avoided in favor of the earlier term from the Greek, *mysterion*, *mystery*, which in the letter to the Ephesians (chapter 5) describes the saving activity of God in raising Jesus Christ. The union of husband and wife when interpreted as exemplifying the love between Christ and the Church is understood to be anchored in the *mysterion* of God's resurrecting love. In the 1979 prayer book, this language of *mysterion* appears in the opening address, one of the readings, and the second prayer of blessing.[4]

The opening address asserts that marriage as an institution was established at creation by God. This is rather a stretch of the Adam and Eve story but a venerable church tradition supported by the interpretative note in Genesis 2:24 ("a man leaves his father and his mother and clings to his wife, and they become one flesh"). Marriage is also said to have been approved by Jesus in its then-current Jewish form ("our Lord Jesus Christ adorned this manner of life by his presence and first miracle at a wedding in Cana of Galilee," BCP, p. 423).

Marriage is to conform to the laws of the state (BCP, p. 422). In fact, when presiding at a marriage, clergy are acting as functionaries of the state, a rather peculiar, even inappropriate, but little-contested role for clergy! Given that there are marriages characterized by violence, selfishness, naivete and the like, which the Church should properly refuse to sanction but the state may license, and that there are relationships which may be godly, mutual, self-giving, kind and hospitable that the state may refuse to license (for example, between persons not deemed competent to give legal consent) or that would cause the couple intolerable hardship if legalized (elderly persons who might lose Social Security income), a strong case can be made for having legal marriages licensed and solemnized by the state and godly covenants of relationship, including some civil marriages, witnessed and blessed by the Church. I confess to being a proponent of getting the Church out of the "marrying business" and into the "blessing business" where it belongs, properly separating Church and state.

Marriage must also conform to the canons of the Episcopal Church (BCP, p. 422). Together with the rite, this establishes several assumptions or expectations:

- Marriage is assumed to be for the purposes of mutual joy, help, comfort and the procreation and nurture of children in faith if God provides them.

- Marriage is required to be without coercion, an act of free will.

- The couple marry one another, the priest or bishop presides, and the community witnesses and promises to uphold the couple.

- Marriage is faithful, monogamous and of lifelong intent. It is activated by having, holding, honoring, loving and cherishing.

- Marriage endures through changing circumstances and should not be dissolved by illness, financial reverse or other "worse" times.

- Marriage makes one flesh; sexual consummation is intended by this rather archaic metaphoric formulation. The couple also become one heart and soul, metaphorically.

- Mutual affection is expected to spill over in hospitality to others.

- Marriage is a sign to the world of healing and reconciliation. It is characterized by growth.

- Witnessing a new marriage is assumed to strengthen other married couples.

Theology

The dominant theological images underlying the Episcopal marriage rite are the relationship between Christ and the Church, and the Genesis imagery of gender complementarity and covenant.

Is the Christ-Church language of the key text of Ephesians 5:21-33 salvageable for the Church of the twenty-first century? Apologists for Ephesians point out that the text begins generously: "Be subject to one another out of reverence for Christ." Indeed, this postulates an unexceptionable mutuality of relationship which might be a fine foundation for understanding marriage. The text goes on, however, to sketch a hierarchy of relationships: "Wives, be subject to your husbands as you are to the Lord. For the husband is the head of the wife just as Christ is the head of the church..." Though the delicate syntax of the next sentence makes a distinction between Christ's role as savior and the husband's as ruler and wishes to point to the simple subjection of women to men as the Church to Christ, the nuance is largely lost in English: "For the husband is head of the wife just as Christ is the head of the church, the body of which he is the Savior. Just as the church is subject to Christ, so also wives ought to be, in everything, to their husbands." The relation of man and woman described is the relation of ruler and subject. That the text goes on to instruct husbands to "love your wives, just as Christ loved the church and gave himself up for her" may indicate that husbands are to be benign rulers, even self-sacrificing ones, but does not alter the fundamental inequality of spouses.

Worse still, the text connects the role of the husband with that of Christ as the consecrator and cleanser of that which formerly was stained, wrinkled and blemished. After two thousand years of description of the feminine as unclean, unholy and only of value insofar as it is unwrinkled, young, without blemish and beautiful, the text adds to the sexual objectification of women. Further, the text goes on to ask husbands to love women as they love their own bodies, emphasizing the age-old reduction of women to physicality devoid of spirit and the capacity for holiness. Men are to "nourish and tenderly care for" their spouses, making women not only their possession, but one which seems passive and dependent upon the protective activity of the male mind and will.

The author of Ephesians exegetes the scriptural injunction "a man will leave his father and mother and be joined to his wife, and the two will become one flesh" as "a great mystery... [applied] to Christ and the church," an interesting metaphorical reading of Genesis 2:24. To the author of Ephesians, the reference to Christ and the Church is its primary meaning; only by extension is it descriptive of marriage: "each of you, however [literally, 'nevertheless, also you'], should love his wife as himself, and a wife should respect [literally, 'fear'; Greek, *phobetai*] her husband."

The proper relationship of the Church to its Savior—gratitude, dependence, reverence and fear, as well as love—is hardly a useful model for the relationship of a wife to her husband in an age where women and men are seeking equality, mutuality and nonviolent partnership in marriage. Nor is it helpful for men to see themselves as Christlike in terms of the power relationship of Christ and the Church, which is inseparable from *agape*, self-giving love. It does neither men nor women any good to see women's holiness and cleanness as derived from male prerogative, or women's relation to Christ as through the mediation of their husbands. I do not believe this text can be salvaged as casting any light on Christian marriage in our time.

The two Genesis texts offered as primary authority for marriage

(1:27-28; 2:21-24) are also problematic. The first is so less because of what it says about the relation of the genders and more because of its language about creation: "be fruitful and multiply, and fill the earth and subdue it; and have dominion over" it. In the twenty-first century, as we endeavor to shape a new environmental ethic, Christians wrestle with the painful heritage of dominating and subduing the earth and its creatures and multiplying without limit. As life expectancy has increased and remarriage or older first marriage becomes more common, fewer couples find liturgical mention of fruitfulness and procreation fitting as a theological base for their covenant.

Mark 10:6-9 recapitulates Genesis 2. It has always seemed ironic to me that this excerpt from a conversation about divorce has become a standard at weddings! Most problematic in this text for modern ears is the description of two becoming one flesh. The New English Bible and the Revised English Bible exacerbate the difficulty by translating the repetition literally rendered "so as no longer are they two but one flesh" as "it follows that they are no longer two individuals: they are one flesh." A text that in its initial meaning emphasized the protection of wives from being left socially and financially out in the cold through their husbands' freedom to divorce them, and further stressed that the passionate physical union sanctified by God overcomes the right of law to separate spouses, now suggests that the individualism of the partners is lost in their marriage; not a helpful reading! While Christians do well to confront the rampant individualism of our time, this is not usefully done through language which suggests a merging that diminishes the distinctiveness of gifts and identities of marriage partners. Two becoming one in the institution of marriage has been tarnished by a history of marriages in which the identity of women was often subsumed into that of their husbands in name and action.

With the decline in usefulness of these traditional foundational texts for the marriage liturgy, how might scriptural images be drawn forth to take their place and strengthen the institution of marriage as a mutual, faithful, nonviolent, generative and loving covenant? What other readings might we choose? On what shall we found a reformed theology of marriage? Let me suggest some themes and texts.

Potential Theological Themes

We are made a new creation by baptism. Through baptism all old categories and rivalries are transcended. Christian marriage is not about rigid sex roles but about living into the fullness of this radical remaking of human nature. The image of new creation is profoundly eschatological; it leans into the vision of the fullness of the reign of God.

> ...for in Christ Jesus you are all children of God through faith. As many of you as were baptized into Christ have clothed yourselves with Christ. There is no longer Jew or Greek, there is no longer slave or free, there is no longer male and female; for all of you are one in Christ Jesus. (Galatians 3:26-28)

Our baptismal covenant is the foundation for all covenants, including marriage, which receives a renewed meaning through Christ. The couple delighting in God's reconciling presence between them become ambassadors of Christ's new creation to the world.

> From now on, therefore, we regard no one from a human point of view; even though we once knew Christ from a human point of view, we know him no longer in that way. So if anyone is in Christ, there is a new creation: everything old has passed away; see, everything has become new! All this is from God, who reconciled us to himself through Christ, and has given us the ministry of reconciliation; that is, in Christ God was reconciling the

> world to himself, not counting their trespasses
> against them, and entrusting the message of recon-
> ciliation to us. So we are ambassadors for Christ,
> since God is making his appeal through us; we
> entreat you on behalf of Christ, be reconciled to
> God. (2 Corinthians 5:16-20)

Based on the baptismal covenant, marriage becomes the place
where the Good News of Christ is both heard and proclaimed to
others by word and example. Marriage epitomizes the seeking and
serving of Christ in all persons as the couple celebrate the image of
God in one another and love each other as themselves. Marriage
strengthens each partner for doing justice, making peace and
respecting the dignity of all people; what begins at home spreads
outward into the world. In its constantly reconciling and forbear-
ing love, marriage resists evil within and is schooled for reconciling
work in the world. In marriage, scripture is opened and valued,
and bread is broken at the eucharistic table with the wider Church
and at the family dinner table.

The royal banquet table and the wedding feast. These are the signs of
the hospitable reign of God and models for the Church and
Christian household. Far from being an impediment to charity,
marriage is a relationship of hospitality one to another which overflows into a welcome for others and in particular for the poor and
lonely and needy.

The wedding feast at Cana in John 2 is one scriptural option on
this theme. It is interesting that although Cana is cited in the
opening address of the marriage liturgy as evidence that marriage
was a state of life "adorned" by Jesus, it is not among the offered
readings. There are a variety of possible interpretations of the miracle at Cana, but in fact none of them has much to do with marriage.

Perhaps a more provocative reading on the theme of feasting is
this:

> One of the dinner guests, on hearing this, said to

[Jesus], "Blessed is anyone who will eat bread in the kingdom of God!" Then Jesus said to him, "Someone gave a great dinner and invited many. At the time for the dinner he sent his slave to say to those who had been invited, 'Come; for everything is ready now.' But they all alike began to make excuses. The first said to him, 'I have bought a piece of land, and I must go out and see it; please accept my regrets.' Another said, 'I have bought five yoke of oxen, and I am going to try them out; please accept my regrets.' Another said, 'I have just been married, and therefore I cannot come.' So the slave returned and reported this to his master. Then the owner of the house became angry and said to his slave, 'Go out at once into the streets and lanes of the town and bring in the poor, the crippled, the blind, and the lame.' And the slave said, 'Sir, what you ordered has been done, and there is still room.' Then the master said to the slave, 'Go out into the roads and lanes, and compel people to come in, so that my house may be filled.'" (Luke 14:15-23)

This is not a gentle text, but a stern admonition to respond to the welcome of God as a first priority. If the marriage partners do not make God and their covenants with and before God a priority, their relationship is likely to founder.

Friendship with God as a basis for friendship with one another.
This is my commandment, that you love one another as I have loved you. No one has greater love than this, to lay down one's life for one's friends. You are my friends if you do what I command you. I do not call you servants any longer, because the servant does not know what the master is doing; but I have called you friends, because I

have made known to you everything that I have heard from my Father. You did not choose me but I chose you. And I appointed you to go and bear fruit, fruit that will last, so that the Father will give you whatever you ask him in my name. I am giving you these commands so that you may love one another. (John 15:12-17)

Self-giving friendship after the pattern of Christ is a powerful image for marital partners. In this text we hear it free from the hierarchical associations of Ephesians. Friendship strengthens friends to go forth and live productively, generatively.

Further, on the theme of friendship, one might wish to read excerpts from the book of Ruth, "Where you go, I will go; where you lodge, I will lodge; your people shall be my people, and your God my God" (Ruth 1:16). Can the relationship of a mother-in-law and daughter-in-law provide a model for marital union? Or perhaps the friendship of David and Jonathan, "Jonathan made a covenant with David, because he loved him as his own soul" (1 Samuel 18:3), might provide an appropriate model. If friendship is accepted as a theological basis for marriage, why not? These friendships describe just the sort of self-giving love on Jesus' lips in John 15:17.

The Trinity as the model for all community. At the very heart of God there is diversity in relationship, a dynamic movement of love and hospitality. Each person is distinct, yet all are one.

For all who are led by the Spirit of God are children of God. For you did not receive a spirit of slavery to fall back into fear, but you have received a spirit of adoption. When we cry, "Abba! Father!" it is that very Spirit bearing witness with our spirit that we are children of God, and if children, then heirs, heirs of God and joint heirs with Christ—if, in fact, we suffer with him so that we may also be glorified with him. (Romans 8:14-17)

The exodus as sacred journey. God is always leading the people of God out of captivity and toward the land of promise. Marriage also is a holy journey with its wilderness and grumbling, its joyful vision, its awareness of God's leading presence, its fulfillment of promises made.

> Then the cloud covered the tent of meeting, and the glory of the Lord filled the tabernacle.... Whenever the cloud was taken up from the tabernacle, the Israelites would set out on each stage of their journey; but if the cloud was not taken up, then they did not set out until the day that it was taken up. For the cloud of the Lord was on the tabernacle by day, and fire was in the cloud by night, before the eyes of all the house of Israel at each stage of their journey. (Exodus 40:34-38)

The covenant of God with the people. The covenants of God with the chosen people iterated both to Abraham and to Noah offer models of the faithfulness and mutual responsibility required of marriage partners. Indeed the language of married love, and adultery, was commonly used by the prophets to describe the relationship of God and the people.

Omissions of the Current Rite

Vocation. Remarkable by its absence from the liturgies and writings about Christian marriage is the concept of marriage as a *vocation.* Bernard Cooke writes, "married life was denied full participation in Christian faith for it was neither clerical nor monastic. Marriage was second-best; the idea of 'vocation' was appropriated to those Christians who were called to a 'higher way of life.'"[5] Is it time for the Church to honor marriage by considering that it is a godly calling to service and self-giving? When we speak of "what God has joined together" are we not speaking of vocation? I believe so. For those so called, Christian marriage is a vocation founded in baptism and following the way of the cross.

The single state. Also absent from the marriage liturgy is any acknowledgment of the single state. In the prayers of the people, biddings are offered for other married couples but not for those who are single. If we begin to consider in what way marriage may be a vocation just as worthy of respect as a vocation to holy orders or any other work of life to which Christians may be summoned, then how shall we include those who are joyfully called to singleness, as well as those who may find themselves single not by choice or calling? The Gospel reconstitutes the meaning of "family," which is no longer "mother, sister or brother" or spouses, but rather the community called together to hear and to do the will of God (Mark 3:33-35). Christian marriage takes place in this context.

Previous marriage. The marriage liturgy does not include any mention of previous marriage which may have ended in divorce or death. For several decades, divorced Episcopalians have been permitted to remarry in the church, with the proviso that the counseling have demonstrated that the previous relationship has been properly terminated and any continuing obligations fulfilled. An entire congregation may gather for the celebration of a second marriage, knowing and remembering a previous marriage, and the liturgy should offer some options that assist the people to pray and the couple to acknowledge whatever grief, disappointment or sense of failure they may have worked through. Children of a previous marriage also deserve the dignity of recognition of a former union. Silence on this matter resembles the proverbial denial of the family with the dead elephant in the living room!

Some couples might find a special form of general confession useful; others might wish to make a statement of having learned and grieved the errors or weaknesses of the past; some might wish to bid prayer for a previous spouse and existing children. Perhaps the divorce decree might be laid on the altar with a prayer for healing and then removed. The Orthodox guide to Holy Matrimony notes that after divorce "the rite of the second marriage possesses a marked penitential character."[6] The unfortunate absence of any rite for the dissolution of a marriage makes the need for some observance of divorce more urgent in the marriage rite.

Community role. Another deficiency in the current rite is the role of the community as witnesses to the covenant. The community is asked to pledge to uphold the partners in their marriage. There is no detailing of what this might entail. Nor is there any direction concerning the composition of the "community" for this important liturgy. Commonly, the community has been an *ad hoc* assembly of various friends and relatives of the couple. Might it not be appropriate to direct, since Christians are expected by baptism to "continue in the apostles' teaching and fellowship, in the breaking of bread, and in the prayers" (BCP, p. 304), that the marriage be celebrated at a gathering of the parish in which one of the partners is a regular communicant? Or if an out-of-town wedding is desired for strong pastoral reasons, might the parish in which the rite is celebrated ask for a letter from the home parish(es) and speak for them by proxy?

In a smaller parish, the role of the community might be emphasized by celebrating marriage within the normal Sunday eucharist. The betrothal and exchange of vows might take place suitably after the Creed and before the Prayers of the People, which could be adapted for the occasion. In a large parish, the number of weddings might make this unworkable unless more than one couple were married at one eucharist. Nonetheless, marriage is not a private rite but a public liturgy of the Church. John Meyendorff writes, "in the early days of the Church, marriage was not celebrated, as today, during a special ceremony or rite which one attends by special invitation. It took place...at the solemn Sunday eucharistic liturgy. The whole community was gathered together as the Body of Christ."[7]

My experience has been that within Sunday worship, the marriage rite assumes proper proportions, with the eucharist taking precedence, and the use of overly elaborate costuming and hosts of attendants (at great expense) tends to seem out of place to the congregation and dwindles naturally. Additionally, the couple may go off for a fancy reception somewhere, but first there is a modest festive coffee hour to which the whole parish is invited, including visitors and the poor of the streets who might have come into the church; thus the eucharistic banquet table is extended into the world through the hospitality of the new family and their friends.

Furthermore, the marriage rite might spell out some of the duties of the community witnessing the covenant: to pray for the new family, to intervene if there is evidence of covenant violation or other difficulty, to extend hospitality to the couple as they begin their new life together, to rally round in times of loss or crisis, and to celebrate with them in times of joy. Some parishes have asked premarital couples to select a sponsoring couple from the congregation to meet with them and discuss frankly each others' relationships, to pray with and for them privately and publicly, to befriend them through their first year of marriage, and to make a declaration at the wedding service that they discern the relationship to be godly and well-founded. One such declaration reads, "As members of the parish of *N.*, we testify that in our conversations and relationship with *N.* and *N.* we discern the presence and activity of God in their life together," to which the congregation responds, "Amen!"

Family roles. The role of the family is similarly underdefined in the current rite. As a result, many couples cling to the old practice of having the bride "given away" by a male relative, usually her father. Couples feel a deep need to include the family. Even greater is the need of the nuclear families to recognize the newly constituted family: husband and wife who become each other's first priority and the extended combined family with its complex relationships.

For one couple, the bride came from a multigenerational clan with a great-grandmother who was matriarch. It was very important for all concerned that she be invited to give her blessing to the couple as part of the liturgy. For another, an intrusive set of in-laws were presenting difficulties, and the couple wrote a promise to honor and respect the boundaries of their relationship and asked the in-laws to make it as part of the service. Perhaps the rubrics might suggest that each couple consider what sort of statement of support or blessing they might ask relatives, stepchildren or other particular friends to make as part of the community witness section of the liturgy. Alternatively, this might be the place for parents to come forward and embrace their children and greet the other in-laws, symbolizing the reconstituting of relationships. Then the couple could enter in procession side by side as co-ministers of the marriage, instead of the bride with father, with other family members being left out of the liturgy. That old ceremonial did not originate in the church, but "goes back to ancient Rome, where the conception was that women were owned by their fathers and husbands, and the ritual enacted an exchange of property" from one to the other.[8]

Theology of the Cross

In the twentieth century, the tradition of Christian love and marriage has become sentimentalized and trivialized. Couples may choose a church because the building is pretty for their photographs. There is a popular belief that "love will overcome all adversity" but little emphasis on Christian discipleship, including relationship, following the way of the cross.

> The "in-love" experience is fairly new as a primary reason for marriage. It is compounded of a number of factors among which are sexual attraction and emotional dependence. Persons seeking marriage in the context of the Gospel need to evaluate carefully the factors which have led to their being in love in order to determine those which are primarily the result of psychic and emotional dependence.[9]

Any revision of rite must take seriously the need to form couples and congregations in the rigors and depths of our theology of marriage.

Unfortunately, over time, the opening address of the liturgy has fallen prey to sentimentalization. Unchurched Americans can recite the words they have seen on the television soaps and in films: "Dearly beloved: we have come together in the presence of God to witness and bless the joining together of this man and this woman in Holy Matrimony." The address no longer serves its formational purpose; indeed, the content is hardly heard!

Opening Ceremonial and Eucharistic Context

The marriage rite is unusual in starting with a didactic monologue. Even in the Ordination of a Bishop, the didactic address is tucked into the liturgy as part of the examination. Opening the marriage rite with the customary opening acclamation of the eucharist, followed by a collect for marriage, might help to bring the rite into conformity with other rites. If the marriage rite is to continue in eucharist, as is *normal* (unless there is particular pastoral need otherwise), such an opening would emphasize the eucharistic context of the couple's life together. Since The Book of Common Prayer includes "An Order for Marriage" (pp. 435-6) which can be tailored to particular needs, perhaps it is time to have the standard rite assume that the marriage will take place in the context of eucharist and say so.

The Declaration of Consent

The Celebration and Blessing of a Marriage contains two older rites: the betrothal, now the declaration of consent, and the marriage. Anciently, the two parts might be separated by many years. Betrothal sealed the pact between two families that their children would eventually marry, with the exchange of property they had arranged.

Perhaps in our time, betrothal might be resurrected to serve newer purposes. For a couple intending to marry but not yet ready for significant reason such as interruption by school or work or finances, betrothal might allow them to express their intent, earn the prayer and support of their community for the time of preparation and further discernment, and publicly identify them as a couple set apart for each other and not available to others. Where the couple is ready to marry but torn between locations for the rite, because of, for example, an elderly or infirm parent unable to travel or two much-loved parishes, a betrothal might be celebrated at one location and the marriage at the other.

One of the functions of the declaration of consent is to determine that the couple are coming to the rite without coercion or impediment. The Orthodox Church asks this in a wonderfully explicit way which we might consider: "Do you have a good, free, and unconstrained will and a firm intention to take as your wife/husband this woman/man who is here before you, having promised yourself to no other?"[10]

The Vows

Should the marriage vows remain unchanged? They have evolved over the generations, equalizing the promises of man and woman in both betrothal and marriage and moving toward a more contemporary vocabulary.

Perhaps "An Order for Marriage" should allow more latitude for verbalizing the promises. I have found it immensely helpful during premarital preparation to ask the couple to write separately, and in their own words in detail, all those things which they would like to promise their beloved and what they would like their partner to promise in return. Then the two share their lists and together formulate vows which express their priorities in a brief, clear fashion. The indispensable ingredients that the vows must include are the qualities of love and faithfulness, monogamy, fidelity through change of circumstances, the presence of God, and lifelong intent. The vows couples have produced have been remarkably eloquent and sometimes included in some fashion in the liturgy. When the traditional words of promise are spoken, the couple then understand the range and depth of expectation they bring to them. To allow such personal vows to be used in place of the traditional ones seems reasonable and desirable.

Conclusion

There is much room for deepening the theological understanding of Christian marriage to include the dimensions of eschatology, baptism, the cross, social justice and mission. We might be edified by the bold statement of our Lutheran neighbors: "theologically, marriage between persons without reference to racial and ethnic differences and background is a witness to the oneness of many under the one God, and as such should be fully accepted in both church and society,"[11] or the thoughtful observations of the United Church of Christ: "we are called to realize that our New Testament witness has limitations in giving a realistic portrayal of human sexuality and is not an unerring guide to marriage and the family. The biblical tradition is authoritative in revealing that the covenant nature of relationships must have a center of focus in the Lord of history."[12]

Most importantly, in this age of individualism, the marriage rite must in every aspect build and strengthen community and embed the marrying couple within the eucharistic community which will nurture, form and sustain them over time.

Notes

1. Marion J. Hatchett, *Commentary on the American Prayer Book* (New York: Seabury, 1980), p. 429.
2. *The First and Second Prayer Books of Edward VI* (London: J. M. Dent & Sons, 1910), p. 252.
3. Ibid., p. 410.
4. Bernard Cooke, *Alternative Futures for Worship*, Vol. 5: *Christian Marriage*, (Collegeville, MN: Liturgical Press, 1987), p. 42.
5. Ibid., p. 37.

6. *Holy Matrimony* (Orthodox Church of America, Department of Religious Education, 1975), p. 38.

7. Ibid., p. 33.

8. Cooke, *Christian Marriage*, p. 34.

9. *The Celebration and Blessing of a Marriage: A Liturgical and Pastoral Commentary* (Alexandria, VA: Associated Parishes, 1987), pp. 2-3.

10. *Holy Matrimony.* (Orthodox Church of America)

11. *Ecumenical and Pastoral Directives* (Massachusetts Consultation on Church Union, 1980).

12. Ibid.

Death: Appearance and Reality A Consideration of the Burial Rites of the 1979 BCP

Gregory M. Howe

Introduction

The opportunity to comment on the burial rites of the 1979 Book of Common Prayer was welcome on several grounds, not least because it provided a chance to clear up some unfinished business. Before and during the early days of the 1976 General Convention there was a series of long meetings between the Standing Liturgical Commission and the legislative committees of the House of Bishops and the House of Deputies. These proceedings provided an exhaustive examination of the contents of *The Draft Proposed Book of Common Prayer* (*DPBCP*), leading to thirteen pages of proposed changes which subsequently were accepted by both Houses as part of the Proposed Book of Common Prayer, 1976.

The last of these meetings ended at about eleven o'clock one night, cut off by the pressing necessity of getting everything to the printer by six a.m. Since there remained scores of small details to be fixed, a series of *ad hoc* committees were formed to tidy up the remaining issues in time for the printing deadline.

That is how it came about that the last editorial work on the Pastoral Offices, Marriage through Burial, was done in my rather box-like hotel room by five members of the House of Deputies Committee on Prayer Book and Liturgy between the hours of 11:30 p.m. and 5:30 a.m. on that last night. Since the largest

130

amount of negative mail received by the Standing Liturgical Commission about *DPBCP* concerned "The Celebration and Blessing of a Marriage," we spent the majority of our time in that area. However, we made it through "The Burial of the Dead: Rite One," and the clock stopped us about halfway through Rite Two.

Against this background I would suggest that the burial rites of the 1979 prayer book represent two full services and an attached agenda which are distinct, separate and not especially equal. This is an attempt to raise questions and make suggestions which others may consider at a later date, offered from the dual perspective of the experience cited above and thirty years experience as a parish priest.[1]

Concerning the Service

A careful reading of the general rubrics "Concerning the Service" (BCP, pp. 468, 490) might suggest that this is trying to do two rather different things. The first four paragraphs state general principles of Christian custom which seem to grow in importance as the practices of the Church diverge more and more notably from secular customs. The last six paragraphs constitute practical instructions for those who preside at Christian burial rites.

In the future it might be useful to separate the general principles of Christian custom from the directions for officiants. One possibility might be to provide an introductory statement "Concerning the Service" using the material for pastoral guidance which is now found in the concluding "Note" ("The liturgy for the dead is an Easter liturgy...", BCP, p. 507). The last six paragraphs of the current "Concerning the Service" could be printed by themselves as an appendix to the burial rites, with a final line in the introductory rubrics directing readers to the appropriate page. If the material in the "Note" on page 507 does not wear well, there are interesting possibilities in the more elaborate statements offered in the Canadian *Book of Alternative Services* (1985; pp. 565-9), or *A New Zealand Prayer Book* (1989; pp. 811, 826).

The guiding principle here is that many people come upon the first funeral they need to plan rather suddenly and relatively unprepared; thus the impulse to put general instructions up front and file technical instructions where those who need them can find them.

Rite One

Do we need this rite at all? The view from here is, in the short term, yes. At least through the first decade of the next century this office will remain useful. Since the general time-frame for a new proposed revision of The Book of Common Prayer seems uncertain at this time, this question should be answered then. We are a pilgrim people, always on the road, always moving, but we need to carry our totems with us—as a reminder of who we are and where we have been. "The Burial of the Dead: Rite One" will probably be the last part of the 1979 prayer book to cease being useful. It would be helpful to let it die a natural death, rather than to remove it by committee action only to precipitate another unnecessary church fight. I would venture to suggest that there will be a significant percentage of Episcopalians who would prefer to be buried according to "The Burial of the Dead: Rite One" (with its clear echoes of the 1928 prayer book) well into the teens of the next century. They should have that right.

Collects

If we are to retain anything like Rite One, why not allow "O God of grace and glory..." (BCP, p. 493) as a permissive alternative, as in Rite Two?

In Rite Two, the comparatively generous choice of options is welcome. However, in most other cases the makers of the 1979 prayer book adhered firmly to the principle of using only one collect at the eucharist. The option of an additional collect (BCP, p. 494) is one of several items that slipped through due to the time pressure described above and should be reassessed as the prayer book is revised.

Scripture

Since 1976 we have restricted ourselves in matters of scripture. One would hope future revisers would look very carefully at the lectionary for the Burial of the Dead with an eye to possible revision and additions. I have found several passages to be particularly useful:

- Isaiah 40:28-31 (Even youths will faint and be weary);
- Daniel 12:1-3 (Your people shall be delivered, everyone who is found written in the book);
- Psalm 25 (My eyes are ever looking to the Lord);
- Psalm 103 (He redeems your life from the grave);
- 1 Thessalonians 4:13-18 (Even so, through Jesus, God will bring...those who died);
- 1 Peter 1:3-9 (A new birth into a living hope through the resurrection of Jesus Christ).

Both the Canadian *Book of Alternative Services* (pp. 604-5) and *A New Zealand Prayer Book* (pp. 864-5) list these and other choices—including imaginative abridgments of the great classics Romans 8 and 1 Corinthians 15—which may prove useful.

The Creed

If something like Rite One is to be retained, print the appropriate version of the Creed in the text as in Rite Two.

The Lord's Prayer

When the burial rite is a eucharist, the Lord's Prayer comes in a familiar place. In a noneucharistic context, I find the placement of the Lord's Prayer rather jarring. To be sure, there is precedent going back at least as far as 1549. But that was partly dependent on the presumptions of the daily office. In the current situation this seems to be one of the few contexts in which the Lord's Prayer introduces substantial intercessory prayer rather than being placed in a summary position. Is this good enough reason to continue an exception to otherwise standard usage and placement?

The Prayers

Even if Rite One is not retained in a future revision of the prayer book, one hopes that something like the prayers (BCP, pp. 480-1) will be kept. They have a kind of Anglican *gravitas* which is badly missing from the non-Anglican form of intercession in Rite Two. Certainly, *gravitas* is not what is always wanted, but what we have printed in the two rites seems an unnecessary dichotomy. One might even suggest that one reason for the persistence of "The Burial of the Dead: Rite One" is focused at this point.

A possible solution for a future revision might be to place all intercessory prayer in an appendix of its own, as the 1979 prayer book does with the majority of intercessions for The Holy Eucharist. Such a section might include the current primary choices (BCP, pp. 480-1, 497), perhaps with other possibilities such as "Prayers for a Vigil" (BCP, pp. 465-6) and prayers found in other Anglican prayer books. Consider, for example, this form in *A New Zealand Prayer Book* (p. 833):

> God our Father, we pray for the family and friends of *N.*, that they may know the comfort of your love.
> *Lord, hear our prayer.*
> We pray that you will use us as bearers of your love, to support them in their grief. We also remember before you all who mourn and all who suffer.
> *Lord, hear our prayer.*
> Give us patience and faith in this time of our loss, so that we may come to understand the wonder of your mercy and the mystery of your love.
> *Lord, hear our prayer.*
> Increase our faith and trust in your Son, Jesus

Christ, that we may live victoriously.
Lord, hear our prayer.
Give us such a vision of your purpose and such an
assurance of your love and power, that we may ever
hold fast the hope which is in Jesus Christ our
Lord.
Lord, hear our prayer.

Another possibility is a prayer originally written by Huub
Oosterhuis and included in the first draft of the 1979 burial rite.[2]
While this prayer did not make it into *The Draft Proposed Book of
Common Prayer*, it was adapted and included in the Canadian
Book of Alternative Services (pp. 602-3):

God of grace and glory, we thank you for *N*, who
was so near and dear to us, and who has now been
taken from us.
We thank you for the friendship *he/she* gave and for
the strength and peace *he/she* brought.
We thank you for the love *he/she* offered and
received while *he/she* was with us on earth.
We pray that nothing good in this *man's/woman's*
life will be lost, but will be of benefit to the world;
that all that was important to *him/her* will be
respected by those who follow; and that everything
in which *he/she* was great will continue to mean
much to us now that *he/she* is dead.
We ask you that *he/she* may go on living in *his/her
children*, *his/her* family, and *his/her* friends; in their
hearts and minds, in their courage and their con-
sciences.
We ask you that we who were close to *him/her* may
now, because of *his/her* death, be even closer to
each other, and that we may, in peace and friendship here on earth, always be deeply conscious of
your promise to be faithful to us in death.

We pray for ourselves, who are severely tested by this death, that we do not try to minimize this loss, or seek refuge from it in words alone, and also that we do not brood over it so that it overwhelms us and isolates us from others.

May God grant us courage and confidence in the new life of Christ.

We ask this in the name of the risen Lord. *Amen.*

At the Eucharist

Both the preface of the "Commemoration of the Dead" (BCP, pp. 349, 382) and the postcommunion prayer (BCP, pp. 482, 498) seem to work and wear well, and I hope that something like them will be retained. On the other hand, future revisers may wish to consider promising alternatives from other branches of the Anglican Communion. As in other areas, both the Canadian *Book of Alternative Services* and *A New Zealand Prayer Book* offer some particularly interesting possibilities.

The Commendation

Readers under the age of forty may not realize that the ending of both burial rites in the 1979 prayer book is heavily dependent upon one of the most interesting kinds of liturgical revision: a massive, spontaneous movement from below. The tepid, abrupt quality of the ending of the 1928 burial rite led many clergy on many occasions to borrow the last part of the rites for the dying (included in "The Order for the Visitation of the Sick," BCP, 1928, pp. 317-20) and insert them at the ending of the burial office. This was the immediate predecessor of the present form of conclusion, especially important in a noneucharistic rite where there is no immediate move to the committal. In the same context, one or more forms of a final blessing would be welcome.

I would also hope that Professor Talley's recessional anthems (BCP, pp. 483, 500) would be retained in a future revision. They seem to have power and authenticity.

The Committal

In general terms, this seems to work very well. Herewith, some small personal quibbles. The theological direction of the two opening anthems in Rite One seems to be significantly divergent. I could cheerfully omit "In the midst of life..." (BCP, p. 484), but friends have cautioned me that such action could result in significant unrest in other parts of the country. However, we make a significant statement by the order in which we print items (especially to "Canon 9" clergy and lay officiants). So in the next revision, which will be printed first?

A second personal issue is the ending of the committal prayer. In our funeral rites we are always cutting something off short and thus confusing the faithful. For generations it was the Lord's Prayer. In the case of the 1979 prayer book, it is the Aaronic blessing (pp. 485, 501), most versions of which conclude with something like "now and for evermore." One hopes that future revisers might consider restoration of the familiar form.

Finally, it seems strange that the first prayer printed after the Lord's Prayer is a very general statement. To continue the argument that what we print is important, I would argue that the first prayer printed after the Lord's Prayer should provide for some final personalization of the deceased. We are burying a person, not a concept. However, I would hope that "rest eternal..." and the final blessing would be retained in a future revision.

The Consecration of a Grave

In thirty years as a parish priest, I have had occasion to use this prayer just once. It should be put back into *The Book of Occasional Services.*

Additional Prayers

One hopes that some thought might be given to special prayers for those in the Armed Forces and for those who died while holding public office or as civilian public-safety employees (police, fire, ambulance, etc.). Although these categories frequently provide our most public funerals, it often appears that we have nothing to say or must borrow it from unofficial sources.

An Order for Burial

There would seem to be serious grounds upon which to question whether or not this item has any further utility. In 1976-1979 do-it-yourself eucharists and marriage services were relatively popular, and the agenda forms for those services were offered in large part to provide some order and a greater certainty that no vital items would be overlooked. If memory serves, there was no such fashion in burial rites, and "An Order for Burial" was intended primarily to provide for alternative use of the burial office from the 1928 prayer book. By the time of the next revision of the prayer book, one would presume no great concern for continued use of the 1928 book. Since *The Book of Occasional Services* as well as several unofficial sources carry material for "Burial of One Who Does Not Profess the Christian Faith" (*The Book of Occasional Services 1994*, pp. 175-8), "An Order for Burial" might be omitted in a future revision of the prayer book.

The Burial of a Child

There is one item which was omitted in 1976 which ought to be restored in any future revision: a separate and quite distinct rite for the burial of a child. In 1976-79 there was a general pattern of recasting prayer book material previously geared to children (baptism, the catechism) for adults. Whether this was the reason for dropping the previously distinct burial rite, or a burst of sixties' optimism believed that few children would die in the future because of medical advances, I cannot tell. Twenty years of pastoral experience suggests that one collect and a brief list of the least unhelpful scripture passages is not even barely adequate. Our current position is rather like that of the pre-Renaissance painters who faithfully rendered the baby Jesus as a miniature adult in his mother's arms.

With the very slim resources currently provided, we end up treating children as miniature adults when they die. Unfortunately, too many children die as victims of adult abuse, as accidental targets of urban gunfire, and as unintended victims of drunken drivers on country roads. In all such cases, and the majority of others where violence is not a factor, children tend to die suddenly and long before their allotted time for whatever actuarial scale one chooses.

This is to suggest that the shock, surprise and horror of the death of children presupposes psychological and theological issues significantly different from those of an adult funeral, however painful. These different circumstances deserve a discrete, clearly separate and different liturgical framework. One hopes the next group of revisers might recognize this.

Afterword: The New American Way of Death

In conclusion: two stories from the past and a question about the future. One of the most engaging and cautionary tales of the making of the 1928 Book of Common Prayer is the story of how air travel as a subject of prayer crept in at virtually the last minute. A friend of some of the revisers had a rather scary flight from London to Paris and lived to tell the tale. Thus did travel by air enter the concerns of The Book of Common Prayer.

Readers not familiar with the constitutional requirements of the Episcopal Church might look at the 1979 Book of Common Prayer without realizing that because of those requirements it had been frozen in place since 1976, and that much of its concepts, design and words were already in place by 1970. Those of us who started our work in the meetings of Associated Parishes and the Standing Liturgical Commission during the late 1960s and early 1970s often felt that we were in the middle of a vital and exciting movement. We didn't realize we were at the end of a chapter. It was only in a conversation with a rather radical Benedictine monk while on sabbatical leave in Rome in 1980 that it suddenly hit me that no one in that hotel room on the last night in 1976 had ever heard of inclusive or expansive language, much less tried to apply it to the Pastoral Offices of what was about to become the Proposed Book of Common Prayer, 1976. Future revisers would do well to check the burial rites of the 1979 prayer book very carefully for language problems. No one else did.

In another life this writer is an active bio-ethicist who has drafted state statutes on death and dying and helps to lead a general hospital ethics committee. That experience leads to a final suggestion for future revisers of the burial rites. The rites of the 1979 Book of Common Prayer still reflect a classical view of death—a fixed point at the end of life. From the viewpoint of bio-ethics, death is becoming something of an elective, a moveable feast.[3]

During clinical training in the mid-sixties a primary metaphor for death was "ceased breathing." Today, people who can't breathe on their own can be maintained for months or years with the latest medical technology. In such cases death is a matter of negotiation between family members and physicians to withdraw hi-tech treatment judged to be futile. In most cases death follows withdrawal, but sometimes it doesn't.

In another direction, there are major legal struggles about physician-assisted suicide for the terminally ill. This brings into the open a long-term open secret. As long as physicians have been administering heavy-duty pain killers to the terminally ill, we have had a form of physician-assisted death, if not suicide. At some point heavy-duty pain killers tend to depress respiration to a point where the patient ceases to breathe, that is, dies. Today some localities already have laws which hold harmless both physicians and patients in cases of mutually agreed suicide in the Dutch model.

Urgent questions for future revisers of the prayer book include:
- Does death as a negotiated process involving only others than the deceased indicate a need for change in our burial rites? If so, how and in what direction?

- Can those who choose assisted suicide be buried by the rites of the prayer book? A number of my smartest clergy friends are deeply divided on this issue. Some argue that ecclesiastical opposition to suicide began comparatively late (within the last four hundred years) and that it was unopposed before that time.

- Finally, are we to make distinctions between those who are victims of bad pain management and the terminally bored? As death changes presentation and meaning, how will these changes influence the Church's liturgy?

In posing such questions, a line is crossed from liturgical commentary to bio-ethical speculation. However, the foundation of my argument is the conviction that those who in the future may be asked to revise the Church's rites for the dead may find themselves confronting one of the most profound paradigm shifts placed in the way of liturgical scholars: from a classical view of death as the set termination of a physiological process called life (as reflected in our current rites), to death as the flexible, negotiable conclusion to the termination of a mechanical process generally known as heroic measures.

In the decade from the mid-eighties to the mid-nineties vast amounts of medical skill, technology and energy were devoted to terminally ill patients during the last sixty to ninety days of their lives at very high emotional and economic cost but to no significant positive effect. Rushed in and out of hi-tech intensive care units on short visiting hours, confronted by a bewildering array of machines and sounds and a series of wires and tubes more frightening than anything imagined by Mary Shelley—the general population has a high degree of fear and loathing of the current process of critical-care medicine. Clearly it is not the fear of death that has stimulated interest in Dr. Kevorkian, the Hemlock Society and physician-assisted suicide. Rather, it is the dread of a fate perceived as worse than death: an indeterminate sentence to a medical purgatory between life and death.

One reason I am reluctant to make specific suggestions is that the advance of managed care principles and urgently needed medical economic reform may push the process of dying back to more traditional forms for all but the very rich. However, since the habit of technology is to continue to develop, this may turn out not to be true.

At the very least, the rubric which reminds clergy to remind their congregations to make wills (BCP, p. 445) should be amended to include encouragement to prepare advance directives for the terminally ill and durable powers of attorney where applicable for the unconscious but non-terminally ill. For centuries the Church has been very responsible about reminding people to exercise due care in the guardianship and disposition of property. With the advent of increasingly hi-tech and relatively anonymous medicine, the Church needs to be just as responsible about living wills and other forms of advance directives. In other words, we need to be as careful about persons as we are about property.

Recent studies suggest that only twenty percent of the population have executed an advance directive to tell physicians and relatives what major options they expect when terminally ill. Many states now require the execution of advance directives as part of the hospital admissions process. In my view a hospital admissions office is one of the least promising places to execute an advance directive. This is an area in which the Church has a very important ministry, that is, helping people to understand a bewildering variety of complicated concepts. The current position of the rubric in question—at the conclusion of "A Thanksgiving for the Birth or Adoption of a Child"—has a certain logic, since it is focused on responsible provision for minors. It might be even more useful if an amended form was repeated as part of the prefatory material of the burial rites.

The use of advance directives represents the best defense against the over-enthusiastic application of medical technology at the end of life. Careful teaching and preparation in these areas are also an urgent necessity for the Church in the next century, as it continues to lead its people from death to life in Jesus Christ our Lord.

Notes

1. What follows also presumes familiarity with Marion J. Hatchett, *Commentary on the American Prayer Book* (New York: Seabury, 1980), pp. 477-500.
2. *The Pastoral Offices*, Prayer Book Studies 24 (New York: Church Hymnal Corporation, 1970), p. 128.
3. There is a vast amount of literature on this topic. Following are some items which have been especially helpful to me:
   R. Hamel, ed., *Active Euthanasia, Religion and the Public Debate* (Chicago: The Park Ridge Center, 1991).
   "Dying Well? A Colloquy on Euthanasia and Assisted Suicide," *Hastings Center Report* 22 (March-April 1992).
   G. Meilaender, "*Terra es Anima* on Having a Life," and D. Callahan, "Pursuing a Peaceful Death," *Hastings Center Report* 23 (July-Aug. 1993).
   J. D. Lantos, "Bethann's Death," *Hastings Center Report* 25 (March-April 1995).
   "Assisted Suicide," *Hastings Center Report* 25 (May-June 1995).
   "Improving Care at the End of Life," *Journal of the American Medical Association* 274 (Nov. 22/29, 1995).
   "Dying Well in the Hospital: The Lessons of SUPPORT," Special Supplement, *Hastings Center Report* 25 (Nov.-Dec. 1995).

EPISCOPAL SERVICES

The Shape of the Ordination Liturgy

Paul F. Bradshaw

When the ordination rites of the 1979 Book of Common Prayer first appeared, they set a new pattern within the Anglican Communion, one that has been followed to a greater or lesser extent by nearly every revision which has subsequently been undertaken in other Anglican provinces.[1] Experience has shown that this pattern has generally been welcomed, has worked well, and has helped to articulate a theology of ministry more in accord with current Anglican thought than the older rites were able to do. However, in the course of time it has also become evident that in some respects it really needs to be taken further still. More recent research into ordination practices in the early centuries of Christianity, together with current theological reflection on the nature of sacramental rites, points to a number of conclusions that were not as clearly recognized when the previous work of revision was undertaken. These would include:

1. That in all ordinations the true ordainer is God,[2] working through the whole Church and not just through the bishop or other ministers alone.

2. That ordination is a process accomplished over time and not just in a brief sacramental moment, a process that begins with the Church's ratification of the discernment of God's call to an individual for a particular ministry within a specific Christian community, continues with the community's prayer for the bestowal of the gifts and graces nec-

essary for the effective discharge of that office, and culmi-
nates in the acceptance by the people of the new minister's
role among them, expressed in their assent to his or her
performance of the liturgical functions belonging to the
particular office.

3. That baptism is the fundamental sacrament that admits a
   person to a life of Christian ministry and that confers
   membership in the royal priesthood of the Church (1 Peter
   2:9). Ordained ministry is therefore a particular leadership
   role within the varied ministries exercised by the different
   members of the body of Christ, and not the only ministry
   of the Church. Similarly, the ordained priesthood exists to
   lead and serve the baptismal priesthood of the Church,
   and not to replace it.

Such conclusions call for some reconsideration of the shape of the
1979 ordination rites.

The Role of the Church in the Act of Ordination

The 1979 rites do not bring out as clearly as they might the essential role that the whole Church plays in the act of ordination. On
the contrary, at a number of points they give the unfortunate
impression that those present are little more than spectators at
what is essentially an episcopal action, the friends and family who
have come to support the ordinand on his/her big day, rather than
the baptized people of God who are intimately involved in the
process. It is small wonder, then, that the way in which ordinations are actually performed in some dioceses bears a closer resem-
blance to a successful graduation than to the humble prayer of the
Church for the divine grace needed to accomplish what is, humanly speaking, an impossible task. This style of celebration, moreover, helps to perpetuate the unfortunate attitude held by many
people in previous generations, in which ordination and not baptism was equated with "going into the church."

   Changes could, therefore, be made at three points in the rites to
reduce this tendency:

(a) The Presentation

While the directions for the presentation of the candidate at the ordination of a bishop in the 1979 rite state that the presenters are to be "representatives of the diocese" (BCP, p. 513), the directions in the ordination of priests and deacons merely require them to be "a Priest and a Lay Person" (BCP, pp. 526, 538). Nevertheless, in these latter two cases the presenters do act "on behalf of the clergy and people of the Diocese," as they state in their presentation, and indeed on behalf of all who have been involved in the process of discerning the validity of the ordinand's call, since they must then attest that the selection has been in accordance with the canons of the Church and that he/she is qualified for the order. For that reason it is not appropriate for the presenters to be the friends of the ordinand, still less that his/her spouse should be included, as sometimes happens. It would thus be helpful for the directions in the text to be more specific. For example, more suitable presenters would be members of the Diocesan Commission on Ministry and the Rector and a Warden of the parish in which the ordinand is to serve.

Some changes are also needed in the words of presentation. First, it is desirable that they should specify the place where the ordinand is to minister. Ancient Christian tradition always insisted that someone could not simply be ordained as "a bishop and chief pastor" in the Church at large or as a priest or deacon "in Christ's holy catholic Church," which is all that the 1979 rites state. Instead, ordination had always to be to a specific ministry in a particular place or Christian community, and so this ought to be included in the statement. Second, in the rite for a bishop, the presenters currently ask the Presiding Bishop "in the power of the Holy Spirit to consecrate" the candidate. If the understanding that ordination is an act of God which is exercised through the whole Church is accepted, then these words need to be amended to reflect that.

(b) The Prayer of the People

It is vital that the important place belonging to the prayer of the people in the rite be more strongly emphasized. Currently, the Litany for Ordinations forms the conclusion of the section headed "The Presentation," and then there is a second opportunity for prayer immediately prior to the ordination prayer itself, where the hymn *Veni Creator Spiritus* or *Veni Sancte Spiritus* is sung and a period of silent prayer follows (BCP, pp. 515, 520, 527, 533, 539, 544). Duplicating the prayer of the people in this way may serve to diminish its significance, and in neither case is the action given much prominence: it does not have its own heading in the text, nor is it introduced by a solemn bidding of the type found in classical ordination rites (except in the case of the rite for a bishop, where the bidding from the traditional Anglican ordination rite has been retained before the first of the two periods of prayer). This lack of emphasis appears to encourage the commonly held view that it is the ordination prayer alone that matters, and that the prayers of the congregation are merely incidental to the rite. Early ordination rites, however, would challenge that way of thinking. The prayer of the whole assembled community of baptized Christians is an invariable feature of such rites, and the ordination prayer constitutes the climax and conclusion to this central action.[3] It would be desirable therefore to give greater emphasis to the period of prayer that immediately precedes the ordination prayer. It could be given its own heading in the service and should certainly be introduced by a substantial bidding affirming its importance.

(c) The Peace

The 1979 rites direct that at the Peace the newly ordained should greet "family members and others" (BCP, pp. 522, 534, 546). This suggests the idea that ordination is primarily something personal or familial rather than ecclesial. While there is nothing wrong with the newly ordained exchanging a greeting with family and friends, this should not be at the expense of the exchange of the Peace between the new minister and the lay people and clergy among and with whom he/she is to serve. For the same reason, it is questionable whether it is really "appropriate," as the 1979 rites say, for the bread and wine for the eucharist to "be brought to the Altar by the family and friends of the newly ordained" (BCP, pp. 511, 524, 536). What follows is not a semi-private celebration of the eucharist for the newly ordained, family and friends, but the liturgy of the local Christian community, and persons who better represent that body would be more suitable for this role.

The function of the Peace in relation to the rest of the rite also calls for further examination. In ancient ordination practice, the bishop presiding over the rite always exchanged a kiss with the newly ordained at the conclusion of the ordination and before the eucharist continued.[4] This was not merely the normal greeting of Peace which occurred in every eucharistic celebration but a "sealing," as it were, of the ordination process: the bishop thereby signalled his acceptance of the new minister, and the rest of the clergy and people then did likewise. In other words, it was they who initiated the greeting to the newly ordained. The 1979 rites, however, exhibit some confusion.

In the rite for a priest, the bishop is directed to greet the newly ordained first, but then the new priest initiates the Peace before the other priests present greet him or her, and afterwards the new priest in turn is said to initiate the greeting of family members and others. The confusion of roles here seems to have arisen because the compilers probably did not see the Peace as part of the ordination itself but as one of the liturgical functions within the regular eucharistic rite that properly belonged to a priest, and so wanted the newly ordained to be able to exercise it. But even so, the giving of the Peace belongs to the person presiding at the eucharist, and it is the bishop and not the priest who then goes on to fulfill that role in the eucharistic prayer.

The rite for a bishop is slightly more logical in this regard, in that the new bishop initiates the Peace and also presides over the rest of the eucharistic rite. But there is a similar confusion of roles surrounding the Peace as there was in the case of the priest: without having greeted the new bishop, the Presiding Bishop presents the newly ordained to the people; the new bishop initiates the Peace; the Presiding Bishop and the other bishops greet the new bishop; and the new bishop then initiates the greeting of "clergy, family members, and the congregation."

The rite for a deacon follows a somewhat different order. The bishop does not first greet the newly ordained but instead initiates the Peace, and then the bishop and clergy (but not the lay people) greet the newly ordained, after which the new deacon exchanges greetings with family members and others. In all three cases, everything would be much clearer if the newly ordained were the recipient of the greetings of the bishop(s), clergy and people present.

The Ordination Prayer and the Imposition of Hands

One of the most welcome features of the 1979 revision was the restoration of the ancient tradition of locating the imposition of hands within an ordination prayer that asked for the Holy Spirit to be poured out upon the ordinands. Those responsible for compiling the rites wanted to give liturgical expression to the conviction that ministers are not ordained merely as the result of the recitation of a particular formula, a view which the older Anglican rites had implied. But at the same time, they were conscious of the Roman Catholic condemnation of Anglican Orders in 1896, which had criticized the imprecision of the "form" (i.e., what it regarded as the essential words) of ordination in the earliest Anglican ordinals;[5] and they also faced the problem of what to do when more than one person was being ordained to a particular order on the same occasion.

As a result, they adopted an arrangement already pioneered in the Church of South India in 1958 and followed in the 1968 draft ordinal of the unsuccessful attempt at Anglican-Methodist reunion in England, in which hands are laid on the ordinand only during one sentence of the ordination prayer—the one that asks God to send down the Holy Spirit upon the person for the particular order—and this sentence is repeated over each ordinand in turn before the bishop then goes on to complete the rest of the ordination prayer. Unfortunately, this way of doing things—which has no precedent in any other Christian tradition—tends to reinforce the very idea that the compilers were trying to avoid, since it gives the impression that ordination is effected by the recitation of this particular set of words alone, and that the rest of the prayer is relatively unimportant.[6]

It is highly desirable, therefore, for the imposition of hands to be continued throughout the whole petitionary section of the ordination prayer, and for a different arrangement to be adopted when there is more than one person to be ordained at a time. If there were a only very small number of candidates, the whole prayer could be repeated over each one of them, or perhaps better still, the bishop could move along the line of ordinands, laying hands briefly on each one in turn, while the prayer itself was said only once; this would make it clearer that no particular set of words in the prayer needed to be recited over each person. If numbers were too great for this method to be practicable, there is the arrangement adopted in the current Roman Catholic rites, where the laying on of hands on each person takes place in silence immediately before the prayer, and then the prayer is recited once over them all. Although this procedure does force a separation between the prayer and the ritual gesture, the two remain in very close proximity to one another. But even better than any of these options might be a return to the practice of the early church, where a candidate was usually ordained in the particular local congregation in which he was to serve, rather than the medieval custom of ordaining a group of candidates at some more central location for the convenience of the ordaining bishop. To this day, the rule has been retained in the Orthodox churches that not more than one person may be ordained to each ecclesiastical order during any one service.

In relation to the text of the ordination prayers, two other factors need to be considered. First, the appropriateness of what is now part of the central petition of the prayers for the presbyterate and diaconate, "fill *him* with grace and power, and make *him* a priest/deacon in your Church" (BCP, pp. 533, 545), may be questioned. Not only does it emphasize authority rather than service as the primary characteristic of the ordained ministry, but the request for God to make someone a minister is not a common feature of the earliest Christian ordination prayers. On the contrary, those prayers generally understand the person to have already been appointed to the office through the election which has preceded this rite. Thus they ask God for the bestowal of the particular qualities and gifts necessary for the fruitful discharge of that office upon which the new minister is embarking, in a somewhat similar way to the act of prayer and blessing in a traditional marriage rite, which follows—rather than precedes or effects—the joining of the couple in matrimony.[7]

The second factor that warrants consideration is the continued use of a version of the prayer from the so-called *Apostolic Tradition* of Hippolytus as the ordination prayer for a bishop. Although the Roman Catholic Church has adopted the same prayer, recent scholarship has begun to cast doubts on the traditional identification of the document in which this prayer occurs as actually being the *Apostolic Tradition* of Hippolytus, and hence an early-third-century description of liturgical practice at Rome. It now seems more likely that the document may be a composite work containing elements from different time periods and even different geographical regions, and thus in its extant form be representative of no single ecclesiastical tradition.[8] Moreover, it is quite untypical of other ancient ordination prayers in its strongly authoritarian and sacerdotal language, and those same characteristics have also limited its appeal to most other provinces of the Anglican Communion: only Scotland in its 1984 rite has followed the lead of the USA in adopting it as the ordination prayer for a bishop.

The Vesting and the Bestowal of Symbols of Office

Although from the perspective of the theology of ordination, the ceremonial acts of vesting and the bestowal of symbols of office may be considered as peripheral to the central ritual of ordination, in actual liturgical performance they are often the most prominent and so largely responsible for the tendency to view ordination as graduation or promotion. Currently, the vesting comes immediately after the conclusion of the ordination prayer itself and so seems to constitute the climax of the rite, resembling the "hooding" of the recipient of an academic degree. It would be preferable, therefore, if it were to follow the Peace instead, so that the newly ordained could be more clearly seen to be vesting in order to carry out the liturgical functions of their new order in the eucharistic celebration that follows, or even if the ordinands were already vested when the service first began, as was the practice in the ancient Roman ordination rites. Similarly, the encouragement in the directions for the ceremonial bestowing of "other instruments or symbols of office" after the presentation of the Bible (BCP, pp. 521, 553) may need to be reconsidered. A chalice and paten, for instance, are more appropriately brought to the altar along with the bread and wine to be used in the community's celebration of the eucharist than given to the priest as though they were his/her personal property.

Conclusion

Many of the criticisms and suggestions in this essay may seem to be of minor importance. But details of the way that we do things ceremonially often speak volumes about our real beliefs, and this is no less true in the case of an ordination than it is in other ecclesiastical rites. The manner of celebration and the roles assigned to different individuals and groups within it symbolize and communicate our understanding of the interrelationship of the different parts of the body of Christ. Thus, to get the shape of the ordination liturgy right is to help bring clarity to our theology of ministry.

Notes

1. See Colin Buchanan, *Modern Anglican Ordination Rites*, Alcuin/GROW Liturgical Study 3 (Bramcote, Nottingham: Grove Books, 1987).

2. This concept was articulated in the Constitution of the Church of South India and reiterated in the preface to its 1958 ordination rites, which formed one of the principal sources of the 1979 American revision.

3. See Paul F. Bradshaw, *Ordination Rites of the Ancient Churches of East and West* (New York: Pueblo, 1990), pp. 26-32.

4. Ibid., pp. 34-5.

5. See Paul F. Bradshaw, *The Anglican Ordinal: Its History and Development from the Reformation to the Present Day* (London: S.P.C.K., 1971), p. 143.

6. See further Paul F. Bradshaw, "The Liturgical Consequences of *Apostolicae Curae* for Anglican Ordination Rites," *Anglican Theological Review* 78 (1996): 75-86.

7. Ibid.

8. See Paul F. Bradshaw, "Redating the Apostolic Tradition: Some Preliminary Steps," in John Baldovin & Nathan Mitchell, eds., *Rule of Prayer, Rule of Faith: Essays in Honor of Aidan Kavanagh, OSB* (Collegeville, MN: Liturgical Press, 1996), pp. 3-17.

"Gentle as a Dove, Living, Burning as Fire": Images and Language in the 1979 Ordinal

Richard G. Leggett

Paul Bradshaw, prior to becoming a member of the faculty of the University of Notre Dame, gave a public lecture on the use and abuse of patristic texts. In the course of that lecture he quoted the petition for the gift of the Holy Spirit from the rite for the ordination of a bishop in the 1979 prayer book:

> Therefore, Father, make *N.* a bishop in your Church. Pour out upon *him* the power of your princely Spirit, whom you bestowed upon your beloved Son Jesus Christ, with whom he endowed the apostles, and by whom your Church is built up in every place, to the glory and unceasing praise of your Name. (BCP, p. 521)

Dr. Bradshaw then asked the assembled students and faculty what it meant for a church serving in a twentieth-century republic to ask that a share of God's "princely Spirit" be given to its bishops.

This question still echoes in my thoughts and remains a question for all North American Anglicans. While I give thanks for the work of those responsible for the 1979 ordinal, their work cannot be enshrined as the ultimate nor even penultimate word in the revision of Anglican ordination rites. Canadians took this ordinal and, with significant revisions, made it the basis of the 1985 rite in *The Book of Alternative Services* (pp. 631-66). Anglicans in New

Zealand drew from the American rite as well as others in the creation of a unique and distinctive set of ordination rites as part of *A New Zealand Prayer Book* (pp. 887-924). Revisers in Canada and New Zealand, however, were not content to make structural changes alone; both rites make significant contributions to the development of new language and images for ordination as well as the recovery of older language and images that the tradition has covered with dust.

The task before us now is to ask whether our present understanding of the relationship between ordained ministry and the ministry of all the baptized is as clearly articulated in the language and images of the 1979 ordinal as we desire. In the twenty-five years between the publication of the trial ordinal and the present, significant changes have occurred in the life of North American Anglicanism. The ordination of women to the episcopate and presbyterate is no longer theory but fact. The exploration of the boundaries of liturgical language has pushed us beyond the patristic age into our own. New models of ministry, including the growth of the diaconate as an order with its own integrity, have begun to change our ways of engaging in our mission.

Ordination rites are ecclesial structures that give shape to the sacrament of order. Through the sacrament of order we are able to catch a glimpse of the nature of the reign of God. This mystery finds its clearest expression, perhaps, in the epistle to the Ephesians (4:11-13):

> But each of us was given grace according to the measure of Christ's gift.... The gifts he gave were that some would be apostles, some prophets, some evangelists, some pastors and teachers, to equip the saints for the work of ministry, for building up the body of Christ, until all of us come to the unity of the faith and of the knowledge of the Son of God, to maturity, to the measure of the full stature of Christ.

Ordination rites attempt to give concrete historical and cultural expression to this mystery. On the one hand, rites make use of language and images which can help us experience the mystery which the sacrament of order signifies. On the other hand, rites can become so culturally and historically limited that they obscure the sacrament and, as a consequence, hinder participation in the mystery.

One approach to the revision of the 1979 ordinal would be to begin with the existing ordinal and make changes to it. Such an approach would be fundamentally conservative. The presumption would be that the 1979 ordinal has served us well and requires only fine tuning rather than complete revision. A different approach would start with basic principles. This second approach does not preclude us from making use of texts and structures from the existing ordinal, but it does require us to establish principles rather than toy with texts and structures.[1]

The first principle established by the drafters of the 1979 ordinal was that "All Christians, as members of Christ's Body, participate in his royal priesthood; we are a priestly people, a living temple consecrated by the Holy Spirit." In ordination some members of this priestly people are given grace to perform the responsibilities of preaching the Gospel, pastoral care and sacramental presidency:

> The Christian clergyman [sic] is not being assigned to witness to the gospel, to care for the poor, or to pray, so that other members of the Church can be dispensed from these activities. Rather, the pastor is to help his people in the fulfillment of what is their vocation as well as his. Seen in this light, the mission of the ordained minister is related organically to the mission of all the baptized. The ordained ministry finds its fulfillment in the enabling of the entire Christian community to exercise its ministry in the service of God and man [sic].[2]

More recent reflections on the relationship between ordained ministry and the ministry of all the baptized have tended to support the understanding of this relationship as articulated by the drafting committee.

A similar view of the relationship between lay and ordained ministry is found in *Baptism, Eucharist and Ministry*, an ecumenical statement seeking to identify the convergence of the churches' teaching on contentious issues which continue to divide us:

> The word *ministry* in its broadest sense denotes the service to which the whole people of God is called, whether as individuals, as a local community, or as the universal Church.[3]

This ministry is exercised through the mutual ordering of gifts which allows for a collaboration between lay and ordained ministries:

> All members of the believing community, ordained and lay, are interrelated. On the one hand, the community needs ordained ministers. Their presence reminds the community of the divine initiative, and of the dependence of the Church on Jesus Christ, who is the source of its mission and the foundation of its unity. They serve to build up the community in Christ and to strengthen its witness.... On the other hand, the ordained ministry has no existence apart from the community. Ordained ministers can fulfil their calling only in and for the community. They cannot dispense with the recognition, the support and the encouragement of the community.[4]

The affirmation given by the Episcopal Church to this convergence document and the absence of any criticism of the above statements in the official response of the Episcopal Church leads to the conclusion that the "Ministry" section of *Baptism, Eucharist and Ministry* expresses the mind of the Episcopal Church regarding the ministry of ordained and lay Christians.[5] This affirmation provides some guidance for future revision.

A second principle articulated by the drafters of the 1979 ordinal was that "Leadership requires within itself certain differentiations of function and rank." This assertion leads to a definition of the bishop as the leader of the Church's mission and ministry. Presbyters are the bishop's associates in the exercise of leadership, deacons the bishop's assistants.[6] *Baptism, Eucharist and Ministry* supports this perspective:

> ...the threefold ministry of bishop, presbyter and deacon may serve today as an expression of the unity we seek and also as a means for achieving it.... In the fulfilment of their mission and service the churches need people who in different ways express and perform the tasks of the ordained ministry in its diaconal, presbyteral and episcopal aspects and functions.[7]

The exercise of these ordained ministries requires certain guiding principles to ensure the proper working of the body of Christ:

> The ordained ministry should be exercised in a personal, collegial and communal way. It should be *personal* because the presence of Christ among his people can most effectively be pointed to by the person ordained to proclaim the Gospel and to call the community to serve the Lord in unity of life and witness. It would also be *collegial,* for there is need for a college of ordained ministers sharing in the common task of representing the concerns of the community. Finally, the intimate relationship between the ordained ministry and the community should find expression in a *communal* dimension where the exercise of the ordained ministry is rooted in the life of the community and requires the community's effective participation in the discovery of God's will and the guidance of the Spirit.[8]

The threefold ordained ministry and the exercise of authority within personal, collegial and communal spheres of life find strong affirmation in the official response of the Episcopal Church. However, Episcopalians criticized the document for not being clear enough in describing (a) the relationships between bishops, presbyters and deacons, (b) the relationship between bishops and presbyters, and (c) the participation of presbyters in the councils of the Church.[9] These criticisms emerge out of the Episcopal Church's liturgical experience, yet there is a recognition of the need to move further in the Church's incorporation of its theology into its life:

> We acknowledge that the whole of BEM radically challenges us. We confess that we ought to practice more fully what we say we believe. This church has, for example, already implemented most liturgical changes indicated or implied in BEM, including its implications for our liturgies of ordination.[10]

Despite the disclaimer, there are still dimensions of the ordination rites that require revision in order to express more fully and clearly the implications of the Church's theology.

The principles described above help shape the ordination rites. Ordained ministry is *derivative* of the ministry of the whole people of God, not *constitutive* of that ministry. Ordained ministry is a *representation* of the ministry of all the baptized, not a *substitute* for that ministry. Ordained ministry is inherently *collegial*, relying upon the collaboration of ministries, lay and ordained.

In addition to these principles, the revision of the language and images of the ordinal must be guided by norms which help give form to the principles themselves. First, "worship must be shaped to fit the needs of actual people in a specific time and place."[11] Imagery and language arise from the collective experience of a given community over time, and express both the universal and particular aspects of that community's condition. For example, to those of us living near the sea and mountains, "Saint Patrick's Breastplate" (370 in *The Hymnal 1982*) evokes familiar images.

These images, however, may not be as evocative for those of us living on the prairies. Liturgical rites must allow for images particular to the gathered community to be expressed in central liturgical texts and actions as well as in hymnody.

Fidelity to this norm requires that the liturgical texts and rubrics must be revised in ways to dispose of gender-specific language. Throughout the ordinal, when the candidate is referred to in the third-person singular, the masculine singular is used. Whenever the candidate is addressed directly, the form of address is "My brother." Although the masculine singular pronouns and the term "brother" are printed in italics, indicating that these terms are to be changed when the gender or number of the candidates requires it, the overall effect of the continued use of exclusively masculine language is to suggest that the normative candidate is male. In the Canadian rite, the convention is to use "he/she" when required and to address the ordinand by his or her baptismal name rather than by "brother" or "sister." The New Zealand convention is to use "s/he" and to address the ordinand by name as well.

A second norm is theological: "what we do must reflect Christian faith."[12] If liturgical rites are to be faithful articulations of the sacraments of the Christian mystery, then images and language which are not expressive of this mystery, despite their antiquity, have no place in the rites.

> If at any point circumstances should force us to choose faithfulness to the gospel and faithfulness to any other aspect of the tradition—church, ordained ministry, doctrinal definitions, or whatever—the only authentically Christian choice is to prefer the gospel over everything else.[13]

Finally, in tension with the previous norm, is the statement that "we cannot make decisions independently from the worship experiences of millions of Christians around the world over the course of twenty centuries."[14]

> The past is basic to adult human identity. All of us may have some areas of selective amnesia; but, on

the whole, we think of the victims of amnesia as unfortunate because they have lost massive parts of who they are. Still, the past is never a full or sufficient definition of a person, that is, until a person is dead. Sometimes taking the next step in our lives demands turning our backs on some aspect of our past or, at the very least, recognizing the ways in which our past hinders us and choosing to build on some parts of it rather than others.[15]

While history is not prescriptive, it is not irrelevant. The practice of designating chosen individuals to serve in roles of public ecclesial leadership by the laying on of hands with prayer by those authorized to do so did not spring full-grown from the forehead of the first-century church. Christians have found and continue to find that this action has served the mission and ministry of the Church.

For the sake of this discussion of the future revision of the language and images of the ordination rites, I have chosen to consider the ordination rites as consisting of five liturgical units: (1) the presentation of the candidate, (2) the readings, (3) the examination of the candidate, (4) the consecration of the candidate, and (5) the explanatory rites.

1. The Presentation of the Candidate

In all three rites of the present ordinal, the language and images of the presentation of the candidates for ordination seek to hold before us the derivative nature of ordained ministry. It is significant to note that the ordinal specifies that the candidate for any ordained ministry begins the liturgy without any vesture signifying ecclesiastical or academic rank or order (BCP, pp. 511, 524, 536). The candidate arrives as a member of the people of God who has been called to a new ministry.

Candidates for the episcopate, presbyterate and diaconate must be presented by lay and ordained representatives of the community in which the candidates are to serve (BCP, pp. 513, 526, 538). While no directions are given regarding the identity of lay presenters, the appropriate rubric in all three rites specifies that the ordained presenter is to be a presbyter.[16] Yet if the lay and clerical presenters are to be speaking on behalf of the Church, then their identities are not a casual concern. The ordinal in *A New Zealand Prayer Book* (p. 922) is more specific than the 1979 prayer book in describing the selection of presenters:

> The presenters for deacons and priests shall be chosen by the candidates in consultation with the bishop.
>
> The priest and lay representative who present the bishop-elect shall be appointed by the Standing Committee of the Diocese concerned. The bishop who takes part in the presentation shall, after consultation with the bishop-elect, be appointed by the presiding bishop on behalf of the Province.

Presenters should be persons who have had an actual role in the selection and/or training of the candidate. In this way one may more clearly see that ordained ministry arises from an individual's response to the community's call.

A second issue arising from the existing rubrics is the specification that presbyters are to be the clerical presenters. This perpetuates the image that the ordained ministry consists only of bishops and presbyters, thus diminishing the stated intent of the original revisers that ordained ministry be envisioned as a collaboration of orders. Presently in the Anglican Communion, deacons are among the presenters of candidates for the diaconate in Scotland and the presenters of bishops in Canada.[17] Given the growth of the diaconate as a full and equal order among North American Anglicans, the exclusion of deacons from the ordained presenters of candidates for ordination provides a diminished image of the ordained ministry into which the candidate is entering.

2. The Readings

The scriptural texts used in the ordinal are, at times, exclusive of women. The appointment of 1 Timothy 3:8-13 for the ordination of a deacon, although translated in the New Revised Standard Version as "Let deacons be married only once" instead of "Let deacons be the husband of one wife," poses the question as to whether a section of a household code is an important image for the diaconate. Likewise, 1 Timothy 3:1-7, among the appointed readings for the ordination of a bishop, is based upon a household code in which women are under the authority of their husband or father. As an image for the episcopate in an age in which we are striving to restore a collegial and communal aspect to the exercise of authority, the use of texts based upon a Greco-Roman *pater familias* is problematic.

With the restoration of readings from the Hebrew scriptures come new problems as well. Both of the texts from Isaiah appointed for the ordination of a bishop have messianic associations and are not necessarily descriptive of the Church's expectations of its bishops.[18] In the rite for the ordination of a presbyter, Isaiah's vision and appointment as a prophet (Isaiah 6:1-8) is moving and significant in the life of the people of God. The question for the Church, however, is whether it expects its presbyters to assume the prophetic role in the Church.

Psalm 99, a kingship psalm appointed for the ordination of a bishop, raises various specters, including the appropriateness of associating the ministry of bishops with monarchy. Psalm 40:1-14, also appointed for the ordination of a bishop, is a plea for vindication by one who has experienced persecution and rejection by those among whom the psalmist has ministered. In the rite for the ordination of a presbyter, Psalm 43 begins by invoking God: "Give judgment for me, O God, and defend my cause against an ungodly people; deliver me from the deceitful and wicked" (BCP, p. 644). One is almost immediately forced to ask, "Who is this ungodly people?"

The stiffest challenge comes in finding new scriptural texts which celebrate the ministry of women. If we seek texts which indicate that women have held positions of authority in the life of Jewish and Christian communities, then we find the list somewhat limited.

In the Hebrew scriptures, several texts come to the fore. The first is Exodus 15:20-21, in which Miriam, the sister of Moses, is described as a prophet. Another is Judges 4:4-10, which describes the beginning of Deborah's judgeship in Israel. In the deutero-canonical books, Judith 15:12-14, 16:13-16 tells of Judith and the women of Israel leading the people in celebrating their victory and in praising God.

In the New Testament our task is to discover texts in which women are shown to be exercising ministries traditionally ascribed to men. The first and foremost example is Mary Magdalene, the first Christian apostle, a woman to whom the risen Christ appears, to whom Christ gives a commission to proclaim his resurrection, and who fulfills this commission (Matthew 28:1-10; Luke 24:1-10; John 20:11-18). There is the unnamed woman who anoints Jesus and whose faith will be celebrated wherever the Gospel is proclaimed (Matthew 26:6-13; Mark 14:3-9). Among the first to know and proclaim that Jesus is the messiah are the woman at the well in Samaria (John 4:4-42) and Martha, the sister of Lazarus (John 11:17-27). Although Romans 16:1-2 has been appointed for use in one Anglican ordinal, it is worth considering expanding the passage to include verses 3 to 16 with its list of the men and women who shared with Paul in the apostolic work. Other women gave the Church its first places of meeting and were considered among its leaders and teachers: Lydia of Philippi (Acts 16:11-15), Priscilla of Ephesus (Acts 18:1-4,24-26) and the "elect lady" of 2 John (2 John 1-9).

Equally important as the restoration of texts which celebrate the ministry of women is their use. It is not sufficient that these texts make their appearances only at the ordination of women. If these texts have value as celebrations of the ministry which God gives to the Christian people, then their value extends beyond simple gender equality into the realm of texts which remind us that all of us, men and women, are called into ministry. A sign of the full integration of women into the Church's ministry will be occasions when the decision to use one or more of these texts is not determined by the gender of the ordinands.[19]

As Anglicans begin to recover a baptismal theology of ministry, other necessary revisions of the use of scripture in the ordinal emerge. Among these revisions is whether we should continue to use a typological approach to ordination readings, i.e., providing a list of appointed readings or limiting ordinations to specific days, or instead should follow present baptismal practice. This latter practice identifies major feasts on which baptisms are most appropriate, but also permits baptisms to occur at other times and appoints the readings of the day whenever baptism is celebrated as the principal service on a Sunday or other feast (BCP, p. 300). It seems appropriate that the ordination rites follow a similar pattern. Certain Anglican ordinals, for example, that of the Canadian *Book of Alternative Services* (pp. 632, 642, 651), have moved in this direction and this should be encouraged throughout the Communion.

One advantage to using the scriptures of the day is that it frees the preacher to set the ordination in the broader context of God's activity rather than the narrower typological framework provided by an appointed list. In addition, the continuing revision of lectionaries to include texts celebrating the place of women in God's economy of salvation offers the preacher new opportunities to link the occasion of the ordination to the work of God in creating a whole people.

3. The Examination of the Candidate

In simplest terms, the question that I want to pose is "What do we think we are doing when we ordain someone?"

> When, therefore, we come to ask what is meant by
> "ordination," we are concerned...with the interrela-
> tionship between a group and the leadership of
> that group.... On the one hand the group, in order
> to continue its life and develop its concerns, calls
> for certain sorts of leadership; on the other, differ-
> ent members of the group contribute their own
> particular aptitudes. In choosing and appointing its
> leaders...the group authorizes them to employ
> these talents to further its purposes, and clothes
> them, as it were, with its own characteristics. Thus
> ordination presupposes both a vocation, "directly"
> from God, in the sense that he endows an individ-
> ual with certain gifts, and mediately "through the
> Church" in its selection of him [sic] to exercise cer-
> tain of its functions.... The ordination itself is first
> a prayer that God will endorse this choice by
> enabling the ordinand to fulfil and persevere in the
> functions allotted to him, and secondarily, and by
> implication, the public authorization and commis-
> sion of the man concerned.[20]

Ordination is the public recognition of God's gifts for ministry
already present in an individual and the community's prayer that
this individual might be empowered to use these gifts in a lifelong
commitment to support the community's ministry and mission.[21]
The examination, with its prologue and subsequent questions and
answers, provides an opportunity for the Church to declare its
convictions and to establish the parameters within which it expects
the ordained to act.

The language of the present ordinal reveals a tentative recovery
of a baptismal theology of ministry. The rites speak of the ministry
of the whole people of God, and images which tend to subordinate
the laity to the clergy are being replaced by ones which uphold the
call of God to all the baptized. This shift, however, has not yet

been fully reflected in the roles that laity take in the ordination rites nor in the language used to describe the relation of the ordained priesthood to the priesthood of all the faithful. In order to reflect the appropriate role of the laity, future revision of the ordinals must begin from the presupposition that "Christians...do not ordain to the priesthood, they baptize to it."[22] This presupposition will lead Anglicans to question whether it is appropriate for ordination rites to outshine baptismal rites in their complexity.

> [I]t seems that the ritual power of the ordination rite exceeds in practice that of baptism. At no step in our comparison does the action of baptism (as conventionally practiced) speak more loudly than ordination at a comparable point.... It may seem harsh to say it, but on the basis of this comparison, what we want to claim about baptism and "the principal order of ministry" is ritual nonsense. And so long as that remains true, our teaching, however wise and faithful, however substantive and compelling, will be defeated by our ritual actions, which by this test contradict our theology.[23]

Reform of the provisions regarding presenters is only part of the solution. Lay persons might also be permitted to join with the bishop in asking the questions put to the candidates. Some ordinals already permit other bishops to join in asking the questions of a bishop-elect; perhaps the time has come for this practice to be expanded, in appropriate ways, to include laity, presbyters, and deacons. Such a revision might help to emphasize the communal dimensions of the ministry into which a candidate is entering.

The communal dimension of the exercise of authority is treated unevenly in the manner in which the ordination rites describe the ordained as sharing with the laity in ministry and decision-making.[24] For example, the 1979 ordinal does not describe the bishop as sharing the government of the Church with the laity, although the presbyter is challenged to labor "together with (those whom you are called to serve) and with your fellow ministers to build up the family of God" (BCP, p. 532). Since synodical government characterizes the Anglican Communion and shapes its practice of authority, then it is incumbent upon the ordinals to reflect that the ordained ministry exercises whatever authority it possesses in collaboration with the baptized.[25] An example of a liturgical articulation of this reality is found in the rite for bishops in *A New Zealand Prayer Book* (p. 917):

> *Presiding Bishop* Will you uphold the authority of
> the General Synod and the Constitution of the
> Church of this Province?
> *Bishop-elect* Yes, I will. I am under that authority,
> and will exercise it in partnership with my sisters
> and brothers in Christ.

Language such as this makes it clear that bishops, while exercising personal authority, do so within a community who share in dimensions of decision-making.

4. The Consecration of the Candidate

In the 1979 ordinal the consecration of the candidate consists of three parts: (a) the singing of *Veni Creator Spiritus* or *Veni Sancte Spiritus*, (b) a period of silent prayer, and (c) the ordination prayer with the laying on of hands (BCP, pp. 520-1, 533-4, 544-5). While it is significant that this liturgical unit is parallel in all three rites, future revision will need to address at least two of these parts.

First, the singing of the hymn *Veni Creator Spiritus* or *Veni Sancte Spiritus*, while of some antiquity, cannot be assumed to be a *sine qua non* of the ordination rites.[26] In his speech to the governing body of the Church in Wales, Keith Denison speaks of that revision committee's proposal to omit the *Veni Creator Spiritus* completely:

> [W]e have to consider the historical and theologi-
> cal context of the use of this hymn.... As long ago
> as 1932, scholars were pointing out—and here I

quote the tome *Liturgy and Worship*—"The introduction of the *Veni Creator* into the medieval rite
of ordination...could not but have the effect of
obscuring the significance of the imposition of
hands." In the Edwardian and 1662 Ordinals,
moreover, the *Veni Creator* was the *only* place in the
rite, quite divorced from the act of ordination
itself, where the Holy Spirit was invoked. But in
most primitive rites, it is the Holy Spirit who is the
giver of Orders. So also, in the services before you,
the invocation to the Holy Spirit comes in the
Ordination Prayer itself, a point which would be
obscured if the *Veni Creator* were to be retained.[27]

An analysis of the content of the hymn suggests that it has the
character of a petition for purgation and enlightenment rather
than empowerment. If the purpose of the hymn is to invoke the
power of the Holy Spirit upon the gathered community so that the
community might accomplish the task that God has given to it,
then the *Veni Creator Spiritus* may not be the best choice. In this
regard, the New Zealand ordinal of 1989 (*A New Zealand Prayer
Book*, pp. 896, 907, 920) might provide a model for future revision:

> *After a pause, the bishop continues*
> Like the first disciples waiting for your coming,
> empowering Spirit, we watch and pray.
> *The congregation prays in silence for the candidates.*
> *Silence*
> *A hymn invoking the Holy Spirit may be sung.*
> *Bishop* Holy Spirit of God, meet us in this moment
> as you met the apostles of old. Be with us, Holy
> Spirit,
> *People* bring faith and hope, we pray.
> *Bishop* Come Holy Spirit
> *People* be present in your power.

Our present ordination rites and the language of the ordination prayers tend to convey the impression that the rite confers upon the person being ordained "something" that he or she did not possess before the rite. What is not always clear is the identity of this "something." Is it the authority to act publicly on behalf of the Church? Is it some indelible character that represents an ontological change in the person being ordained? Is it the release of a charism to be used on behalf of the Church?

Most Anglican ordinals continue to use language for the laying on of hands which suggests that through the imposition of hands the candidate is being given gifts which he or she did not possess prior to the ordination rite. Our ordination rites do not always reflect a theology of "giftedness," a conviction that the person being ordained has the charism for the office to which he or she is being ordained. Here I associate myself with Paul Gibson's thoughts as he writes about blessing in *Occasional Celebrations*, a liturgical publication of The Anglican Church of Canada.

> We bless people not to increase their spiritual dignity but to give thanks for the role they have been called to play within the reign of God and thus to release them to play their part. Every eucharistic prayer is such a blessing: we give thanks for the mighty acts of God and pray that those who gather at the table may be "one body and one holy people, a living sacrifice in Jesus Christ our Lord." Of course our traditional forms of blessing people may continue (e.g., "Almighty God...bless you"), but we should remember that they are prayers of thanksgiving for God's goodness and grace already received, and for its completion in these people.[28]

What would happen to our ordination rites if we were to accept the premise that the ordinand already possesses the necessary gifts of the Spirit for office and that the ordination rite is an elaborate blessing, a rite which releases the ordinand's gifts to be used on behalf of the Church?

At the present time the three ordination prayers of the American ordinal share a common structure. Each begins with an act of praise and thanksgiving to the First Person of the Trinity which includes allusions to scriptural passages thought to be appropriate to the order. This paragraph is followed by the laying on of hands and prayer for the Holy Spirit to be given to the ordinand. The prayer then concludes with a series of petitions for the grace necessary for the faithful exercise of the order to be given to the ordinand.

The prayer for the ordination of a bishop, adapted from the analogous prayer in the *Apostolic Tradition* attributed to Hippolytus of Rome, associates episcopal ministry with "prophets, kings, and priests" (BCP, p. 520). Is episcopal ministry prophetic, monarchical and sacerdotal, or is a bishop "given authority to speak and act as the Church's representative, to be a focus of unity for the diocese" (*A New Zealand Prayer Book*, p. 919)? Later in this same prayer, the presiding bishop asks that God pour out "the power of (God's) princely Spirit" upon the ordinand (BCP, p. 521). While not disputing the accuracy of the translation of a patristic prayer, we have an obligation to ask whether this petition accurately expresses what we are asking God to do when a bishop is ordained. Do we not perhaps want to ask something more like this: "God of grace, through your Holy Spirit, gentle as a dove, living, burning as fire, empower your servant *N.* for the office and work of a bishop in the Church" (*A New Zealand Prayer Book*, p. 921)?

Questions must also be raised with regard to gender. In the Examination, the presiding bishop speaks of the faith of "patriarchs, prophets, apostles, and martyrs" (BCP, p. 517). Likewise, the ordination prayer describes the people of God as inheriting "the covenant of Abraham" and God as raising up "prophets, kings, and priests" to serve the temple, and in the petition for the Spirit asks that God pour out "the power of (God's) princely Spirit" upon the candidate (BCP, pp. 520-1). These texts alone point out the need for any future revision to include complementary feminine images and to revise existing texts in the direction of greater inclusivity.

Revisions to the ordination prayer for a deacon are also necessary. By using Philippians 2:5-11 and Matthew 20:20-28 as the dominant scriptural allusions, the rite tends to emphasize the diaconate as "the servant ministry" of the Church. Yet as contemporary experience of the renewed diaconate in the United States and Canada indicates, the scope of diaconal ministry may be better understood as a ministry of agency, advocacy and empowerment. In this context, the present prayer provides inadequate scriptural referents for the ministry being undertaken.

Ordination prayers might also be revised along the lines of the 1989 New Zealand rites to permit a significant involvement of the laity in the recitation of the prayer. This step has already been taken in various Anglican revisions of the thanksgiving over the water in baptism and the eucharistic prayer. Extending this to the ordination prayer does not seem to be an inappropriate step.

5. Explanatory Rites

Despite the antiquity of the presentation of symbols of office and the implicit acceptance of the Roman Catholic criticisms in *Apostolicae Curae* that the proliferation of this practice in Anglicanism reveals, this practice is increasingly problematic, especially in the rites for the ordination of presbyters, where such symbols range from giving chalice and paten to anointing the hands of the newly ordained. Whereas the symbols given to bishops tend to be items of vesture and regalia, those given to presbyters tend to be associated with the eucharist and stress the role of the presbyter as eucharistic president. Likewise, the giving of the Bible alone perpetuates reformation debates and seems to forget that Anglican authority rests upon the interaction of three sources: scripture, reason and tradition.

Future revision of the ordinal might take its model from the early Roman practice rather than the Gallican. In the Roman model, before the service began the candidates were already vested according to the order they were entering. After the ordination prayer, the newly ordained publicly exercised their ministry in the context of the ordination eucharist. The Gallican practice extended into the major orders the practice of giving symbols of office to candidates for the minor orders. This *traditio instrumentorum* came to be considered as more important than the laying on of hands with prayer. In accepting the Gallican pattern, Anglican ordinals have missed an opportunity to stress the entry of the candidate into an episcopal, presbyteral or diaconal college and the implications of collegiality for the exercise of ministry. By relying upon vesture and upon the exercise of the liturgical responsibilities of a new office in the context of the ordination eucharist, Anglicans could model a liturgical pattern which parallels the baptismal liturgy itself.[29]

Conclusion

The present ordinal will not last the centuries of its spiritual progenitor, the English ordinal of 1662 in its American guises. On the contrary, the ecumenical convergence towards a shared theology of ministry, the renewal of a baptismal theology of ministry, the ordination of women, and the restoration of the diaconate as a full and equal order are but a few of the movements in the Church that will require Anglicans in North America to revise the ordinal once again. This future revision will bring even more to the fore the question of Anglican identity and how that identity might be preserved in the midst of a multicultural and multiracial communion. Whereas the present generation was inclined to dress Hippolytus in tweed, the coming generations will join with Ambrose and, while honoring our ancestors in the faith, will assert in the many voices of Anglicanism that this new generation has common sense, too, and will order its life in the light of that gift.

Notes

1. Bryan D. Spinks and Gianfranco Tellini, "The Anglican Church and Holy Order," in Kenneth Stevenson and Bryan

D. Spinks, eds., *The Identity of Anglican Worship* (Harrisburg, PA: Morehouse Publishing, 1991), pp. 117-18.

2. *The Ordination of Bishops, Priests, and Deacons*, Prayer Book Studies 20 (New York: Church Hymnal Corporation, 1970), pp. 7-8.

3. *Baptism, Eucharist and Ministry*, Faith and Order Paper 111 (Geneva: World Council of Churches, 1982) M 7b. Hereafter cited as *BEM*; citations will be according to section and paragraph, e.g., M 7b = Ministry section, paragraph 7b.

4. *BEM*, M 12.

5. "The Episcopal Church," in Max Thurian, ed., *Churches Respond to BEM: Official Responses to the "Baptism, Eucharist and Ministry" Text*, vol. 2 (Geneva: World Council of Churches, 1986), pp. 57-62.

6. *The Ordination of Bishops, Priests, and Deacons*, pp. 8-10.

7. *BEM*, M 22.

8. Ibid., M 26.

9. *Churches Respond to BEM*, 2:60.

10. Ibid., 2:61.

11. James F. White, *Sacraments as God's Self Giving* (Nashville: Abingdon, 1983), p. 121.

12. Ibid., p. 122.

13. L. William Countryman, *The Language of Ordination: Ministry in an Ecumenical Context* (Philadelphia: Trinity Press International, 1992), p. 24.

14. White, *Sacraments*, p. 123.

15. Countryman, *Language*, p. 4.

16. At the ordination of a bishop, the lay presenters are presumably "representatives of the diocese" (BCP, p. 513).

17. *Scottish Ordinal 1984* (Edinburgh: The General Synod of the

Scottish Episcopal Church, 1984), p. 16; *Book of Alternative Services* (1985), p. 634.

18. In Luke's Gospel, Jesus' reading of and commentary on Isaiah 61:1-8 (Luke 4:16-21) is a revelation of his messianic identity. Isaiah 42:1-9, the so-called First Servant Song, has generated strong scholarly debate as to whether the Servant is an individual or the nation of Israel.

19. I am indebted to my former colleague at Vancouver School of Theology, the Rev. Dr. Janet Cawley, for this observation.

20. Victor De Waal, "What is Ordination?," *Theology* 71 (1968): 554.

21. Everett Ferguson, "Laying on of Hands: Its Significance in Ordination," *Journal of Theological Studies*, new series 26 (1975): 1-12; Geoffrey J. Wainwright, "Some Theological Aspects of Ordination," *Studia Liturgica* 13 (1979): 143; "Church of North India," *Churches Respond to BEM*, 2:72-3; "Church of England," in *Churches Respond to BEM*, 3:60.

22. Aidan Kavanagh, "Christian Ministry and Ministries," *Anglican Theological Review*, Supplementary Series 9 (1984): 39; Wesley Frensdorff, "Holy Orders and Ministry: Some Reflections," *Anglican Theological Review* 59 (1979): 284; Wainwright, "Some Theological Aspects," p. 132.

23. William Seth Adams, "Decoding the Obvious: Reflections on Baptismal Ministry in the Episcopal Church," in Ruth A. Meyers, ed., *Baptism and Ministry*, Liturgical Studies 1 (New York: Church Hymnal Corporation, 1994), p. 10.

24. Peter Dixon, "Mutuality and Episcopacy in the Body of Christ," *The Modern Churchman*, new series 24 (1981): 25-6.

25. "Church of England," *Churches Respond to BEM*, 3:59, 77.

26. H. Boone Porter, "The Theology of Ordination and the New Rites," *Anglican Theological Review* 54 (1972): 77; Spinks and Tellini, "The Anglican Church and Holy Order," p. 118.

27. Keith M. Denison, "Ordination Services," speech made to the Governing Body of the Church in Wales, September 1982.

28. *Occasional Celebrations of The Anglican Church of Canada* (Toronto: Anglican Book Centre, 1992), pp. 119-20.

29. In the baptismal liturgies of the Anglican Communion, participation in the exchange of the peace and reception of the eucharist are increasingly the first "ministerial" acts which the newly baptized perform. Their status as members of the faithful is celebrated by their full participation in the eucharist rather than by the presentation of various symbols.

Celebrating the Ministry of All the Baptized at the Welcoming of New Leaders into the Continuing Life and Ministry of Congregations

Steve Kelsey

I am deeply grateful personally for how the 1979 prayer book has enriched our spiritual life in the Church. Coming into adulthood as the book was finally approved, it represented for me that my Church was serious about treating me as a capable, mature, responsible adult who is called, by virtue of my baptism, to continual, lifelong growth in Christ as a disciple and a minister in the midst of the community of faith. I am to *participate* fully in the ministry of Jesus Christ *in every component of my life*, in companionship with many others who share in that ministry. Discipleship and ministry are discovered, nurtured and practiced *in community*, never in isolation. And the work of *"bringing out the best" in one another* is at the heart of how we do this. When I was ordained, I understood my calling to be to continue that growth personally, even as I gave and received support to and from others (ordained or not) who were also growing, day by day, in Christ.

There is much in the 1979 prayer book to support all of this. But there is a liturgical moment in the lives of many congregations which sends a mixed signal in regard to these things: the "Celebration of a New Ministry."

We know that baptism, not ordination, is the source of ministry and that those who are called to leadership in the community of the faithful are called to *support* and not *replace* the ministry of all the baptized. We know that the gifts of all are crucial to the life and ministry of the Church, even those which seem most modest and small (cf. 1 Corinthians 12). So we have learned in our congregations not to focus attention exclusively on one member's contributions, lest we be distracted from remembering Christ as the center of our life together. But isn't that precisely what we have been doing in the "Celebration of a New Ministry"?

The welcoming of new leaders is an exciting moment in the life of a congregation. Many have high hopes for the new beginning. Old feuds and disappointments are put aside as members reaffirm their commitment to the source of their common life and mission. Often, the arrival of a new leader has been preceded by a time of self-examination and planning by the congregation, a time which can bring considerable healing and reconciliation. Relationships are restored with neighboring congregations, and new leadership often emerges. Many discover a renewed sense of self-esteem as they celebrate what they have accomplished together while others labeled them "vacant." It can also be a time when the people of a congregation remember who they are called to be, not just in relation to one, prominent, usually clerical personality, but as a community of the baptized in their own right: *"a ministering community, rather than a community gathered around a minister,"* as Bishop Wesley Frensdorff liked to say.[1]

For others, it is a traumatic time. Some encounter unresolved personal issues as they grieve the loss of things as they have been. Does affirmation of new leaders involve betrayal of those to whom we were committed before? Leaders, ordained or not, remaining in the congregation may be uncertain as to whether in this new chapter in the life of this congregation their contribution will continue to be welcome. Similarly, the new leader, while excited about the new start, may be uncertain as to how his or her relationship with the members of this new congregation will emerge. Who could live up to all these expectations?

At this crucial moment, the congregation gathers with the bishop and representatives of other congregations and community organizations for a "Celebration of a New Ministry" to mark the beginning of a new chapter in their life together. In the context of this swirl of anxious energy and emotions, all attention, typically, is focused upon the new leader. Even the title of the liturgy encourages this: "celebrating the new ministry" (i.e., the new "cure") of the new leader him or herself, rather than the continuing life of that ministering Christian community. Is the local congregation considered significant primarily as an arena in which professional clergy may ply their trade? The liturgy is planned and observed with a passion often reserved for marriages or coronations. In the background, one can almost hear variations on the theme from *Mighty Mouse*: *"Here he comes, to save the day!"*, so intent is everyone on convincing themselves and one another that they have found the one and only person appropriate to lead this congregation into a new day!

The rite for the "Celebration of a New Ministry" can easily take such a turn. Engraved invitations are sent out, honoring both the new leader and the congregation on their marvelous good fortune in finding one another. The analogy to marriage is not lost, with many thus assuming that the relationship is meant to last until death, retirement... or until something goes wrong. Thus the dissolution of any pastoral relationship tends to carry with it a suspicion of blame or shame for someone. I can remember being welcomed into a new congregation as rector while, simultaneously, another family arrived. There was no fanfare or special liturgy for them, although they were at least as serious about their faith as was I and were to contribute equally to the life and mission of the congregation over the next few years. But it seemed so important to everyone that the arrival of the new cleric be marked with grandeur. I left the ceremony with a clear understanding that by virtue of my ordination and institutional status, my ministry was considered crucial to the life of the congregation, while that of others was merely supportive or incidental.

This practice is not intentionally mean-spirited toward anyone. The anxiety of forming new relationships in the congregation can encourage an escalated effort to make the new leader and his or her family feel welcome. But it raises a question as to whether our practice in inducting new leaders perpetuates the notion that ministry is primarily the province of the ordained, with others being either recipients or, if they are extraordinary, supporters of the ministry of the ordained. Can we, in the excitement of the arrival of a new leader, reaffirm the ministry of *all* the baptized as the foundation of the life of the congregation? How are we in this liturgy to make it clear that this new leader has arrived not to *replace* but to *support* the continuing ministry and leadership of all the baptized in this congregation?

As we grow in our understanding that baptism, rather than ordination, is the primary sacrament of ministry, we will want to reconsider the shape that this liturgy takes. So many cultural forces around us impose expectations and advice as to how "*the* minister" should behave and be treated. In Christ, we are called to reach beyond those expectations to pattern a life in which no one member or segment of the community, no matter what their status within the Church or in the world at large, dominates our attention or activity; in which the gifts and contributions of *all* the baptized are known to be equally precious, equally necessary to the life and mission of the Church. What will it look like when all members of the community of faith are successful at bringing out the best in one another, engaging and supporting all people in ministry, both within the Church gathered and in the Church dispersed, in their daily lives? This we seek to rehearse, to "practice" now in our liturgy.[2]

Why Do We Need a Liturgy for Welcoming New Leaders?

Consider an occasion of the welcoming of a new leader in a congregation when this liturgy would *not* be necessary: the ordination of a "local priest" or "local deacon" (using "Canon 9"). In this case, the new leader is a member of long standing in that community, called by that community to serve among them. There is a natural integrity to such an ordination, as the leader and the people have had years of experience supporting one another in living their baptismal vows. The local congregation is presenting "one of their own" to the bishop to be ordained to a new role. The acclamation by the congregation, "He [or she] is worthy!" is clearly from the heart and carries much weight. There is no question about mutuality and continuity within the life of the local congregation. The action of the bishop and the participation of those from other congregations add a dimension of continuity with the Church universal to the new relationship being forged by the Holy Spirit between these persons locally.

A service of "welcoming" or "inducting" a new leader will be necessary primarily when a congregation is calling as leaders those who have *not* been ordained or commissioned locally—when these leaders are being "imported" rather than emerging naturally from the local community. The bishop is present to assert his or her affirmation of the new leader's role in this community and the connectedness of that person's ministry to the bishop's and hence to the Church universal. But, in addition, there is a need to establish a mutual pastoral relationship between the new leader and this congregation. The presenting crisis is that these people have no "track record" together. They have not lived together long enough for the people to be able to assert *from their own experience* that "This person is a leader *for us*, one who speaks for us and represents who we are and what we are about." What, then, is an authentic role for the congregation under these circumstances?

Consider another moment when a congregation welcomes a new member who has not had a lengthy history in that congregation: the baptism of an infant. It is expected that sufficient effort is extended toward the parents and sponsors of the infant to prepare them for their role in supporting the baptismal life of the child. The congregation is also involved in the process of preparation (*catechesis*) and continuing support (*mystagogy*). Still, even without a lengthy period of preparation of the infant-candidate him or herself, we can baptize with confidence for several reasons. First, this new birth in Christ is accomplished by the action of the Holy Spirit, not by our response to that action. Certainly, we take seriously our responsibility to support the spiritual life of the newly baptized, but it is not our actions alone that make the sacramental action "valid." Rather, we rely upon the action of the Holy Spirit to accomplish what we fail to complete.

Second, we assume that this child will be learning and growing as he or she participates in the life and mission of the Church in the years to come. It doesn't all have to happen before the actual baptism, as long as we continue the process of formation in the years that follow.

Third, in the case of the baptism of an infant, great emphasis is placed upon the intention and commitment of the parents and sponsors and, indeed, of the entire congregation. In many congregations, the question: "Is this candidate prepared to receive this sacrament?" is being voiced in the same breath with another question: "Are *we* prepared, as a community of faith, to administer this sacrament?" This concern is addressed by including in the baptismal liturgy a renewal of baptismal vows for all who have just promised "to support these persons in their life in Christ" (BCP, p. 303). It is a serious, if also a joyful, business to baptize. The sponsors and witnessing congregation are assuming at least as much responsibility as the candidates themselves; for the integrity of the life of the local congregation (the context for the spiritual growth of the newly baptized) is vital to effective support of these persons. *"It takes a village to raise a child,"* the African proverb declares!

Returning to the liturgy of welcoming a new member (this time a new leader) to the life and ministry of a congregation, the liturgy should rehearse the role of the entire congregation in the mutual life and mission they will share. It is appropriate that all the baptized be recalled to their role in supporting the life and mission of this congregation, responsibility which the new leader will now share with them. This makes plain to everyone that the new leader is here not to replace but to support the continuing ministry and leadership of those who now greet him or her!

But another question emerges. In his article in *Liturgical Studies 1*, William Seth Adams asks us to consider how things might be different in the Church if our leaders saw themselves as standing primarily as members of "the blessed company of all faithful people," rather than as "successors of the apostles."[3] Can we, should we, be speaking of this new leader as we speak of any other member? In what way is our relationship with this person different from our relationship with others?

The Relationship of the Baptized to Their Leaders

> Jesus called [the disciples] and said to them, "You know that among the Gentiles those whom they recognize as their rulers lord it over them, and their great ones are tyrants over them. But it is not so among you; but whoever wishes to become great among you must be your servant, and whoever wishes to be first among you must be slave of all. For the Son of Man came not be served but to serve, and to give his life as a ransom for many." (Mark 10:42-45)

> Let the elders who rule well be considered worthy of double honor, especially those who labor in preaching and teaching; for the scripture says, "You shall not muzzle an ox while it is treading out the grain." (1 Timothy 5:17-18)

There has always been some degree of tension within the life of the Church as to the appropriate relationship between leaders and the rest of the community. Leaders significantly represent us and recall us to those aspects of our life together which are central. Were we to arrange our lives around a romantic notion that we need have no leaders, leaders would emerge anyway, perhaps wielding power in inappropriate ways. Clearly, we wish to embrace the ministry of leadership in the Church and incorporate that ministry into our life together in ways that do not inhibit but rather promote powerful participation by all members in the common life of the community.

In *Being Clergy, Staying Human: Taking Our Stand in the River*, Dorothy McRae-McMahon points out that it is easy to think of the clergy's role as being called to "heroism," being experts in every aspect of church life, "extra-special" people. An obsessive pursuit of such a role can easily destroy both cleric and congregation. Instead, McRae-McMahon prefers an image for leadership in the Church from a passage in Joshua (Joshua 3:6,8). As the people of Israel wait on the banks of the Jordan River to enter the Promised Land, God commands Joshua to tell the priests as they carry the ark of the covenant and pass in front of the people:

> When you come to the edge of the waters of the
> Jordan, you shall stand still in the Jordan.

Leaders in the Church, says McRae-McMahon, are those who take the initiative to "step first into the river," to show others what can be done, to encourage them to follow.[4] While I do not agree that it should *always* be the ordained who are "the first to step into the river," I do believe that the primary call of any church leader is to live and act with personal integrity and courage. What leaders stand for and *where* they stand affects the entire congregational system. Sometimes a leader will take the first step him or herself. Other times he or she will be supporting others as they make their move. In either case, the effectiveness of leadership is judged by whether the presence and activity of the leader(s) issue in more participation by all the baptized in the ministry of Christ.

By baptism, all share in the eternal priesthood and servanthood of Christ, but some stand among us as "signs" of these things. What does that mean? A "sign" is that which points to a reality beyond itself, participating to some extent in that reality but not exhausting that reality. The gift of a wedding ring, for example, is a sign of love shared in a relationship, a reminder of that love. It is not in and of itself all that is loving in the relationship. It does not exhaust the couple's love. But it is, to some extent, also a source of that which it signifies. *Gifts cause what they signify to take place.* The giving of a wedding ring is both a sign of love shared and the occasion of more love being generated. In the act of the giving of the ring, more love is added to the relationship.

We can speak of ordination as a gift to the Church so that the Church can be a gift to the world. The deacon, for example, points toward and reminds us of the call of all the baptized to participate in the servanthood, *diakonia*, of Christ. The deacon does not exhaust the ministry of servanthood in and of him or herself, but, if effective in that ministry, causes more of that which the office signifies to take place: more participation by all the baptized in the servanthood of Christ. The deacon, then, is one of the leaders of the diaconal ministry of the congregation, who stands *among* those leaders to remind all the baptized of the ministry in which they all share. In doing this, he or she causes more participation in that ministry to take place.[5]

A liturgy for welcoming new leaders should recognize not only the work to be pursued by that individual but also the ministry *signified* by that minister's role or order (if ordained) and how the entire community of the baptized participates therein.

The Mystery of Continuity

The arrival of a new leader also raises the issue of *continuity* in the life of the congregation. At a time of transition, many are asking: will this continue to be the same congregation for me? Will our local traditions continue to be honored? How will this new chapter in our congregation's life be connected to what has gone before?

In Anglicanism, one sign of the mystery of continuity is the tradition of "apostolic succession" through ordination. Ignatius of Antioch described the bishop as a sign of unity and continuity

within the eucharistic assembly. Irenaeus saw the bishop as providing unity of apostolic teaching; Cyprian taught that the bishop unified the local church community with the Church universal.
Ordination of leaders in a local community celebrates connectedness with the larger Church in all these ways, but that is only one
way in which continuity and coherence are achieved through ordination. Ordination also celebrates a continuity that exists internally
for a community, continuity with its own unique local history and
tradition. This is why it has always been essential that a candidate
for ordination be presented to the bishop by the people as one
whom they affirm as a leader. Relationship to a local community is
essential to the regularity of the sacrament of ordination.

Thus, we need both bishop and local congregational leaders to
take significant roles liturgically at a "Celebration of a New
Ministry." The bishop, in conferring authority upon the new
leader(s) to function in that community (specifically by the reading of the "Letter of Institution"), is rehearsing the continuity
between this community and the Church universal. But the affirmation of the new leader's authority by the local community is
equally important. This new leader will stand among the continuing leaders of this congregation as a sign of the ministry which all
share. If the leader is seen as a focus of church unity, it is unity
both locally and with the Church universal. Both the tradition of
the Church universal *and* local church tradition need to be preserved and handed on.

This last point is often overlooked in considering the work of
passing on the tradition of the Church. In an illuminating discussion of this issue, *Constructing Local Theologies*, Robert J. Schreiter
describes how through the ages, local church communities have
wrestled with a tension: how to be faithful both to the contemporary, local experience of the Gospel and to the tradition of
Christian life that has been received, "the deposit of the faith."[6]
This tension is obvious when Christianity encounters extremely
diverse cultures, but it is also true of the encounter between "the

great Christian tradition" and any local Christian community, in that every congregation can be understood to possess its own distinctive culture, norms, traditions and values.[7]

For tradition to have power, Schreiter asserts, it must have credibility, intelligibility and authority for those who share it. In order for tradition to have life and breath, it must be received and appropriated by a local community, or it is lost. Thus, we can speak of a conversation between "the great Christian Tradition" and local experience, in which the action and reflection of the local community is at least as important as the work of those designated officially as "bearers of the tradition" of the Church.

These insights herald a radical shift in the roles of the "professional theologian" and "the people" in the life of the Church. Rather than being seen as the primary source of theological information or authority, the professional theologian serves as an important resource, "helping the community clarify its own experience and relate it to the experience of other communities, past and present." It is an indispensable but limited role of "creating the bonds of mutual accountability between local and world church."[8] On the other hand, members of the local congregation, whether or not ordained, must be seen not as empty receptacles to be filled with the theological truth dispensed by experts, but as partners in theological dialogue. As Ian M. Fraser puts it:

> The proper subject-matter for theological reflection is [not] the preoccupations of the church.... The proper "reflectors" are [not] academically trained specialists, as if God had not equipped a body of people with gifts of the Spirit for discerning and expressing his will.... People in the thick of life, struggling to make sense of it in complex, difficult/hopeful situations, who search the scriptures together as a source of light, have the equipment to do theology. They have to learn to do so, and be given confidence to do so.[9]

The local leaders of a Christian community, then, require a relationship of continuity with the larger Church, acted out in this liturgy by the presence of the bishop. But the new leader must also clearly share authority and credibility locally to be effective in "bearing" or "handing on" the tradition. Otherwise, he or she may actually inhibit, rather than promote, the preservation of church tradition! Opportunity for the community to commit itself to helping the new leader(s) establish such local credibility is of utmost importance at this time.

"It Takes a Village..."

Our discussion of the mystery of continuity, then, leads to the mystery of mutuality. If *"it takes a village to raise a child,"* it also *"takes a village"* to establish effective leadership, continuity and courageous innovation in the life of any congregation. Ministry is exercised by the entire community of faith. The participation of each and every member, including the new leader, is essential to its effectiveness. The new leader will play a significant role in the life and mission of the congregation not by replacing people in their ministries, but by helping them to share ever more powerfully in the leadership of the congregation. A "Celebration of a New Ministry" is not to be an occasion of people gathering to proclaim hope and faith in what the new leader can do among these "his or her new people." Rather, it should be an occasion of an entire community gathering to proclaim faith and hope in what Christ is already doing among them. The mystery is not just that Christ can work through the ministry of those ordained or designated as new leaders but that Christ can and does work through the ministry of *all* the baptized! And when we have that in focus, a far more honest and healthy relationship emerges between those who lead and all other members of the body.

It is essential that leaders in the Church not define their entire identity and sense of self-worth in relation to their formal role within the institution. When clergy or other church leaders forget that they share an essential identity and common life with all the baptized, they lose perspective. When one is caught in a set of relationships within the Church in which mutuality is replaced with a one-way, "trickle-down" flow of information or spiritual nurturing, not only is our life together diminished, it is, in fact, dangerous to the leader's own spiritual life.

Instead, church leaders need to be recalled to the roots of their Christian lives, that is, that their highest calling is the same as anyone baptized: *to live with integrity in response to their own baptismal vows.* All sacraments are but occasions for this, including ordination.

Many seem to have the impression that the professional church leader is somehow diminished when all the baptized are empowered to share more powerfully in the leadership of the Church. The mystery of mutuality is that the opposite is the case. For whenever anyone in the body of Christ is empowered to act more boldly, with more personal authority, *every* member is honored and strengthened. Never is the seminary-trained professional more valued and useful than when a local community is filled with people who are empowered to preach and teach and engage in every facet of the ministry of the Church and, even more significantly, engaged in powerful witness and service in every component of their daily lives!

Clearly, we need to avoid any notion that the new leader has arrived to "deliver ministry services" to congregants, the passive consumers. Perhaps it is also time to move beyond the idea that the professional church leader is to "develop" the ministries of the others. Instead, let us remember that in our spiritual friendship, it is Christ who is "developing" each of our baptismal ministries. It is a two-way relationship in which both new leader and congregants discover their ministries further "developed" in the context of their life together. Those with graduate education bring that into the conversation, not to replace dialogue with pronouncement but rather to listen first and then respond. With such humility, the received tradition will be far more effectively heard and incorporated into people's lives. "To each is given the manifestation of the Spirit for the common good" (1 Corinthians 12:7), and as *all* share what they have been given, each one grows in faith.

It is important that the new leader be recognized not only as a leader but also as a companion in faith, in need of pastoral ministry from the congregation as well as a dispenser of the same. Dorothy McRae-McMahon, who, as discussed earlier, takes as an image for church leadership "stepping first into the river," writes:

> I ask myself, "could it be that the bravest and truest way to lead people into life is to be authentically human ourselves?" ...Experience has shown me that the world is waiting for a human church—where people can be honest with one another, in which leaders give clear evidence of going through universal human struggles.[10]

It is, in fact, a gift to the entire congregation when leaders share their personal struggles appropriately with other baptized members of the congregation. To maintain a false persona as one who never struggles is a disservice to the congregation, promoting a standard for Christian living which is both unrealistic and ultimately unfaithful, since it is born of fear of how we will be received if we appear less than perfect.

"It takes a village to raise a new leader," for the entire community plays a role in affirming and responding to the new leader as *their* leader. Continuing local leaders who already possess local authority and credibility, who already have the trust and confidence of the local community, will need to invite the newcomer into relationship with them and establish a collegial and mutually supportive spiritual friendship. To hold the new leader off at a distance, as if the substance of his or her spiritual life were of a different character than their own, will leave the new leader starving for spiritual support. To hang back, waiting for the new leader to take the lead, rather than continuing to pursue their ministry with spirit and zeal, will only leave the new leader to make misinformed choices,

regularly frustrating the needs and expectations of others. Instead, the new leader needs direct and honest feedback and to be invited to engage in community life, not only in his or her official role but also as a fellow person of faith in search of spiritual and personal support. The new leader, of course, also needs to embrace the assertiveness of other leaders in the congregation rather than trying to orchestrate everyone's every move.

Several years ago, when I moved to the Diocese of Northern Michigan from New York (where I had received my primary formation in baptism and ordination), it was clear to me that I needed "catechesis" from the people there. I had a good idea of what it meant to be Christian and Episcopalian in New York and how to be a "rector" in a conventional sense. But now I was to serve as a "missioner," supporting the development of ministry in a number of small, remote communities, in which people were taking responsibility for their own life and mission, rather than relying predominantly upon help coming in "from outside." I needed to learn what it meant *for them* to be Christian and to participate in the life of the Church in their communities. I needed people to act, as it were, as "sponsors," praying with me, sharing their stories of how the Holy Spirit had been and still was active in the lives of their congregations. I needed to learn the local traditions, even, at times, the language! (What is a "Yooper" or a "Pastie" or a "Troll"?) In the congregations I served there, it was clear that my capacity to serve was strengthened where that ministry of "catechesis" was taken seriously. In the communities which assumed that I was arriving with all the expertise, that they were there to be formed by me (with little mutuality in the process), in those places I found my presence and activity far less effective. Imported leaders, even those with a seminary education and years of experience, need to be *catechized* by the communities in which they serve, no less than those preparing to be baptized.

In fact, those of us who have spent the bulk of our adult lives (starting at an early age) being called "Father" or "Mother" by people of obviously deeper maturity and spiritual depth, know how powerfully all the baptized do minister to their leaders. This is done in so many ways: by example of Christian living, by gentle questioning, or by bold and prophetic action. Jean Haldane has pointed out that it is not that church members are reluctant to minister until clergy talk them into it. Mature, responsible adults are already engaged in significant ministry all the time! Rather, so much of the ministry which members pursue is undervalued or ignored by the Church. She writes:

> The Church offers warmth of relationship, common purpose, and a chance to do those neighborly things we find difficult in society. In contrast, laity's ministry in the world is complex, often difficult and unclear. Many experience struggles of conscience, tensions and worry in their work, loneliness in the gray areas of public conduct and practice. So, they collude with the clergy to keep themselves focused within church programs.[11]

How easy it is to steer church program toward those issues and matters in which seminary-trained clergy have expertise, deftly avoiding the thorny issues with which most baptized members are truly struggling. Leaders in the Church who spend too many waking hours on "church work" need help in lifting their vision to issues with which others in the community are also concerned. When church members refuse to allow the Church to devote so much time, energy and resources internally, then their leaders are truly being ministered to by their brothers and sisters in Christ.

"Mutuality" involves all members of the congregation inserting their insights and concerns and questions into the fabric of church life, so that the entire faith community is called out of narcissistic self-absorption into fuller participation in the life of the world. It is appropriate, then, that a rite which celebrates the beginning of a new chapter in the life and ministry of a congregation, marked by the arrival of new leadership, celebrate the many dimensions of ministry in which all the baptized are engaged.

Reflections on the "Celebration of a New Ministry"

The occasion of the "Celebration of a New Ministry" might be used to raise such issues within a congregation as it prepares to welcome new leaders. A "Celebration Committee," representative of the congregation, including continuing congregational leaders and the new leader, could meet to discuss the shape and message of the service. Here are some issues which might be considered:

What is the purpose of this liturgy? The new leader, whether ordained or not, has been called by the people for a special purpose. They are gathering to welcome this person as a companion in faith, as well as to recognize him or her formally as a leader among them. A new, mutual pastoral relationship is being established between them.

Increasingly, congregations are choosing different patterns of ministry. Many continue to pursue a "one-priest, one-parish" model but work collegially with a team of persons sharing formally in leadership ("lay pastors," deacons, locally ordained persons, etc.). Others choose to participate in "clusters" or regional ministries, led by ministry teams. Alterations in the service need to be made accordingly. When it involves a "multi-point" setting, for example, provision should be made for involvement of all congregations and persons who are engaged in the ministry which the new leader is joining. While the arrival of the new leader marks a turning point in their life together, the local community has a history rich with its own traditions and customs which ought to be considered when planning the celebration. Work which has gone before and work which is continuing ought to be acknowledged. Continuing leaders who function regularly liturgically should be included as much as possible in those roles so that continuity within this local community of faith is affirmed. The new leader will be supporting, not replacing, the ministry and continuing leadership of those who now greet him or her.

The title of the service: When we speak of a "Celebration of a New Ministry," what exactly is being celebrated? Is it the new position of a professional cleric (his or her latest "career move")? Certainly not! Is it the ministry of the entire congregation that is now considered "new"? While there is definite newness in the life of this congregation with the arrival of a new leader, the essential ministry of the congregation is continuing in the ministry of the people of that place. Let us assume that the ministry of this congregation remains strong and vital, sturdy enough to welcome new leadership without having to be dismantled to make it easier for the new leader to adapt.

With these thoughts in mind, some congregations have chosen to call this service: "A Celebration of the Life and Mission of *N*. Church, at the Welcoming [or Induction] of *N*. as [Rector]."

The entrance: Too often, the entrance to this rite is orchestrated like an ordination, built around the person and new status of the ordinand: processing in a place of special honor, surrounded by special ministers and sponsors. Clergy are set apart, processing in vestments, then seated in a prominent location to support a colleague on his or her new beginning. But this service is not an ordination. It *is* the establishing of a new, mutual, pastoral relationship between people of faith as they begin to pursue ministry together. Unfortunately, the structure of the existing service (opening as it does with "The Institution") encourages the parallel between the opening of this service and an ordination. Perhaps a "Celebration Committee" could reflect upon how to arrange the entrance to communicate the collegial dimension of the relationship between the new leader and those continuing in roles of leadership in the congregation.

In fact, if the intent is to welcome a new leader to stand among and minister with others who are continuing to participate in ministry in this place, why not have the service begin as usual—just as any principal act of worship would on a Sunday morning, without any more pomp and circumstance. The eucharistic assembly would be gathered as always, with many visitors seated in the congregation as well. At the Institution and the Induction, those involved would step forward to perform the appropriate actions and then return to their usual places in the assembly, as the liturgical life of the congregation proceeds. This is our current practice when we baptize, so as to communicate that whatever is being accomplished here will continue to be nurtured and grow in the context of the ongoing liturgical life of this faith community. Why wouldn't it be appropriate to welcome and induct new leaders in similar fashion?

The Institution: It is important at this service to affirm the connectedness of the new leader with both the bishop and the local congregation. Preceding the reading of the Letter of Institution, the warden might read a brief letter of agreement between the new leader and the vestry which states plainly, in their own words, the nature of the relationship and the duties which this new leader is assuming. This would affirm the role of the local congregation in establishing the authority of the new leader to function locally, just as the bishop is affirming the authority of the new leader to act on his or her behalf. It would also be in order for the Vestry to review carefully the Letter of Institution (BCP, p. 557) to insure that it is consonant with their understanding of this person's role among them. Both letters should be discussed with the bishop well in advance to address any questions or concerns they may raise.

If it has been decided to play down the connection between ordination and this gathering, consider replacing the "Litany for Ordinations" with a different form of Prayers of the People, such as one of those provided in *Supplemental Liturgical Texts (Prayer Book Studies 30).* These underscore the essential involvement of all the baptized in the ministry of the Church, a good theme to recall at this moment in the liturgy. The "Celebration Committee" may wish to work with the new leader(s) to write their own litany. Be sure to include petition for all the world and not just the local congregation. It is essential at this moment that we be reminded that as grand as all this may be, we *are* called to a life and mission beyond the church walls as well!

Consider whether the appointed collect (BCP, p. 560) describes the relationship intended between the new leader and the congregation. (Does the "patience and understanding," the "love and care" flow only one way in this relationship?) Perhaps the collect used at ordinations (BCP, pp. 515, 528, 540) might be substituted.

The Liturgy of the Word: In addition to the lessons appointed (BCP, p. 560), the following lessons may be appropriate to the situation: Exodus 19:3-8; Isaiah 61:1-8; Psalm 121, 15, or 34:1-8; 1 Peter 2:4-10; 1 Peter 4:7-11; Acts 6:1-7; Mark 10:35-45.

The Induction: Consider what is happening here. Symbols are being presented to the new leader to recognize the nature of the ministry and the mutual pastoral relationship being established between these people. For symbols to be given exclusively to the new leader may send the message that "We are handing over the ministries of this congregation to you. Here: now *you* do it!" We want to recognize the new leader's gifts of leadership and his or her functioning according to the order in which the new leader is ordained, but it should be done in a way that reminds us that there will be a sharing of leadership here. In effect, we might think of this moment as installing the new leader into a new position: standing *among* the continuing congregational leaders—taking his or her place in the eucharistic assembly. When others will share directly in leadership in the ministry represented by a symbol, they should be standing with the new leader as the symbol is presented. This would rehearse the mutuality and collegiality of leadership and the fact that the new leader has come to support, not replace, the continuing ministries and leadership of the persons who now greet him or her.

Instead of giving the symbols directly to the new leader, consider having them placed where the community has been and will be using them: the Bible on the lectern, water poured into the baptismal font, oil presented to the new leader standing with others who will be sharing in a ministry of healing, the bread and wine placed upon the altar.[12] All symbols should be large enough to be visible to all (e.g., using a sizable flagon of baptismal water) and should remain in the sight of the congregation during the Induction. The vestments and bread and wine may be used in the eucharist which follows (BCP, p. 565).

Some congregations have experimented with having both the new leader and other leaders of the congregation receive symbols to affirm and authenticate their various roles in the ministry. In some places, the new leader him or herself has made some of the presentations. This works best when it is done in a manner that clearly proclaims how the new leader will relate to those persons and their work. Are we saying that all authentic ministry in this place will flow through this one person, or that the charisms for ministry are his or hers to bestow? Those engaged in various ministries should consider carefully which symbols to present, so that the items presented are not trivial but point toward and participate in a greater reality. Reflect carefully upon what is being said by each symbol, who gives it and who receives it. If you were visiting or new to the Episcopal Church, would it be clear to you what is happening here and what is the nature of the relationship being established?

In some places, words have been added to rehearse the share of the entire congregation in these continuing ministries.[13] Consider this alternative:

(Bible)	N., the ministry we share is founded in and upon God's Holy Word.
All:	*Join us in proclaiming the word of God.*
or:	*Support us as together we proclaim the word of God.*
(Water)	N., it is our privilege and responsibility to share the Good News of Christ with all people of God's creation, that they might be restored to unity with God and each other in Christ.
All:	*Join us in baptizing in obedience to our Lord.*

(Priest's stole, or leading a new priest to stand behind the altar)

> *N.*, in baptism we were anointed by the Holy Spirit that we might all participate in Christ's eternal priesthood.

All: *Be among us as a priest and lead us in pastoring in Christ's name.*

(Deacon's stole or paschal candle [*if the new leader will be serving primarily as a deacon*])[14]

> *N.*, in baptism we were anointed by the Holy Spirit that we might all participate in the servanthood of Christ.

All: *Be among us as a deacon and lead us as we carry Christ's light into the dark corners of the world.*

(Prayer Book) *N.*, the apostle Paul reminds us that we are to pray unceasingly.

All: *Join us in offering the prayer of Christ daily in this place.*

(Oil)   *N.*, Jesus came among us to bring healing and wholeness to our broken world.

All: *Join us in being healers and reconcilers in Christ's name.*

(Keys)   *N.*, this church building stands as a symbol of Christ's presence in the midst of our world.

All: *Join us in opening the doors of this place to all people.*

(Canons)   *N.*, as members of the body of Christ, we are responsible to and interdependent with one another.

All: *Join us in obeying these canons and sharing in the councils of this diocese.*

(Bread and Wine)

> *N.*, in the Eucharist, we gather constantly to be nourished and sent forth in ministry.

All: *Join us [lead us*] in the breaking of the bread, as we offer our gifts in praise and thanksgiving to God.*

* If the new leader will be serving as a presbyter

Such statements will need to be adapted depending upon the circumstances. If the new leader will serve in a specific role, the words accompanying these presentations should make that clear. But it should be equally clear how others will be sharing in that work.

The opportunity for other symbols to be added (BCP, p. 561) could be used creatively:

- to affirm the ministries of members of the congregation in their daily lives and clarify how the new leader will be involved in supporting them in that work;
- to involve children in the liturgy;
- to affirm local history and customs;
- to acknowledge the work of those who have gone before and those who will continue as leaders in ministry in this community;
- to recognize the ministry in which the new leader was engaged previously, perhaps including a presentation from the community of faith which the new leader has just left;
- to involve representatives of other religious bodies and community organizations;
- to acknowledge the work of the search committee and interim pastors and consultants.

But we should not get carried away with the addition of more presentations. I have been wondering recently how we would react if the family of one just baptized wanted to shower gifts upon the neophyte just after the welcoming of the newly baptized. The current trend in "Celebrations of a New Ministry" is to add more and more, in hopes that no one feel left out. In fact, *fewer* symbols, carefully chosen and specific to the new leader's particular gifts and responsibilities, would be more powerful liturgically. The rubric on page 561 notes that any of the presentations may be omitted. Perhaps the most effective way to tone down the "coronation theme" is to keep this section brief and crisp, moving on quickly to the passing of the peace and the eucharistic feast.

For the prayer following the presentations: It may be appropriate to have the new leader lead the congregation in prayer rather than pray by him or herself. In that case, a prayer such as the Prayer of St. Francis (BCP, p. 833) might be appropriate.

Postcommunion prayer: This adaptation to the appointed prayer (BCP, p. 564) might emphasize the celebration of shared ministries:

> Almighty Father, we thank you for feeding us with the holy food of the Body and Blood of your Son, and for uniting us through Him in the fellowship of your Holy Spirit. We thank you for calling us to be a ministering community in your redeemed world, and for raising up among us faithful servants for your ministry. We pray that we may be to one another effective examples in word and action, in love and patience, and in holiness of life. Grant that we may serve you now, and always rejoice in your glory; through Jesus Christ your Son our Lord, who lives and reigns with you and the Holy Spirit, one God, now and for ever. Amen.

Notes

1. Josephine Borgeson and Lynne Wilson, eds., *Reshaping Ministry*, Chapter 1.
2. Some of these ideas were explored in the address of Richard Norris to the 1984 Trinity Institute Symposium on the Mission of the Church.
3. William Seth Adams, "Decoding the Obvious," in Ruth A.

Meyers, ed., *Baptism and Ministry*, Liturgical Studies 1 (New York: Church Hymnal Corporation), pp. 4-5.

4. Dorothy McRae-McMahon, *Being Clergy, Staying Human: Taking Our Stand in the River*, pp. vii-2.

5. Many of these ideas were developed by Bishop Richard Grein in addresses to the clergy of the Diocese of New York in 1991.

6. Robert J. Schreiter, *Constructing Local Theologies*, p. xi.

7. For more on this, see James F. Hopewell, *Congregation: Stories and Structures.*

8. Schreiter, p. 18.

9. Ian M. Fraser, *Reinventing Theology: As the People's Work*, p. 9.

10. McRae-McMahon, p. 3.

11. Jean Haldane, "Toward a Totally Ministering Church," *Crossings* (Church Divinity School of the Pacific, Winter 1987), p. 4.

12. This practice is suggested in "Celebration of a New Ministry," *Occasional Celebrations of The Anglican Church of Canada* (Toronto: Anglican Book Centre, 1992), p. 83.

13. Liturgies included in the *Total Ministry Notebook* developed by the Episcopal Diocese of Nevada during the episcopate of Wesley Frensdorff contain examples of this.

14. The new leader who will serve the congregation primarily as a priest should not be presented with a deacon's stole, even if he or she has been ordained a deacon transitionally in the past. It is important to keep the focus in this liturgy upon the function that this person will now play in this congregation, not supplanting the ministry of others.

Bibliography

Allen, Roland. *Missionary Methods: St. Paul's or Ours?* Grand Rapids, MI: Eerdmans, 1962.

Occasional Celebrations of the Anglican Church of Canada. Toronto: Anglican Book Centre, 1992.

Baptism, Eucharist and Ministry. Faith and Order Paper 111. Geneva: World Council of Churches, 1982.

Borgeson, Josephine, and Wilson, Lynne, eds. *Reshaping Ministry: Essays in Memory of Wesley Frensdorff.* Arvada, CO: Jethro Publications, 1990.

Donovan, Vincent J. *Christianity Rediscovered.* Maryknoll, NY: Orbis Books, 1978.

Episcopal Diocese of Nevada. *Total Ministry Notebook.* 1985.

Fraser, Ian M. *Reinventing Theology: As the People's Work.* Glasgow: Wild Goose Publications, 1988.

Haldane, Jean. "Toward a Totally Ministering Church." In *Crossings* (Church Divinity School of the Pacific, Winter 1987).

Hopewell, James F. *Congregation: Stories and Structures.* Philadelphia: Fortress, 1987.

McRae-McMahon, Dorothy. *Being Clergy, Staying Alive: Taking Our Stand in the River.* Washington, DC: Alban Institute, 1992.

Mead, Loren. *The Once and Future Church: Reinventing the Congregation for a New Mission Frontier.* Washington, DC: Alban Institute, 1991.

Merriman, Michael W., ed. *The Baptismal Mystery and the Catechumenate.* New York: Church Hymnal Corporation, 1990.

Norris, Richard. "Baptism, Christian Identity and the Mission of the Church," an address to the Trinity Institute Symposium on the Mission of the Church, 1984. Tapes available from The Episcopal Radio-TV Foundation, Inc., 3379 Peachtree Road, N.E., Atlanta, GA 30326.

Pobee, John S. "Spectrum of Ministry." In *Ministry Formation*, January 1993. World Council of Churches, Unit I: Unity and Renewal.

Schreiter, Robert J. *Constructing Local Theologies.* Maryknoll, NY: Orbis Books, 1985.

Schillebeeckx, Edward. *The Church With the Human Face.* New York: Crossroad, 1985.

THE LECTIONARY

The Lectionary of The Book of Common Prayer: Biblical Texts That Shape the Life of the Church

Joseph P. Russell

A lectionary is a schedule of biblical readings that specifies what texts will be read at a service of worship in the Church. A cycle of liturgical feasts can be traced to the lists of annual festivals outlined in Exodus 23:14-17 and 34:21-23, Deuteronomy 16:1-17, and Leviticus 23:1-44. Early Christians adapted this "liturgical calendar" and shaped it to enhance the proclamation of the Gospel. For example, the Gospel of John may have been written partly as Christian commentary on the Jewish festivals. The Gospels of Mark and Matthew show evidence of having been written, in part at least, to be read as lections in the context of worship. Meanwhile as the synagogue developed, portions of the Torah were prescribed for reading, and texts from the Prophets and the Writings filled out a schedule of selections from the Hebrew Bible. The practice of reading scripture in conjunction with feasts, fasts and festivals came early in the life of the young Church.

The Past

The ancient Roman lectionary was the basis of earlier prayer book lectionaries in the Anglican tradition. Massey Shepherd explained the origins of the eucharistic readings appointed in the 1928 Book of Common Prayer:

The selections appointed are derived for the most part from those drawn up by the Church in Rome in the sixth and seventh centuries and later adopted, with some variations, in the medieval Latin Missals, including that of the diocese of Sarum (Salisbury), which the Reformers used as the basis for the Prayer Book propers. However, the first Prayer Book of 1549, and succeeding revisions of it also, have made numerous changes or substitutions both in the prayers and the lessons.[1]

The eucharistic lectionaries from the first three American prayer books (1789, 1892 and 1928) were based on an annual cycle of readings that included selections from an epistle (or Acts or, rarely, Revelation) and a Gospel for each Sunday and feast day. In the 1928 lectionary, an Old Testament lesson was read in place of the epistle on just a few occasions: the Second Sunday after Christmas Day, Ash Wednesday, the Monday and Tuesday before Easter, the Sunday before Advent, and a few holy days. In some cases there was little relationship between the two readings, because over the generations one of the two lections was changed with little regard to thematic unity with the other appointed text or with the season of the church year. For example, one of the features of earlier lectionaries was a three week "pre-Lenten" season, consisting of texts chosen during the sixth century as the Church in Rome dealt with the harsh realities of the invasion of Italy by the Lombards.[2] The texts spoke more to that terrible period of historic struggle than to the shape of the liturgical year.

Though the eucharistic lectionary lacked Old Testament texts, Morning Prayer with its Old Testament and New Testament lections was part of every Sunday service until the second (1892) American prayer book:

Until the 1892 revision of the Prayer Book, Morning Prayer had been required before the Eucharist. According to the system of the first two

Prayer Books, the congregation would have heard
almost all of the Old Testament read on Sundays
within the course of every seven years, and the
New Testament (except for Revelation) within
every period of two years and four months. The
whole of the Psalter would have been read on
Sundays almost twice every year.... The Sunday service still contained a substantial portion of the
Scriptures until the 1892 revision allowed the celebration of the Eucharist without requiring that
Morning Prayer precede. This left a meager diet of
scripture for celebrations of the Eucharist.[3]

After 1892, congregations using Morning Prayer as the principal
service of the week would have been exposed to considerable scripture, but congregations committed to the celebration of the
eucharist every Sunday were limited to the one-year cycle of readings noted above.

The Present

This practice changed dramatically with the introduction of the
three-year lectionary adapted from the Roman Catholic *Lectionary
for Mass* that resulted from the liturgical revisions initiated by the
second Vatican Council. The three-year lectionary was first published for study and trial use in the Episcopal Church in 1970.[4]
Many Episcopal parishes began using this lectionary on a regular
basis when the Proposed Book of Common Prayer was authorized
by the 1976 General Convention for use beginning on the First
Sunday of Advent 1976.

In 1978 the *Lutheran Book of Worship* was published with its
own adaptation of the Roman lectionary, and during the same
period Presbyterians and Methodists began adapting the Roman
Catholic lectionary for optional use as well. Each denomination
made some changes in the Roman Catholic model. Though the
Gospel lections are virtually the same in the different lectionaries,

there are some variations in the first two readings and psalm texts.

Today, congregations using the three-year lectionary are exposed to semicontinuous readings of all the epistles with the exception of Second and Third John and Titus. The Gospel of Matthew is read in Year A, the Gospel of Mark in Year B and Luke in Year C. The Gospel of John is heard each year during Lent and/or Easter, and the sixth chapter of John is heard in four segments during August in Year B. An Old Testament text and psalm in thematic harmony with the Gospel lection are integral to the propers for each Sunday and feast day.

During the major seasons of the church year, all the lections are in thematic harmony with the season and usually with the other appointed texts:

- Advent: The readings on the First Sunday of Advent point to the coming of Christ at the end of the age. The Gospels on the Second and Third Sundays of Advent speak of John the Baptist, and on the Fourth Sunday of Advent the texts point to the first coming, that is, the incarnation, of Jesus.

- Christmas: Jesus' birth and the significance of the "Word becoming flesh and dwelling among us" (John 1:14).

- Sundays after the Epiphany: From the baptism of Jesus on the First Sunday after the Epiphany, we move on to the calling and preparation of the disciples. This theme is built into the early chapters of Matthew, Mark and Luke.

- Lent: The texts, particularly those of Year A, provide a short course in the meaning of baptism, and thus are designed to lead catechumens through their final preparation for baptism and the whole Church towards the renewing of baptismal vows at the Easter vigil.

- Easter (the Great Fifty Days): During the early church this was a period of "mystagogy," a time to reveal the secrets, or mysteries, of Christianity to those baptized at the Easter vigil. The lections provide theological reflection on the meaning of baptism.

The season after the Feast of the Epiphany and the Feast of Pentecost is described by the Roman lectionary as "Ordinary Time," denoting the counted weeks following the two major cycles of feasts. During Ordinary Time the lectionary makes a shift from reflecting on the themes dictated by the season to semicontinuous reading of New Testament material. The rest of the Gospel of the year is read in semicontinuous segments along with several epistles. Much of what was not heard during the Christmas and Easter cycles is heard in semicontinuous readings during Ordinary Time. The Old Testament and psalm are in thematic harmony with the Gospel, or occasionally with the epistle. Because both the appointed epistles and the Gospel of the year are heard in semicontinuous readings, there is usually no thematic relationship between the New Testament lections.

In addition to the lectionary for Sundays, used at the principal service, whether Morning Prayer or the Holy Eucharist, a new two-year Daily Office Lectionary was created for the present prayer book. Over the course of two years, the lectionary leads the Church through the New Testament twice. All the relevant portions of the Old Testament are read once, and the entire psalter is read every seven weeks.

The Future

The Common Lectionary. In 1983, the Consultation on Common Texts, an ecumenical body representing American and Canadian denominations, published the *Common Lectionary* as a "conservative harmonization of the major variants of the three-year lectionary used at this time."[5] In the process of working to harmonize the variant texts of the lectionaries, the Consultation made the major decision to offer semicontinuous readings from the Hebrew scriptures for the Sundays beginning on the Second Sunday after Pentecost and continuing through the Sunday before Advent. The Hebrew scripture and psalm lections remain in thematic harmony with the Gospel during the Christmas and Easter cycles. The decision for the semicontinuous treatment of the Old Testament during Ordinary Time was "to provide readings that are more completely representative of the Hebrew Bible and not simply prophetic or typological."[6]

The *Common Lectionary* was placed in trial use among member denominations, including the Episcopal Church. Episcopalian, Roman Catholic and Lutheran liturgists objected that with the semicontinuous readings from the Old Testament added to the semicontinuous readings of epistles and the Gospel of the year, any semblance of theme and focus for the Sundays of Ordinary Time was lost. Liturgists feared that congregations would simply leave out the first reading or that the liturgy of the Word would suffer from the lack of cohesive proclamation.

As a result of this evaluation, the Consultation on Common Texts developed the *Revised Common Lectionary*, published in 1992,[7] which beginning with the Second Sunday after Pentecost offers the option of either semicontinuous lections from the Hebrew scriptures *or* lections in thematic harmony with the Gospel of the day. The semicontinuous option provides lessons based on the major narratives from Genesis through Judges in Year A. The Davidic covenant and Wisdom literature form the focus for the semicontinuous readings in Year B. Year C lessons review the stories and writings of the prophets, beginning with Elijah and Elisha in First and Second Kings and continuing with important texts from Amos, Hosea, Isaiah, Jeremiah, Joel and Habakkuk.

Another important contribution of the *Revised Common Lectionary* is the inclusion of texts highlighting the role of women in biblical history, texts which have not previously been heard at the Sunday liturgy.[8] The most notable example of important texts omitted from the present lectionary is Mark 14:3-9, the anointing at Bethany. In this pericope, Jesus responded to the woman who anointed him by saying, "...wherever the good news is proclaimed in the whole world, what she has done will be told in remembrance of her." Ironically that text emphasizing remembrance has been relegated to an *optional* reading on Monday in Holy Week! The text is now included in the *Revised Common Lectionary* as part of the passion narrative read on Palm Sunday in Year B.

The *Revised Common Lectionary* is becoming the standard for a growing number of denominations around the world. In this country, the Presbyterian Church (USA), United Methodist Church, United Church of Christ, Evangelical Lutheran Church in America, Christian Church (Disciples of Christ) and the Christian Reformed Church in North America are among those who have officially adopted the lectionary. The 1994 General Convention authorized the *Revised Common Lectionary* for trial use in the Episcopal Church. The Anglican Church of Canada, the United Church of Canada, the Evangelical Lutheran Church in Canada, the Church of Scotland and the Council of Churches in the Netherlands are other examples of a spreading practice. We are seeing a truly *common* lectionary.

As Christians share the same basic texts over the course of three years, an ecumenical consensus is happening across the Church. United Methodist publishing houses produce lectionary resources. The United Church of Christ publishes a lectionary-based curriculum. Ecumenical lectionary Bible study groups bring preachers, teachers and others together to be formed and informed by the unfolding biblical Word.

Beyond the three-year lectionary, *The Book of Common Worship* authorized by the Presbyterian Church (USA) in 1993 includes a "Daily Prayer" section reflecting the Daily Office tradition familiar to Episcopalians. The Daily Office Lectionary of The Book of Common Prayer was adapted for this book. Ecumenism is alive and well in the practice of the lectionary!

The Joint Liturgical Group. There are, however, other approaches to lectionary structure in use today. The Church of England and several other denominations in Great Britain working together as the Joint Liturgical Group developed a two-year lectionary that in 1990 was revised and expanded to a four-year cycle of readings. The original lectionary of the Joint Liturgical Group matched texts to specific themes rather than offering semicontinuous readings. Their revised lectionary follows the lead of the Roman lectionary and its heirs, including the *Revised Common Lectionary*, and focuses on one Gospel each year, including the Gospel of John.[9] Other lectionaries have been developed over the years, but the three-year Roman Catholic model dominates the field. The Church of England is now seriously considering the *Revised Common Lectionary.*

Weekday lectionaries. The Book of Common Prayer and *Lesser Feasts and Fasts* provide propers for holy days, days of special devotion, and days of optional observance. The practice of assigning lections and collects for specific commemorations, observances and special occasions has a long history. Adjustments to the list of commemorations come with every General Convention. The 1994 General Convention authorized new "Guidelines and Procedures for Continuing Alteration of the Calendar in the Episcopal Church," based on similar guidelines developed by the Anglican Church of Canada. These guidelines, published in the 1994 edition of *Lesser Feasts and Fasts*, encourage local commemorations as a way of remembering persons significant to a particular diocese or province of the Church.

The 1991 General Convention instructed the Standing Liturgical Commission to publish a complete daily eucharistic lectionary for the entire year. The 1994 General Convention authorized readings for the weekdays of Advent through the Eve of the Baptism of Jesus (the First Sunday after the Epiphany), complementing the propers already provided for the weekdays of Lent and Easter. These propers were taken from *The Book of Alternative Services* (1985) of the Anglican Church of Canada, which in turn adapted them from the Roman Catholic daily eucharistic lectionary.

The 1994 General Convention also authorized experimental use of a different approach to eucharistic lections for the weekdays of "Ordinary Time." Instead of semicontinuous readings such as those heard on the Sundays of Ordinary Time and in the Daily Office, thirty-six sets of brief readings are provided to serve "as a corpus of texts and themes available in whatever order the celebrant and worshiping community wishes to use them. Each proper includes two brief lessons and a psalm reflecting the theme of the two texts. The brevity of the lections invites a brief reflective homily, silence, or the reading of nonbiblical meditative texts."[10] Precedent for this experimental lectionary lies in the "votive" propers found in the 1979 prayer book under the heading "Various Occasions" (BCP, pp. 927-31) and the corpus of collects available for use during the Great Fifty Days of Easter (*Lesser Feasts and Fasts 1994*, pp. 65-75).

Collects. Another lectionary-related development is the publication of alternative opening prayers by the International Commission on English in the Liturgy, a joint commission of Catholic Bishops' Conferences from around the world. In *The Proposed Revision of the Sacramentary* (Segment One: Ordinary Time, and Segment Two: Proper of Seasons) opening prayers keyed to the lections of the day are offered.

The collects of The Book of Common Prayer bear little relationship to the biblical texts during Ordinary Time, since they represent a one-year cycle of traditional prayers that are placed alongside the three-year lectionary. In a future revision, the prayers of the revised *Sacramentary* developed by the International Commission on English in the Liturgy may inform a new approach to calling the congregation together in prayer.

Conclusion

The present prayer book is dramatically transforming the Episcopal Church. It is sometimes said that the Church spends too much time and energy worrying about the liturgy rather than thinking about the world that God comes to redeem. However, it is the liturgy that forms the Church. We "see" God's presence in the world through the eyes of the liturgy and the biblical Word. The Baptismal Covenant, for example, propels us out into the world to "proclaim," to "seek and serve Christ," to "strive for justice and peace" (BCP, p. 305). What we say, pray, sing and enact at the liturgy forms us for ministry in the world as well as in the Church. It is the lectionary of the present prayer book that has led directly to a new enthusiasm for the Bible. Congregations immersed in the scriptures are more apt to find themselves immersed in ministry. Continued attention to development of the lectionary is thus vital for the formation of Christians for ministry.

Notes

1. Massey H. Shepherd, *The Oxford American Prayer Book Commentary* (New York: Oxford University Press, 1950), p. 90.
2. Ibid., p. 118.
3. Marion J. Hatchett, *Commentary on the American Prayer Book* (New York: Seabury, 1980), pp. 325-6.
4. *The Church Year*, Prayer Book Studies 19 (New York: Church Hymnal Corporation, 1970).
5. *The Common Lectionary: The Lectionary Proposed by the Consultation on Common Texts* (New York: Church Hymnal Corporation, 1983), p. 5.
6. "Minutes of the Consultation on Common Texts" (Washington, DC, 28-31 March 1978), cited in *Common Lectionary*, p. 9.
7. Nashville, TN: Abingdon Press.
8. For further discussion, see Jean Campbell, OSH, "The Feminine as Omitted, Optional, or Alternative Story: A Review of the Episcopal Eucharistic Lectionary," in Ruth A. Meyers, ed., *How Shall We Pray? Expanding Our Language about God*, Liturgical Studies 2 (New York: Church Hymnal Corporation, 1994), pp. 57-68.
9. John Fenwick and Bryan Spinks, *Worship in Transition: The Liturgical Movement in the Twentieth Century* (New York: Continuum, 1995), pp. 121-5.
10. Joseph P. Russell, ed., *Weekday Readings: A Daily Eucharistic Lectionary for the Weekdays following the First Sunday after Epiphany and the Feast of Pentecost* (New York: Church Hymnal Corporation, 1995), p. iv.

ISSUES IN
PRAYER BOOK REVISION

"O for a Thousand Tongues to Sing..."

Ellen K. Wondra

Editor's Note:
Since 1985 the Standing Liturgical Commission, in accord with directives of the General Convention, has been developing inclusive-language texts for Holy Eucharist and Morning and Evening Prayer. The first set of texts published for use was Supplemental Liturgical Texts, *Prayer Book Studies 30 (Church Hymnal Corporation, 1989), authorized for experimental use by the 1988 General Convention. These texts were revised in view of responses from those who prayed with the texts, and the revised texts were published as* Supplemental Liturgical Materials *(Church Hymnal Corporation, 1991; expanded edition, Church Hymnal Corporation, 1996), authorized for use by the 1991 and 1994 General Conventions. The following essay was written in light of these experimental texts.*

Corporate worship presumes first and foremost that God is self-disclosing, accessible, and involved in human life and history. Because of this, the language of worship focuses on the presence of God, and it uses images that convey what human persons know of God and how our lives may be brought into greater harmony with God's intentions for us. At the same time, it is *God* that we worship; that is, one who is ultimately incomprehensible to us, beyond both our encompassing and our complete understanding. There is, then, a tension between the knowability of God and the mystery of God; and this tension must be maintained in worship, in reflection, and in holy living, if our faith is to be both authentic and effective.

Corporate worship, theological reflection, and contemplative prayer all have their own appropriate languages, which inform but are not identical with each other. In theological reflection and in contemplative prayer, the tension between the knowability and the mystery of God may be maintained by disciplined attention to the "negative moment" of our naming God, in which we recognize that God is hidden from us as well as revealed, in which we recognize that everything we say of God is partial and limited and therefore not-true as well as true. Such recognition of God's incomprehensibility is imperative. Without it, we readily forget the majesty, power, and sheer graciousness of the living God. Such forgetfulness leads to that overreliance on human capacity and knowledge which is part of idolatry.

Corporate worship, by contrast, focuses on expressing and evoking what we know and experience of God's presence. How, then, can liturgical language help us recognize the incomprehensibility of God? One way is through the multiplication of names, images, and forms through which we address and contemplate God in corporate worship. The *Supplemental Liturgical Texts* and *Materials* (along with the process of development, use, evaluation, and reception of these materials) provide just such a multiplication when they are seen in conjunction with The Book of Common Prayer which they explicitly supplement. The rest of this paper will explain what I mean and why I think it is important that this process continue.

The shape, forms, and language (words, images, gestures) of liturgy matter greatly because our praying shapes our believing and our living. Particularly for members of liturgical traditions such as Anglicanism, corporate worship is the forming ground for Christian belief. It is in corporate worship that we come to know the God with whom we desire closer union. It is there that we encounter the ongoing story of our faith through scriptural and liturgical texts, and it is there that we become part of that story through sacramental participation. It is there that we gain the strength, will, and disposition to live that faith in our daily lives. Our individual prayers and lives are embedded in this corporate worship which spans time and place, joining individuals and congregations together as members of one Body.

And yet we can pray, individually or corporately, only in the images and symbols and gestures—the language—available to us. Much of this language is conveyed through corporate worship and its use of scripture, hymnody, prayer, and so on. But our spiritual formation is accomplished not only in church. The world in which we live is also part of the formative context of our faith, and the language of faith derives its meaning not only from our prayer but also from our everyday lives. The Reformation liturgical principle of worship in the vernacular recognizes not only that this is true, but that it has positive value. The basis of that positive value is the fundamental Christian conviction that God meets us in the midst of our history, that is, in the midst of our historical particularities and conditions, and in ways that are accommodated to our contexts and limitations. The Word became flesh and dwelt among us; through that incarnation in human history is our fullest encountering of God.

So it is of great importance that our corporate worship be shaped to recognize the presence of both God and the faithful in particular historical contexts. The revisions leading to the 1979 Book of Common Prayer made great strides in this direction, but more are needed. Some of these are undertaken by the *Supplemental Liturgical Texts* and *Materials*, for example, in recognizing that human sin involves violation of self and of all creation, as well as of other human persons and relationship with God.

The contextual nature of human life is also reflected in the scriptural and liturgical traditions whose continuous use knits together the Body of Christ across both time and space. The fact that these texts and traditions have a historical character may, however, be masked by our conviction that they are important revelations of God who is sovereign over all the elements of time and space. But to say that something is revealed does not mean it cannot be historically shaped, nor does saying that something is historically shaped mean that it may not also be revealed. Indeed, because of the Incarnation—the Word become flesh and living in human history—we can both recognize and embrace the fact that, whatever else our sacred texts may be, they are *also* the work of human persons living in concrete history and responding to the presence of God in that history.

I have already said that God accommodates divine revelation to our conditions and limitations. This is to say that God makes Herself known in ways that are accessible to our recognizing and available to our understanding. God freely limits what He will make known on the basis of what we are able to glimpse and to grasp. God's accommodation is a manifestation of Her own gracious determination that we be able to delight in the one who made us, to know the one who redeems us, and to love God with the love with which He loves us. Again, it is part and parcel of belief in the Incarnation to affirm that our knowledge of God is historically shaped.

It also must be recognized and embraced that all human works, no matter how divinely inspired and guided, are also both limited and fallible, simply because they are human. What it means to be human is that we are finite creatures living in a created world. We are capable of only partial perception, articulation, and reflection, but we are also capable of growth. In our biblical tradition, for example, this reality is reflected in the two different narratives of the creation of the world, each of which reflects a different understanding of the nature of creation, and both of which differ from other understandings with which we are familiar. This does not mean that we recognize these narratives as any the less true.

In addition to this, there is also sin, that human propensity to turn away from God and each other, to distort our own importance, and to suppress our need of others and our reliance on God. These propensities are reflected in texts and traditions as well, and not just in ways that the Bible itself presents and condemns as negative examples. For example, biblical accounts of divine commands to slaughter conquered non-combatants and scriptural warrants for slavery have, in our context, lost all credibility and are even considered abhorrently contrary to "the Word of God"—even though they are found in something that we recognize as the Word of God overall.

So to say that even the most sacred of texts and traditions is humanly shaped (whatever else they may be) is to say that all such texts and traditions may be affected both by human limitation and by human sin. This does not mean that they are no longer sacred; rather, it means that they are not inerrant and infallible. And so they must be read critically, with an eye both to the contexts in which they were formed and to the One to whom they testify. The facts that the church is continuously engaged in reform of its life and belief and that some scriptural materials are given relatively little or no weight in our ecclesial life are age-old recognitions of the human shaping of sacred texts and traditions.

There are a number of ways to proceed once one has said that revelation is both accommodated (or relative) *and* uncompromisedly true. One way is to say that a new revelation has come which modifies, corrects, supplements, or even supersedes the old. The problem here, of course, is one of discernment: how do we know which new "truths" are in fact true? Clearly, continuity with already given-and-received truth is necessary. But continuity does not mean identity; it means both similarity and difference. The prophets, for example, reclaimed a faithful God by representing that God in a recast form and in new images. To them, and to those who contributed to the making of the canon, this newly represented God was recognizable as the same God. (To others, let us remember, it was not a god, but a new idol, one to be rejected.)

The early church, of course, finally went even further in the same process in its separation from Judaism. Our contemporary processes of discernment and reception are basically the same.

Worship, then, makes use of the various elements of our blessed historicalness to articulate the praise of God and to knit together the Body of Christ. It does so by bringing together multiple materials (word, reading, music, silence, prayer) of different genres (narrative, teaching, exposition, vision, poetry, exhortation, song, gesture) from many times and places (ancient and contemporary, near and far). This bringing together is, and should be, polyphonic. It should have the character of a rich symphony whose harmonies are produced by complex arrangements of individual elements and movements and whose discords serve to increase the abundance of the whole.

Worship should be polyphonic because our human ability to articulate the fullness of God's graciousness, glory, mystery, and presence is so limited. No single word, image, concept, or story that we have can encompass or convey the full reality of the divine or the wonder of God's coming among us. In part this is so because of our inherent creaturely limitations and the distorting and falsifying effects of sin.

But even more, it is so because of the grandeur and mystery of the divine life itself. Our God is a living, active God who is first and foremost always much more than what we can know or express, and who is *always* creating, *always* revealing, *always* saving, *always* inspiring. Therefore our relationship with God is not reducible to single or immutable theological or liturgical or pastoral or spiritual formulas and narratives. The diversity of our texts and traditions reflects this conviction as much as it does our recognition that our own ability to give voice to the reality of God is bound by the limits of creatureliness and distorted and perverted by sin.

So the language of praise, entreaty, repentance, conversion, and thanksgiving is polyphonic language. It is also figurative. That is, it identifies God with something with which God is not identical—

with a rock, for example, or supporting hands; or with wisdom, goodness, or love. It is readily evident to most that God is not identical with any concrete, inanimate object. It is perhaps less immediately clear that God is not identical with more abstract characteristics, like wisdom, goodness, or love. But even when we say that God is the ultimate exemplar of these or other qualities, we are still speaking figuratively. For we know these characteristics most directly and immediately through their human exemplars with all their flaws and failings, flaws and failings that are not, we believe, found in God. Further, while we may say that God is the ultimate exemplar of these qualities, we do not know that ultimacy except in partial forms which are mediated through our historical experience with all its particularities and limitations.

Second, figurative language is both positive and negative. It makes a statement about what something is, but also about what it is not (the latter often silently): to *say* that God is like a raging fire, for example, also *implies* that God is not like that. Sometimes the negation is expressed more directly: God is *in*finite—that is, not finite—or *im*mutable—not changeable.

In figurative language, then, there is a tension between positive and negative, between affirmation and negation. There is also a play, a give and take, an interaction, between similarity and difference, between like and not-like. With this interaction, this play, also comes a temptation to resolve the tension by overemphasizing the positive, stated similarity: to say, for example, that God is love without qualifying the meaning of the term so that it moves beyond what is associated with its human exemplars. In this way, figurative images are taken to be literal statements.

Theologians, spiritual directors, and mystics have long recognized the importance of this tension-laden play of similarity and difference. It conveys to us something of the incomprehensibility of God, the beyond-ness of God who nevertheless freely chooses to be self-disclosing to our perception and understanding with all its limitations and faults.

The play of difference is, in some instances, a play of conjunction, of saying that God is at one and the same time two opposite things; for example, God is the supreme ruler of all and the servant who suffers for the sake of all. This conjunction encourages—even forces—language to expand, to signify more than it might otherwise. The conjunction of the images of ruler and servant recasts the meaning of both, not only in relation to divine activity but also in the context of human society. Such expansion encourages the human imagination, challenging us constantly to envision how things might be true and not true at the same time, how apparent contradictories or opposites might coincide in one harmonious unity. Our reflection is moved beyond the primarily rational to a more contemplative stage where rationality and imagination combine to generate insight and resolution for action.

The play of similarity and difference also guards against idolatry, the exaltation of something less than God into the place that only God may rightly occupy. For if we recognize that any image or language we use about God is both true and not true at the same time, then no image can become absolute. We may say truthfully that God is our King, but we also must say truthfully that God's way of ruling is most *un*kingly, in that God is neither temporally bound nor reliant on force or coercion for obedience. When we recognize this, we cannot see any king as divine.

In all, then, the fact that our liturgy is polyphonic helps us worship God more fully and truthfully and also turns our attention more accurately to the well-being of all creatures in this created world. The *Supplemental Liturgical Texts* and *Materials* enter into the play of polyphony by deliberately increasing and enriching the type of images used to give praise to God and to foster our companionship with one another. All of this takes place, it should be remembered, within the normative context of The Book of Common Prayer, whose primary imagery is quite different from that of the supplemental materials.

The expansions of imagery in the *Supplemental Liturgical Texts* and *Materials* have been undertaken to recognize specific changes in the context in which our corporate worship is set. The changes most evident to many have to do with gender. But others, at least as important, are also present. The affirmation that Christ's self-offering is made "for all" rather than "for many," the recognition that human social organization is by "tribe and language" as well as by "nation and people," the acknowledgement of the fragility of creation, and the inclusion of reference to the eschatological "heavenly banquet": all these recognize important theological and historical elements that are underplayed even in the 1979 Book of Common Prayer. Indeed, our process of prayer book revision should go further in incorporating imagery, forms, and traditions familiar to members of African, Asian, Latin, and indigenous cultures who now constitute the majority of the Anglican Communion worldwide.

So far, however, most of the expansions of imagery have focused on correcting the gender imagery of The Book of Common Prayer and, indeed, the bulk of the Christian liturgical tradition. The expansion of imagery goes beyond attention to language about humans and to pronouns referring to God. However, both of these are of great importance.

The language we use to describe humanity conveys significant messages about the relative importance of men, women, and children, not only in the world but in the Church and in the eyes of God. The Rite II texts of the 1979 Book of Common Prayer attend to this concern, by and large, but there is still room for improvement (particularly in regard to children and to creation); the *Supplemental Liturgical Texts* and *Materials* skillfully move in this direction.

The pronouns we use to refer to God either confirm or deny the long-standing theological affirmation that God is beyond "body, parts, and passions," that is, that God is beyond gender, race, age, and the other characteristics that mark human difference and, too often, division. To refer to God only as "He" erodes the credibility of this claim, particularly when our verbal language is seen together with the visual representations that make up such a rich part of our cultural heritage and continue to surround us. The *Supplemental Liturgical Texts* and *Materials* begin to attend to this concern, although (I would argue) they do not go far enough. Use of female-gender pronouns as well as the avoidance of pronouns wherever possible are also needed if we are to convey our conviction that God is beyond gender.

But perhaps of greater importance still is the incorporation of imagery which, though present in our biblical and spiritual traditions, has been omitted from our liturgical usage. The 1979 Book of Common Prayer, like its predecessors, tends to emphasize those attributes of God that are most readily associated with maleness and masculinity in our culture: freedom, sovereignty, reason, and efficacious will, among others. Less evident are attributes like practical wisdom, nurture, loving-kindness, and companionship (particularly in struggle and in suffering), that are most readily associated with femaleness and femininity in our culture. These characteristics, too, are appropriately attributed to God and have been so attributed in both scripture and tradition.

The relative unimportance or virtual absence of some of these attributes from our corporate worship has at least two damaging effects. First, our vision of the reality of God is skewed and obscured, diminishing our ability to recognize and respond to the fullness of what God offers us. If, for example, we overemphasize the reality of God as law-giving sovereign, we may be unable to recognize God's practical wisdom, which made the Sabbath for us rather than us for the Sabbath. We will then be unable to proclaim and embody that same wisdom in God's world. Or, if we overemphasize the fatherliness of God (with the culture-bound notions of authority, jurisdiction, and relative autonomy that accompany it), we may be unable to recognize God's motherliness (with its accompanying notions of intimacy, protectiveness, and presence). It is difficult to say at what point overemphasis becomes idolatry, but it is an ever-present possibility and temptation.

Second, our failure to acknowledge the full range of divine

attributes distorts and falsifies our understanding of humanity as created in and restored to the image of God. When we use images for God which are more readily associated with one group of people than another, what is conveyed is that the former group is already more nearly in the image of God than the other. Particularly when our liturgical usage, or more properly misusage, conforms to the unjust systems and ideologies of our cultural context (as it does in its androcentrism), the effect of this is devastating to the humanity of both groups. It gives the favored an exalted view of themselves. It also reinforces the prevalent degraded and degrading view of the other group, affecting social standing, self-regard, and attributed standing in the eyes of God.

The *Supplemental Liturgical Texts* and *Materials* skillfully attempt to restore the fullness of our understanding of God and redress the bias of our understanding of our own humanity. This is done primarily through the incorporation of scriptural and traditional imagery of divine compassion, nurture, long-suffering, and practical wisdom. When these images are used, gender stereotyping is avoided because God is addressed in the second person rather than the third ("you" rather than "she"). Further, all of creation is identified as one ("we," "sons and daughters") and the experiences mentioned as characteristic of humanity are pluralistic (e.g., "we violated your creation, abused one another, and rejected your love"). This practice provides a powerful corrective to the biases of our customary liturgies.

Less evident in the *Supplemental Liturgical Texts* and *Materials* (and deliberately so) are images drawn from more contemporary experience and from cultures that are not represented in the biblical material (Asian, Latin, Native American) or whose contributions to the Bible are not well recognized (African). The enrichment of Christianity by these cultures and by contemporary experience is great. Why, then, should these riches not be added more explicitly to our publicly shared liturgical heritage? It is my hope that, as the development, study, and reception process continues, these important resources will be more fully recognized and used.

It is not just texts that are important here. The process itself is also significant, and it should continue and be expanded both in scope and duration. The play of polyphony found in the conjoint use over time of The Book of Common Prayer along with the *Supplemental Liturgical Texts* and *Materials* contributes to the Church's growth in faith and faithful life by stimulating our religious and spiritual imagination and sparking our desire to engage in careful reflection. The conjoining of multiple images, forms, and genres brings to our awareness the incomprehensibility of God, the primacy of God over any idols of our making, and both the limitations and expansiveness of the ways available to us to glorify God and imagine our lives as in harmony with the divine. Some of this conjunction serves to modify and enrich familiar images, adding breadth, depth, and sumptuous harmony.

Some of this conjunction is contradictory and even confusing, as is paradigmatically the case in the parables of Jesus. Yet the twists, disjunctions, and intensifications in liturgical language can serve at one and the same time to disclose the limitations of our language and our understanding *and* to force our imagination out of its accustomed modes. This opening of new horizons can lead us into greater receptivity to new and perhaps different glimpses of God and into greater appropriation of divine grace offered to us and through us to the world that God has made and for whose redemption Christ died and rose again. It is important to the spiritual growth of every Christian to live ever more fully into the reality of God.

It is therefore important that this process of development, use, evaluation, and reception of liturgical texts continue to be done with care, deliberation, and sensitivity. It is also important that ample time and resources be given to this phase of liturgical renewal.

Recovery of underutilized and unfamiliar traditions requires considerable research and study. Moreover, it takes time, patience, and cumulative corporate experience for these traditions to become familiar (rather than occasional novelties). And familiarity is a necessary part of the reception and evaluation process. The gradual incorporation of these elements of tradition may give rise to new imagery, which itself must be tested in light of a number of criteria. These include continuity (though not necessarily identity) with already-received tradition and coherence with generally-held beliefs. Fruitfulness for renewed life for both individuals and communities is also important; this, too, requires time to emerge and be evaluated.

Fortunately, the Church recognizes that liturgical reform is an ever-ongoing process, because it is ever needed. The continuing necessity of liturgical renewal arises from a number of areas. Changes in human history, culture, language, and imagery; inherent limitations to human knowledge and the ability to express the reality of the holy; and renewed and expanding relationship to God all affect our worship continuously, both individually and corporately. But our worship is also affected by the certainty we hold that God's grace is beyond our knowledge and our prediction. Therefore, we believe, God's unwavering love toward us will be manifest in ways that will surprise, shock, and unsettle us. But they will also ultimately work our redemption and transformation.

Expansive Language: A Matter of Justice

William Seth Adams

Conversion is a curious business and certainly not all converts are alike. Some converts, for instance, remember the moment, the particulars; some do not. I am in the second batch. I know only roughly when this change of heart occurred. I know there was a time before and a time after—I can document it in my own writing—but as to exactly when and where I cannot say. What I am sure of is that the conversion was serious, thorough so far as I know, and enduring. I came to realize that words and what they declare or ignore are media of justice or its absence, health or harm, nurture or deprivation.

My conversion on the matter of language and justice, firstly with reference to the emancipation of women, was prepared for by a prior awakening, one regarding the ordination of women to the presbyterate. Though I cannot put an exact date to this event either, I recall the circumstances vividly. I was the vicar of a pair of small congregations in the northeastern corner of Missouri, up the Mississippi from Hannibal. At the larger of the two, we had a regular Wednesday morning eucharist, typically (almost always) attended only by women. On one such Wednesday, in the company of five women, I stood reading Luke's gospel: "And Mary said, 'My soul magnifies the Lord . . .'" (Luke 1:46ff). As I proclaimed these verses, the realization passed through me that these extraordinary words of Mary (and Hannah) were *not* words any woman was privileged to read in the eucharistic liturgy of the Episcopal Church. This was 1967 or 1968. I was astounded and awakened in the midst of the Magnificat.

I begin this way in order to declare that I write as a convert, one persuaded that exclusivity can inhere in language, liturgical and otherwise, and that this exclusivity is a sin, particularly in liturgical language. Further, like some converts, I have lost my capacity to understand the perspective of the unconverted. That is, I have lost the ability to understand, or even tolerate, the arguments mounted by those who argue against inclusive / emancipatory / expansive language. And the logic of inclusivity in language is so persuasive, the necessity of justice so compelling as to render me useless in explaining how one could remain unconverted. This is especially true for me with regard to the women in my acquaintance for whom exclusive (and therefore by my terms "sinful") language is "no problem."

It is clear that a concern for just, expansive language has been a part of the process and products of liturgical revision in the Episcopal Church before now, before considering the "next" revision. The current revision of The Book of Common Prayer, within itself, testifies to the existence of this concern and to efforts to respond to it. One need only compare the texts in Rites I and II to see the fruits of efforts on the parts of revisers to be more inclusive in our liturgical language. The same evidence is available, perhaps in greater abundance, in *The Hymnal 1982*. The pursuit of a more just vocabulary and form of expression is a matter with a history. What is needful now, as we look to a rebirth of the formal revision process, is a more thoroughgoing commitment to a more just liturgical vernacular.

Such a vernacular would be characterized by assumptions about uniformity and diversity that are distinguishable from those in the current revision. "Man" and its siblings would not be respected as generic terms for the human community and the experience of men would not survive as normative for the whole of humanity.

With this norm as a first principle, the extension of its logic would be thoroughgoing.

The literature treating this subject matter is extensive and readily available. Most useful to my mind are three sources written by Episcopalians, interestingly enough, and one by a member of the Reformed Church. As an appendix to the *Supplemental Liturgical Materials,* published by the Standing Liturgical Commission in 1991, Leonel Mitchell offered a carefully reasoned and gently written discussion of the nature of liturgical language, the reasonableness of change in liturgical language and the premise for change in our time. He wrote, "To the extent that this traditional usage of English grammar causes worshipers to think of God as male or causes women to feel that their creation in God's image is being denied, it is a serious distortion of the meaning of what is being proclaimed."[1] This line is written with reference to the use of the male pronoun "he" in reference to God, but the same premise could well be cited for the use of generic male terms for all humanity.

The writings of Marjorie Procter-Smith have much to offer as conversion materials regarding the liberation of liturgical language. Two sources in particular are important. In her 1990 book, *In Her Own Rite: Constructing Feminist Liturgical Tradition,* Professor Procter-Smith, an Episcopalian teaching at Perkins School of Theology in Dallas, proposed a schema for a more just vernacular, ranging from "non-sexist" to "inclusive" to "emancipatory." She writes,

> Nonsexist language seeks to avoid gender-specific terms. Inclusive language seeks to balance gender references. Emancipatory language seeks to transform language use and to challenge stereotypical gender references.[2]

Observing that sexist or androcentric language "makes women invisible," she goes on to explain,

> Nonsexist language suggests that God does not

> regard our gender, or that our gender is not rele-
> vant to our relationship with God. Inclusive lan-
> guage implies that God does regard our gender, but
> that both women and men possess equal status
> before God. Emancipatory language assumes that
> God is engaged in women's struggles for emancipa-
> tion, even to the point of identifying with those
> who struggle... [E]mancipatory language must
> make women visible.[3]

It is surely a matter of justice for those who edit and create liturgical texts, including those who translate texts from earlier times and
places, to "make women visible."

In her most recent book, *Praying With Our Eyes Open,* Prof.
Procter-Smith contributes yet another potent observation. In her
chapter entitled "Praying Between the Lines," she reports the experience of women who have found a way of praying "through"
androcentric formulas by "praying between the lines." She speaks,
further, of the necessity of simultaneous translation, rendering the
androcentric text into a more generous, usable vernacular.

> We grow accustomed...to translating as we go,
> reading ourselves into the text from which we have
> been excised, by reading behind the texts, reading
> the silences and the spaces, the absences and the
> omissions. We learn to hear words not spoken
> aloud, see signs unread by others. And we learn to
> keep our readings to ourselves.[4]

Here the author points to two matters of fragmentation, matters
which justice ought to preclude. Firstly, there is the fragmentation
of the gathered community created by the use of a vocabulary (and
its underlying assumptions) which is not the *lingua franca* of that
very community, a vocabulary which is not the natural, native
tongue of the community. This fragmentation would not be tolerated if the community were recognized to be multilingual along
ethnic or national lines.

The second fragmentation derives from the author's final comment, "...we learn to keep our readings to ourselves." Herein lie the seeds not only of fragmentation but also of isolation, the "reading" of the oppressed serving as the "code" among the isolated. Surely, no community, especially the community of the baptized, needs such isolation spawned and supported within itself by its language. Beyond this, of course, is the matter of the ownership and exercise of power, and the creation of continuous power-contests between the "outside" patriarchal language and the "inside" translation and those who "understand" either.

The third writer to receive mention in this setting is Brian Wren, a minister of the Reformed Church in England, now writing and teaching in the United States. Among the books cited in this essay, his *What Language Shall I Borrow?* takes the unique perspective of being written self-consciously for a male readership. In a forthright and literate fashion, Mr. Wren displays and dissects "patriarchy" as a social and theological reality embedded in the way we (men and women) think and talk, and undertakes to find a language to serve as its replacement.[5]

From first reading, I have found this book persuasive in a most captivating fashion. For example, the author ends a section in which he explores male sexual violence by making this simple and profound observation, "We need a new, humane paradigm of manhood in which the 'true man' neither conquers nor protects, but simply behaves as a good neighbor to women, children, and other men."[6] In a later section, considering the life pattern of Jesus as a model for other males, Mr. Wren writes, "Jesus does not merely fail to uphold patriarchal norms or take a different direction. His whole ministry *undermines* those norms and gives us a vision of a different kind of society."[7] The realization of this vision is a task shared by women and men.

These sources, either alone or in combination, along with countless others, provide powerful testimony to the necessities of justice in the reconstruction of our liturgical language. Those who are writing and will write new texts for the future revision of the prayer book are typically persuaded of this necessity, and the emerging texts do and will show forth a deeper commitment to a vernacular that gathers up, one that requires no "translation" as Marjorie Procter-Smith speaks of it. Making the older texts more just, the "received" texts as it were, remains the problem it was in revising the current edition of the prayer book and in the making of the current hymnal, though now the use of biblical texts taken from the New Revised Standard Version will be a boon.

The real struggle in this regard will likely be the matter of the retention of the Rite I formulas, unrelieved of their patriarchal burden. In this case, however, it is not simply a matter of "fixing" the language but also of re-engaging the imagery as well. Though Rite II needs similar re-engagement, Rite I needs it more and more fundamentally. It may be helpful here to recall the convictions about vernacular liturgy held by Thomas Cranmer, the "author" of the first two Books of Common Prayer (1549 and 1552). It was Cranmer's conviction that putting the liturgy in the vernacular was absolutely necessary in order (1) to achieve a higher level of participation among the faithful and (2) to achieve in the Body of Christ a fuller degree of edification.[8] These two necessities, participation and edification, remain central to liturgical revision as much today as in the 1540s. And for Cranmer, as for ourselves, expressing the liturgy in the vernacular is a matter of justice.

What may prove ironic here is that by retaining Thomas Cranmer's convictions about vernacular liturgy, we may find a warrant for letting go some (at least) of Cranmer's language. In any case, it remains true that the crafting of new texts using a more just vernacular will come more easily than the renovation of older ones.[9]

One needs to remember, in all this, that the language of the liturgy is only partially contained in the texts provided in the prayer book. There is a much broader context in which these words serve. The words of the formal texts are joined by other words, those from the Bible, those used to do the congregation's business by way of announcements, those words offered in song, those words employed in the fashioning of indigenous prayers and those used in preaching. Whatever matters of justice are rightly raised about the formal texts, these same matters of justice must also inform these other words. The Church's commitment to justice, when it is shown forth in texts, must find worthy companions in the rest of the language of the liturgy. All our speaking must speak justly.

Extending the context further, we need to recognize that the nonverbal dimension of the liturgical event constitutes a kind of "language," too. Clearly, the critique to which we have pointed and which we have recapitulated in some small measure has most often been aimed at words (and the assumptions that support them). But this critique ought also to call us to be mindful of nonverbal, spatial and gestural justice as well.

When we think of any liturgical event, the Sunday Holy Eucharist for example, what we experience is only partially represented by the prayer book texts and rubrics. Much of the experience is unknown to the texts beyond the rubric's direction. The liturgical space, vesture, furnishings, liturgical objects, gestures and personnel and their actions—this level of the liturgical experience is not "controlled" by the text. If we are to use "expansive" eyes and hearts to assess the texts, such must also be used to determine the justice done and seen to be done in the liturgy as a totality. Do the postures and gestures declare and foster just relationships? Does the liturgical space evince hospitality and invite a just level of participation by all? Pursuit of these questions and others like them ought to describe and direct our thinking about "revision." And if we were to come to some common and clear view as to what makes for justice in these matters, who is to advocate it, teach it, and model it in such a way that the Church at large will see and know?

In the end, it seems to me, the real issue is the matter of power, or better, the twin issues of authority and consent. By whose authority might this more just vernacular be employed and whose consent or pleasure must be sought in the undertaking?

Writing in his fifteen-year-old, yet still challenging book, *The Integrity of Anglicanism,* Stephen Sykes suggested that the real center of authority within Anglicanism is occupied by those who revise the texts and fashion the rubrics in the prayer book. Sykes put it this way, "...the decision-making process whereby liturgies are changed...is the basic seat of authority in the Anglican church, and the basic exercise of that authority is the power to enforce the liturgy."[10] Whatever the truth of this assertion, it is tested every Sunday as texts and rubrics are routinely abridged, reinterpreted or ignored. In any particular place, whatever is customary, "traditional" as it were, is going to contain and exercise the real power, authority and consent, rubrical direction or no, General Convention or no.

But the broader issue is the question of justice itself. The texts and rubrics in The Book of Common Prayer, if they are to promote justice, must also mirror justice. I am persuaded, as many others are, that the ritual life of a community is formative of the heart of that community as well as being expressive of the convictions and story of that community. This being so, the liturgy, while intending the formation of a more just community, must also be expressive of that community's intention to do justice. "Fixing the words" is not the point; justice and godly mercy are. Here we are at the essential matter. Are we (that is, the Church, not just liturgical revisers) able or willing to see the need for a revised liturgical vernacular as a matter of justice at all? Is the dream of a common language sufficiently alluring to elicit from us all a commitment to revision for justice's sake? If we commit ourselves to justice and say "yes" to these questions, we will surely have a wide array of possibilities available to us and a more vivid, hopeful future. A negative answer will bring only loss and despair. The choice is up to us.[11]

Notes

1. New York: Church Hymnal Corporation, 1991, p. 63. This same essay appeared in the earlier publication of some of these "materials" when they appeared as "texts." I once spoke at a meeting of General Convention delegates from the Dioceses of Dallas and Fort Worth. My task was to discuss with them the rationale and substance of the proposed supplemental ("inclusive language") texts. My intent was to commend Prof. Mitchell's essay to them as a clearly written and moderate presentation on the matter. As I listened to the speaker who preceded me, who spoke vigorously against even the idea of the texts, I heard Prof. Mitchell's insightful essay condemned and ridiculed. When it came my turn to speak, I took the floor, so to speak, with that introduction. As one person said to me afterwards, "The floor was not level." Indeed!

2. Nashville: Abingdon, p. 63.

3. Ibid., pp. 66-7.

4. Nashville: Abingdon, 1955, p. 32. Prof. Procter-Smith is relying on Elizabeth Castelli in this instance.

5. New York: Crossroad, 1993.

6. Ibid., p. 43.

7. Ibid., p. 179.

8. These convictions were expressed in his Preface to the first Book of Common Prayer (1549); see BCP, 1979, pp. 866-7.

9. I am reminded of an article written years ago by the late Erik Routley, hymnwriter and composer, in which he struggled with the matter of revising hymns in terms of what we are calling "justice." He set out an array of alternatives, including setting a hymn aside if it could not be "redeemed." See "Sexist Language: A View from a Distance," *Worship* 53 (1979): 2-11.

10. London: Mowbrays, 1978, p. 96.

11. It would be important to recognize that even by shifting the

assumptions about liturgical revision to "expansive" assumptions, there are still significant debates and disagreements to engage and resolve. As one would rightly expect, a common language remains yet a "dream" even among those committed to its achievement. Central to this is the matter of the way older assumptions can be used to test newer ones, while allowing the newer ones to discipline the older ones. How this kind of reciprocity or complementarity among and between assumptions can serve the Church remains for us to explore.

Prayer Book Revision or Liturgical Renewal? The Future of Liturgical Text

Clayton L. Morris

The Problem

Increasingly, over the past decade or so, a variety of concerns have been articulated about the need for renewal of the Church's liturgical language and the structure of its prayer book. Issues include the use of gender-specific (male) language and inappropriate phraseology in reference to disability, color and power. There are specific concerns about the extent to which the 1979 book assumes a role for clergy which places the ordained person in a position of privilege, often as a representative intermediary between the baptized community and God (as in the Celebration of a New Ministry, BCP, pp. 558-65). Communities worshiping in languages other than English object to the direct translation of English forms into another language. They express the need, instead, for liturgical texts which emerge from the community's cultural and linguistic heritage.

The Episcopal Church began its response to these expressed concerns with the publication of a series of supplemental liturgical texts aimed at expanding and to some extent correcting the use of language. These attempts began to address issues that can be corrected by editing and expanding English texts, but the limited scope of the General Convention resolutions authorizing this project[1] leaves other issues unresolved.

The issue of power—how power and authority are expressed liturgically—has been brought into focus, in part, by the supplemental texts. The issue also comes to the fore as increasing numbers of women lead from positions of authority in the Church's political structure and as communities from increasingly diverse cultural circumstances learn to minister from the perspectives of their particular understandings of power and authority. The Church, as it ministers apart from the traditional framework of patriarchal styles of leadership, illustrates the possibilities of a variety of approaches to the exercise of authority within the community.

Black, Hispanic, Native American and Asian communities are struggling to understand what it means to pray in language that simultaneously communicates an orthodox expression of eucharistic theology and reflects the cultural reality of the community in which the liturgy is used. And, in the midst of these conversations and explorations, the Church is coming to grips with the fact that it comprises mostly very small congregations, leading to questions about what sort of liturgical resources are appropriate to small gatherings of Christians.

Meanwhile, there are congregations longing for stability in the life of the Church. In a time of societal, governmental and cultural upheaval, some of these communities declare that the 1979 Book of Common Prayer and *The Hymnal 1982* are all the liturgical resources the Church needs. For them, the liturgical movement has ended. They are less anxious to think of expanding borders than to learn better ways of applying existing liturgical resources in existing communities.

At the General Convention meeting in Indianapolis, the Standing Liturgical Commission was directed to

> prepare a rationale and a pastorally sensitive plan for
> the next revision of the Book of Common Prayer,
> and report to the 72nd General Convention.[2]

The wording of this resolution betrays a bias that will need to be challenged in order to approach the drafting of a "pastorally sensitive" response to the question of prayer book revision.

To speak of "…the next revision of the Book of Common Prayer" seems to make two assumptions which are likely to confuse the Church's consideration of this issue. It apparently assumes that the collection of worship resources authorized for use will continue to be a single document in English. It seems to assume, as well, that a future revision of the Church's liturgical resources will proceed in a style and manner analogous to the previous revision process.

While there are many who understand that renewal of the Church's liturgy must recognize the multicultural identity of the Church, the call for revision seems focused on English-language problems, and it appears that the question of the use of other languages is seen intuitively as a task of translation rather than an issue of inculturation.

A new English redaction of the Church's liturgical texts could deal with the concerns of English-speaking Episcopalians to craft the language of common worship in more inclusive terms. English-speaking Episcopalians for whom the 1979 Book of Common Prayer is problematic have a valid issue with the Church. The Book of Common Prayer functions as a standard for Anglican worship. As a denomination whose identity is expressed in its liturgical life, the Episcopal Church has always looked to the prayer book as the icon of its denominational unity. Thus, when the book articulates claims that are inconsistent with the life of the community, the book must change. For example, those whose concern for revision is focused on women's issues are convinced that the 1979 Book of Common Prayer must be taken from its pedestal to be replaced by a book whose text reflects the emerging identity of the Church as a community whose life and ministry is fully accessible to women. Just as the 1979 Book of Common Prayer, with its renewed emphasis on eucharist and baptism, replaced its 1928 predecessor in order to reflect the growing baptismal consciousness of the denomination, so the 1979 Book of Common Prayer should be set aside in order to reflect the growing consciousness in the Church about the importance of inclusivity.

If correcting the Church's use of the English language and redrafting rites to reorder the relationships among the identified categories of the Church's ministry (i.e., "lay persons, bishops, priests, and deacons," BCP, p. 855) were the only issues to be faced in the process of liturgical renewal, a redrafting of the 1979 Book of Common Prayer could solve the problem. Once again, a new Book of Common Prayer could take its place as the model for liturgical life in the Church and the icon of the Church's unified identity.

But the Episcopal Church is not an exclusively English-speaking denomination. While it is certainly the case that the majority of Episcopalians worship exclusively in the English language, the growing edge of the denomination is in communities whose languages are not English. How are these communities to find their place at the table if the icon of denominational unity is a collection of texts in English?

Is this language issue a problem for non-English speaking communities within the Church, or is it a problem for the denomination as a whole? As the Episcopal Church has rediscovered its baptismal identity and the ministry of service which is so clearly articulated in the baptismal covenant, increasing attention is being given to the notion that the primary task of the Church is the restoration of unity in creation. God created the world as one, global community, and it is the task of the Church to bring *all* persons into relationship with God and into community with one another.

The Episcopal Church is in the process of exploring the implications of a commitment to radical inclusivity. Issues of sexuality and gender, race and culture, for example, all have to do with the question: who is welcome at the Lord's Table? The emergence of communities expecting to worship in languages other than English provides a visible example of the issue of inclusivity, but clearly the question encompasses a host of concerns in addition to the question of how non-English-speaking communities are incorporated into the Church. If prayer book revision is to deal effectively with questions like these which occupy the Church's attention, it must deal seriously with the issue of inclusivity in all of its permutations. And, to be fair, the vision of inclusivity must embrace all Episcopalians; not just those whose culture and values are articulated in the English language, or just those whose habit and heritage has been traditionally represented by the Episcopal Church.

Toward a Solution

Are Episcopalians really "The People of the Book"? The process used to develop the 1979 Book of Common Prayer changed forever the Church's understanding of liturgical planning. Almost thirty years ago, with the publication of *The Liturgy of the Lord's Supper*,[3] Episcopalians began to experience *the leaflet* as a means of placing liturgical texts into their hands on Sunday morning. In many congregations, as a matter of weekly habit, the familiar, leather clad prayer book, often provided by a godparent on confirmation day and carried faithfully to and from church, gave way to the distribution every Sunday morning of a disposable pamphlet.

This shift, encouraged by the experience of "trial use," introduced a new notion into the lives of Christians who had been used to a liturgy "fixed" in print and contained in a venerable book. As congregations began using liturgies variously printed in disposable pamphlets, the sense of the permanence of the liturgy gave way to a more fluid image of the Church's liturgical texts. As the Episcopal Church lived through the process of revising its prayer book, people became aware of the possibility of editing phrases within liturgical rites and, in fact, amending the collections of texts which comprised the rites used Sunday by Sunday, year by year. One imagines that never again will it be possible to think of the Church's liturgy as something so static that it can be held safely between the covers of a book.

In the decade between the arrival of that first trial-use text and the publication of the 1979 prayer book, local liturgical planners became aware of the possibility of creating the weekly leaflet on site, and congregations became accustomed to the use of printed road maps through the liturgy in the particular form celebrated in the local community. Increasingly, these leaflets contained the text for the liturgy as well as hymns to be used in the rite.

Today, the notion of printing week by week everything the worshiper needs to read or sing in the course of a liturgy is taken for granted in many congregations. As this strategy for the delivery of liturgical text becomes increasingly common, the church's expectation of reliance on a bound prayer book decreases.

The prospect of having all the necessary printed material collected in a booklet which can simply be read from front to back is often lauded as an evangelical tool because it simplifies the worshiper's task. There is much talk these days about "user-friendly" liturgy, especially in small worshiping communities and congregations recruiting as new members Christians from diverse denominational experience.

The availability of computerized word-processing and instant-printing, as they emerge and become increasingly available to liturgical planning teams, creates a completely new understanding of the nature of service planning at the local level as well as a new understanding of the process through which liturgical text is developed. Recognizing that the use of these technologies is still developing, the Church should not assume that the result of a process of "prayer book revision" will necessarily be delivered as a single bound volume.

Are Episcopalians really the *People of the Book*? Yes and no. Episcopalians are Christians whose denominational identity is most clearly and accurately articulated in liturgy. But a quick look at the history of Anglican liturgy in the American Episcopal Church suggests that there have always been collections of texts available regionally in the Church. Liturgical unity has never been absolute liturgical conformity. The popular, widespread experience of the editing of liturgical text at the parochial level is fairly recent, but there has always been some degree of local variation in text used for worship.

Perhaps the growing recognition that Episcopalians worship in many languages helps to bring into focus the long-standing diversity which has existed liturgically in the Church. When the Episcopal Church saw itself as an exclusively English-speaking denomination, the icon of the Standard Book of Common Prayer quite naturally suggested the existence of a level of liturgical conformity which never really existed. It was convenient and comforting to assume that everyone read from the same text at 11:00 on Sunday morning. Perhaps, the task of integrating non-English - speaking communities into the community will help the Church come to grips with the idea that some divergence of liturgical text from place to place is justified.

Are Episcopalians really "The Church of England in America"? If the decade-plus between 1967 and 1979 was a period in which the Church developed a willingness to entertain variety in the liturgical texts used in worship, then during the decade and a half since the 1979 prayer book arrived, the Episcopal Church has become increasingly aware of its diversity.

In the context of the liturgical life of English-speaking congregations, a number of issues are coming to the fore: gender issues in language used about persons and about God; choices in the translation of scripture; questions about the lectionary, especially in reference to the absence of stories and images from scripture descriptive of the presence and role of women in the Church; the representation of holy orders in liturgical rites; the expressed need for additional liturgical responses to pastoral circumstance not addressed by The Book of Common Prayer. The issue of diversity is expressed, in this context, by the expectation that all members of the Christian community must be recognized as equal participants in the life and ministry of the Church.

In the larger context of language and culture, the last years have seen an explosion of church growth among non-English-speaking communities. Most Episcopalians would be surprised, for example, to discover that in the Diocese of Long Island, the eucharistic prayer is rendered in at least ten languages every Sunday morning.[4] In the Diocese of Los Angeles, the number is seven.[5] At issue for these communities is not just the question of whether a prayer book is available in the appropriate language. Perhaps more important is the question of whether the liturgical text in a particular language reflects a sense of the cultural circumstances in which the people live and against which they apprehend the message of Christ's Good News.

Christians within the Anglican Communion have become aware over the past few years that Anglicanism is not primarily a northern European expression of the Christian faith. The fruits of British colonialism, coupled with the Church's willingness to indigenize the leadership of colonial provinces, have moved the center of Anglicanism to the southern hemisphere. As the Episcopal Church comes to grips with the realities of its growing edge, the image of the Episcopal Church as the American version of the Church of England in the nineteenth century will slowly fade and disappear.

What would a "revised" prayer book look like? It is not clear what kind of commitment the Church has to the ongoing publication of new liturgical resources. There are some worshiping communities at home and comfortable with the 1979 Book of Common Prayer and *The Hymnal 1982*. There are other communities who have moved far beyond those resources in their exploration of liturgical diversity. Clearly a new English edition of the Church's liturgical texts cannot answer the variety of concerns the Church faces liturgically.

It can be safely assumed that worshipers gathering on any Sunday morning across the country have in hand a variety of printed resources. Some hold The Book of Common Prayer 1979. Others have translations of The Book of Common Prayer into other languages. A few read from copies of The Book of Common

Prayer 1928. As they enter the worship space, many are handed leaflets which contain everything they need to read in the course of the liturgy. Some of these leaflets contain texts reprinted from the current, authorized prayer book. Others contain materials authorized as *Supplemental Liturgical Materials.*[6] Still other leaflets contain materials "borrowed" from other resources or authorized materials edited by the local liturgical leaders. And finally, one imagines a few congregations using leaflets which contain materials crafted by local clergy or liturgy planning teams.

Yes, some of this is unauthorized liturgical behavior. But it has always been so. And if a dispassionate consideration of the Church's liturgical habit and heritage is possible, one realizes, perhaps, that experimentation of the kind alluded to here is a source of creative energy which eventually produces new texts which can, in turn, be made available to the entire Church.

The explosion in the availability of printed material at the local level, created by emerging computer and printing technologies, has encouraged congregations to become testing grounds for new liturgical texts (or edited texts). Recognizing that some of the work of local liturgical designers and editors is not of a quality that would recommend it to the Church at large, nevertheless the Church should probably not expect to curtail the creative impulse of liturgists in the local community. Perhaps, in fact, the goals and purposes of liturgical renewal will be served more adequately if local creativity is encouraged and nurtured.

Thus, there is reason to begin the process of renewing the Church's liturgical text by wondering about moving beyond trial or experimental use. In the process used to produce the current prayer book, drafting teams comprised of experts in a variety of fields were gathered to prepare texts which were then distributed, in a variety of ways, for trial use and evaluation. The Church is currently hearing, especially from its non-English-speaking constituents, that the experts are not always in a position to comprehend the grassroots circumstances that need to be woven into the creative process. Perhaps this witness extends to local communities in general.

It may be time for the Church to take a more permissive attitude about the local development of liturgical texts. To be sure, this position, in order to be authorized by General Convention, will be articulated in such a way as to clarify the need to be governed by the commonly held notions about the nature of liturgical prayer which constitute denominational unity. The proposal will contain workable strategies for development, evaluation and review so that the Church's life of prayer will continually generate material which can, in time, be prepared for general publication.

What would a revised Book of Common Prayer look like? It should be a library of resources, some in English, others in an increasing variety of global tongues. This library will contain much that is familiar, old liturgies as well as new rites on the cutting edge of new inquiry. It will be a growing library, with provision for adding new materials as they are developed and, perhaps, removing materials whose usefulness has waned. Its use will be guided by carefully wrought guidelines approved by General Convention.

How will the vision of Anglicanism united in liturgy be sustained? The rapid development of a new vision for liturgical planning and the techniques and strategies used to organize the worship life of a congregation suggests a basic question: does the unity of the Episcopal Church depend on the existence of a single volume of liturgical texts uniformly accepted and used by the denomination? Should the Church continue to live with the myth of liturgical uniformity?

The unity of Anglican worship has been symbolized, traditionally, by the book itself. In the Episcopal Church, each diocese maintains a copy of the Standard Book of Common Prayer, examined by the Custodian of the Standard Book and determined to be an exact copy of that book authorized by General Convention for use by the whole denomination. In a culture where most Episcopalians owned and used a copy of that "Standard" book in worship, it could be generally assumed that Episcopalians worshiped according to an agreed-upon form. But as congregations currently function, the Standard Book fails as an assurance of compliance to anything.

The time has come for the Church to find a new icon to regard as the symbol of liturgical unity, so central to the Church's identity, an icon which honors, supports and encourages diversity, while at the same time holds congregations accountable to the standard of liturgical prayer which forms and sustains the Church as it proclaims the Gospel and mobilizes the Church for its ministry of reconciliation.

There are at least two concerns standing in the way of a strategy of this sort. One is the question of the formative nature of liturgical prayer: what happens to a congregation if it is exposed to eucharistic prayers whose theology is wanting? Second, what happens to the unity of Anglicanism if the Church abandons the notion of uniform, commonly held liturgical assumptions?

One possible solution to the task of simultaneously addressing issues of unity and diversity in the liturgical life of the Church is a strategy for generating a variety of texts to meet the needs of particular congregations and at the same time constructing a new icon to reflect the reality of the Church's liturgical unity. Perhaps two things need to occur:

1) The General Convention might recognize the extent to which liturgical texts are formed in the praying community and on the basis of that understanding authorize a period of time for and a structure within which congregations could engage in the development of new liturgical texts.

2) The Standing Liturgical Commission might engage in writing a description of liturgical orthodoxy to serve as the "icon" for liturgical unity.

Charting a Path for the Future

Congregational experimentation and development. "The nice thing about being an Anglican is that anywhere in the world I can feel at home in worship!" Yes! Indeed! But the comfort Anglicans feel when they visit their sisters and brothers in other provinces has little to do with the nuances of language. Especially in circumstances where the language in use is not familiar to the visitor, the felt sense of welcome and comfort has to do with the structure of the rite, the use of the building, and perhaps details like movement and vesture.

For faithful Episcopalians, lay and ordained alike, formed in the ethos of prayer book worship, the prospect of granting local communities the freedom to generate and experiment with liturgical text is difficult. The suggestion seems counter to the vision of global unity the Episcopal Church has always valued. But it is instructive to wonder whether or not the canonical prohibitions against local liturgical experimentation actually serve to prevent the local editing and developing of liturgical text. It is even more instructive to imagine the impact local experimentation would have on the richness of the liturgical tradition and the sense of inclusion created by such a process.

Congregations in which baptized persons are challenged to articulate their faith find that people are anxious and ready to develop the ability to speak. The popularity of such programs as *Education for Ministry* demonstrates the willingness of Christians to prepare themselves for the task to which they are invited. Does the Church imagine that the opportunity to participate in the crafting of liturgical resources would find faithful members of the body less enthused? Perhaps it is time to trust the members of Christ's body to take on the tasks they took on in their baptism. Perhaps the formation of liturgical prayer is one of those tasks. Perhaps, in the process of forming liturgical prayer, the Church will itself be reformed. Perhaps, also, it is time to recognize that the Anglican Communion is not unified by a common liturgical text, but rather, unified by a common understanding, expressed liturgically, about the mission and ministry of Christ's body to creation.

A new Icon of unity. The International Anglican Liturgical Consultation, meeting in Dublin in the summer of 1995, articulated this recommendation:

> In the future, Anglican unity will find its liturgical expression not so much in uniform texts as in a common approach to eucharistic celebration and a structure which will ensure a balance of word, prayer, and sacrament, and which bears witness to the catholic calling of the Anglican communion.[7]

A *pastorally sensitive plan* for the renewal of the Church's liturgy will recognize that the liturgical unity which Anglicans cherish as a mark of identity is a common structure, not a common text. The task for the Standing Liturgical Commission, preparing for the General Convention in Philadelphia, is to discern what form a new icon of that unity will take. The task for the Church, in a broader sense, revolves around a question: how can liturgical unity be assured in a church which has license to develop liturgical texts locally? The answer, clearly, is to be found, at least in part, in an accurate description of what the Church means by unity. Such unity is partly found in the care and consistency with which liturgical resources are developed and used at the congregational level.

A Vision

In Native American culture, the shaman is set apart by the tribe to preserve its spiritual heritage and preside over ritual events in the life of the community. This holy person is called by the tribe to spend a lifetime taking into memory and soul the myth, prayer and ritual which comprise the spiritual essence of the community's life and understanding of itself. The formation of the shaman is a lifetime vocation. It is a work which demands the constant and total attention of the one ordained to the call.

Without suggesting that vocation to the Christian priesthood is analogous to the calling of the native holy man, the image of the shaman is compelling in the context of reflections about the future of liturgical prayer. The traditional image for the Episcopal Church is The Book. The presider in liturgy is, thus, one who reads from the approved text. Of course, the bishop, priest, deacon, lay reader or officiant at the daily office is more than one who simply articulates the sacred text. Whatever the liturgical context, the one who presides is the one who gives life to the text in the reading. The presider (or for that matter, the liturgical planner who makes the choices of text, music, gesture and movement which comprise the liturgical event) is the one whose presence engages the attention and imagination of all present, so that the community may gather in celebration and prayer.

Perhaps fifty or a hundred years ago it was appropriate, or at least understandable, for the Church to function as a respected, unchanging institution within the culture. Perhaps it made sense that the recitation of a single, unchanging eucharistic prayer was understood to be one stable element within the life of that Church. But the Church of this last decade of the twentieth century no longer inhabits only a world of privileged stability. The Episcopal Church of this decade, as it prepares for a new millennium, is a church on the move into every corner and culture of American society. As congregations express the Christian faith in the contexts of Anglicanism and the particular cultural heritage each congregation represents, new images of unity will become apparent in the commonalities which emerge among an expanding variety of particular expressions of the faith.

How should the Church prepare a rationale and a pastorally sensitive plan for the next revision of The Book of Common Prayer? That is a question for the Standing Liturgical Commission to entertain and for the General Convention meeting in Philadelphia to consider in 1997. If the response is to be sensitive to the diverse needs of an increasingly eclectic community, and if the pastoral needs of an increasingly diverse constituency are taken seriously, the next decade or more will be a time of gathering the gifts every Episcopalian brings to the Church's celebrations around the Table, so that the prayers and praises of all God's children can sound loudly, clearly, joyfully as a witness to the restoration of the unity of God's creation.

Notes

1. Resolution A095, *Journal of the 68th General Convention,* 1985, p. 605; Resolution A103a, *Journal of the 69th General Convention,* 1988, p. 327; Resolution A121a, *Journal of the 70th General Convention,* 1991, p. 405; Resolution A068, *Journal of the 71st General Convention,* 1994, p. 621.
2. Resolution A051a, *Journal of the 71st General Convention,* 1994, p. 758.
3. Prayer Book Studies XVII (New York: Church Pension Fund, 1966).
4. Interview with The Rev. Canon Roper Shamhart, Diocese of Long Island, 6 Dec. 1995.
5. Interview with The Rev. Canon Carmen Guerrero, Diocese of Los Angeles, 13 Feb. 1996.
6. Expanded edition, New York: Church Hymnal Corporation, 1996.
7. David R. Holeton, ed., *Renewing the Anglican Eucharist: Findings of the Fifth International Anglican Liturgical Consultation, Dublin, Eire, 1995,* Grove Worship Series 135 (Bramcote, Nottingham: Grove Books, 1996), p. 7.

Just Praise: Prayer Book Revision and Hispanic/Latino Anglicanism

Juan M. C. *Oliver*

> ...the job facing the cultural intellectual is...not to
> accept the politics of identity as given, but to show
> how all representations are constructed, for what
> purpose, by whom, and with what components.[1]

In his *Culture and Imperialism*, quoted above, Edward Said has
alerted us to the myriad ways in which, from the French
Revolution on, French, English and now American cultures have
colonized—and continue to colonize—the world. The Episcopal
Church has grown recently in sensitivity to this phenomenon, and
we can begin to unravel the ways in which our representations—in
this case the liturgy—have been constructed in such a way that
they support and effect Anglo cultural ascendancy.

This study explores the challenges in this area brought by the
prospect of a new revision of The Book of Common Prayer of the
Episcopal Church. I employ the cultural context of Latino/
Hispanic (I use the two terms interchangeably) culture for I know
it best; but it is my hope that the gist of my position will find
echoes in the experience of other minority Anglicans—in this case,
any Anglican who is not Anglo. Throughout, I refer to Said's work
as a tool for understanding the cultural power dynamics affecting
our discussions of Anglican liturgy.

In the first section, I place our concern in the framework of
Cranmer's cultural awareness in relation to Rome and the later
development of colonial Anglicanism in the world. A second sec-

tion explores the recent interest in multiculturalism in the Episcopal Church, pointing out some spurious versions of it and endorsing others. Finally, I explore the relation between liturgical studies and cultural justice, concluding with practical suggestions for the articulation, evaluation and dissemination of authentically Hispanic Anglican liturgical elements so that these might in turn form part of an informed dialogue towards prayer book revision.

I. Anglican Cultural Awareness

From Cranmer to Anglophilia

One of the driving forces behind the creation of the first Book of Common Prayer (1549) was the insight that liturgy should be related to the context in which it takes place. In the sixteenth century, this took the form of an emphasis on vernacular language; but it extended, particularly during the seventeenth century, to those aspects of English worship that Puritanism was unable to eradicate and which were reclaimed in the Restoration. If the impetus of the Cranmerian liturgical reformation enjoyed some measure of cultural awareness, it did so within an established, erastian conception of the Church, in which, as John Kater has suggested, "the church's primary identity is drawn from an imperial setting, where the church is understood to be the religious structure of a God-given empire."[2]

In the nineteenth century, however, and for all its cultural awareness of its own English contextual reality, Anglicanism encountered the new frontiers opening up in the world on the basis of this imperial model. Sadly, the cultural awareness of English reality did not translate to the same awareness of other cultures. Instead, Anglicans exported and imposed their cultural forms of theology, polity and liturgy all over the world. Kater has referred to this development and style of ministry as the "chaplaincy model."[3]

It would not be fair to say that these nineteenth-century "chaplaincy" outposts throughout the colonized world were an innocuous minority. They may have been so in numbers, but hardly so in effect. For example, the American colonizers in Puerto Rico following the Spanish-American war had enormous power: the power of invaders to restructure a society. The Episcopalians among them had the power to reproduce locally a specific liturgical sensibility with the resulting ritualization, in the name of God, of their political hegemony. It is one of the glories of Puerto Rican Anglicanism that at a crucial moment in history it opted to evangelize poor rural communities, shifting the meaning of *Episcopal* from a powerful foreign ruling class to a Protestant (i.e., not-Catholic) denomination *of the people*.

But the example of Puerto Rico seems to have been an exception rather than the rule. Throughout the colonized world, Anglicanism was coterminous with British or American ascendancy.

Church colonialism has been a heavy cross to bear for Anglican churches throughout the world. Deprived of, or unwilling to claim, their ability to fashion their own liturgical life, they often developed a foreign sense of themselves, trying to be more Anglican than Canterbury or the Church Center in New York. Their own economic dependence on the "mother churches" may have been a factor in this submissiveness. After the diminution of openly colonial English and American political presence (the colonial presence is now economic and media-based), this native disposition to love things foreign has continued to prevent the development of authentic Anglican liturgical forms rising from the cultural contexts of these churches and has become a major obstacle to evangelization.

Even in the Episcopal Church in the United States, the equation Anglican=Anglo is sometimes so strong that, for example, a bishop of my acquaintance sees no reason for the Episcopal Church to evangelize Hispanics since "they are all Roman Catholic anyway." At the local level as well, many a music director and liturgical planner show marked preferences for an English liturgical aesthetic, romantically evoked in a sad confusion of spirituality with exoticism, tempting to many Anglos who continue in the sad, naive illusion that they have no culture of their own.

We are faced, then, with a situation in which "Anglican" is often employed as a marker for things Anglo, serving only to confuse the nature and scope of Anglican liturgy with Anglo realities and traits. I propose, therefore, that for the sake of clarity, the adjective "Anglican" be employed to refer to essential structural aspects of Anglicanism and the Anglican Communion, such as Hooker's tripod (scripture, tradition, reason), the episcopacy, the Lambeth Quadrilateral (BCP, pp. 876-8), and the *idea* of a Book of Common Prayer rather than specific editions of it. Other aspects of our ecclesial life that derive from the British experience are best termed, well, British; or in some cases, Anglo. And the love of these things Anglo and British might be best referred to as Anglophilia, which like the term "Francophilia" need not be used pejoratively.

The Anglophilia of Anglican worship is a serious barrier to evangelism. To capture the sense of how it feels to live and worship using colonial liturgical forms, the following scenario might be helpful:

> Imagine that a local church is inviting you to join it. You are interested in it and find the people welcoming, but you notice that the English text does not sound like American English (it is a translation of the Guatemalan original because the church's worship had originated in Guatemala). You attend, and find that here the beauty of holiness means a profusion of visual stimuli, gold leaf, statues of saints, huge buildings made of stone, vases of flowers, candles everywhere and the pervasive smell of copal incense. Imagine learning to pray to the saints (sometimes audibly, before a statue) and learning to make a vow if you were praying for help; celebrating a young woman's fifteenth birthday with a grand liturgy and party; presenting

babies at the temple after their birth; exorcising homes; buying and offering amulets, mementos, and *ex votos*; and doing a plethora of holy doings and sayings totally foreign to your (Anglo) American religious experience.

You might grow to love this as "your faith"; but you would weekly run the risk of confusing the reign of God with something exotic, romantic and foreign, however pleasant and beautiful. You might also, I wager, walk away saddened by the immensity of the cultural adaptation you are being asked to make, perhaps suspecting that the church is asking you to convert in more ways than one. You might, consciously or not, embrace this foreign construct as your faith life, particularly if Guatemalan culture were much more powerful than yours and if thinking and feeling in Hispanic ways promised you the chance of economic advancement.

Reverse my example, and you have the experience of Hispanic Anglican congregations both in this country and abroad. It is at times a comforting experience, much the way the Anglophile films of Merchant-Ivory Productions, such as *Room with a View*, can be comforting. But this sort of Merchant-Ivory liturgy is also profoundly unreal. We should not be surprised if the typical Latino were to find it strange and foreign, if not completely unappetizing or demoralizing.

This would not be a problem if the liturgy were a mere addition to the life of the Church—frosting on the ecclesial cake. But the liturgy, as the *Constitution on the Sacred Liturgy* of the Second Vatican Council states, is both the source and summit of church life. It is so, partly because by it we are made as a community, but also because, as Yves Congar pointed out, it is the manifestation of who we are.[4] Thus Anglophile Latino liturgy reveals that the church *is supposed to be* Anglo. In this vision, belonging to this church involves, at least in part, being or seeming to be Anglo. The disastrous consequences of this for evangelization are obvious. (I say evangelization—passing on Jesus' good news—because evangelism—the conscious efforts to share our (Episcopal) faith—is worthless if this faith is not grounded in the Gospel. Church growth in numbers is *not* the proof of its success; conversion to the reign of God and the signs that accompany it, are.)

Liturgy, justice, culture and reign

How does Anglophile liturgy say to the Hispanic that he or she ought to be Anglo? How can a "mere rite" do this? Liturgy, like most rituals, presents what anthropologists, following Geertz, term "worldview," to be internalized and appropriated by the participants.[5]

Liturgy can both perpetuate injustice as well as present an efficacious experience of justice, for it is a communication event presenting in felt (often subliminal) ways an ideal world: the reign of God, preached by Jesus to be around the corner, imminent, among us and surprising. This experience of the reign is the foundation of a Christian worldview.[6]

The literature regarding the reign of God and its relation to liturgy is enormous. Classics such as Geoffrey Wainwright's *Liturgy and Eschatology*[7] point to the textual connections between the eucharistic theology of the early church and the fulfillment of all things. More recently, liberation theologians have reclaimed the concept of the reign of God as a foundation of both Jesus' preaching and Christian identity. One simple way in which the differences between Hispanic and Anglo worldviews may be spotted is by noticing the friction points between the Anglo liturgy and the behavior of Hispanics participating in it, such as delayed arrival, children running loose, or the sporadic reception of communion. Most pastors try to educate the Hispanic so they can fit the Anglo expectations of the liturgy, instead of reshaping the liturgy to embody the worldview of the Hispanic congregation. Since different cultures have different worldviews, it follows that the vision of the reign presented in the liturgy must be crafted from elements of *the culture's own felt sense of God's reign.* In the Hispanic perception of the reign of God, people arrive at their leisure and events start gradually, not suddenly.

Even if the liturgy did not reveal the identity of both God's reign and God's people, the mere fact that rituals always, in some way or other, construct power, would encourage the inspection of the justice aspects of the liturgy. For liturgy, like the Bible itself, deals with power and powerlessness, and so is fundamentally political, not in a partisan way but by concerning itself with the construction—and deconstruction—of power. Students of the liturgy, therefore, are not above Said's rallying call to account for the politics of that which we study.[8] Indeed, the ritualization of foreign hegemony is, not surprisingly, at once both a magnet to those "natives" who would like to climb the power ladders offered by colonial patronage and at the same time a reminder of their own powerlessness. Therefore a Hispanic liturgical theology will be attentive to the political issues raised by our liturgical experience, in much the same way as Justo González has suggested that our biblical hermeneutic is fundamentally concerned with political questions of power and powerlessness.[9]

Thus, the liturgy forms both identity and power. We must briefly look at *how* this takes place. A traditional formulation of sacramental theology, following Thomas Aquinas, is that the sacraments of the Church effect what they mean. They do this precisely by meaning it in the form not only of verbal content but, most especially, through ritual action.

At a foundational level, colonial liturgies—that is to say, liturgies which proceed as if the world were Anglo in the midst of (in our case) Hispanic reality—effect, because they signify, the power of the colonizers over the colonized. Participation in them effects this power by ritually submitting willing bodies to a foreign behavior acted out in a theater of foreign design, informed by a foreign sense of time and a foreign aesthetic. This is the bread and butter of Anglophile liturgical injustice in the Hispanic context. The fact that like all ritual, liturgy communicates worldview *as a set of assumptions about what is desirable or undesirable*, makes this an almost subliminal process. Thus, for example, we assume that it is good to be quiet, pay attention, sit in rows; participate fully and consciously, loudly, in unison; read aloud and sing in public; while assuming conversely that the opposite behaviors, which polymorphously perverse tots have the wisdom to model for us, are profoundly unedifying and undesirable.

Colonial liturgics create injustice, then, by presenting a felt sense that the desirable world is Anglo, thus furthering Anglo power and creating in us a correlative felt sense that our own Hispanic mode of being is somehow not quite cricket.

Liturgical inculturation

The recent interest in theological and liturgiological circles in the development of culturally authentic liturgies has found expression in official and quasi-official Anglican pronouncements.[10] Thus the 1988 Lambeth Conference resolved:

> This Conference (a) Recognizes that culture is the context in which people find their identity. (b) Affirms that...the Gospel judges every culture... challenging some aspects of culture while endorsing and transforming others for the benefit of the Church and society.[11]
> This Conference resolves that each province should be free, subject to essential universal Anglican norms of worship, and to a valuing of traditional liturgical materials, to seek that expression of worship which is appropriate to its Christian people in their cultural context.[12]

Likewise, the International Anglican Liturgical Consultation, at its meetings in 1989 and 1995, advised that

> The incarnation is God's self-inculturation in this world, and in a particular cultural context. Jesus'

ministry on earth includes both the acceptance of a particular culture, and also a confrontation of elements in that culture...[which are] contrary to the good news or to God's righteousness.[13]

The embodied character of Christian worship must be honored in proclamation, music, symbol, and ritual. If inculturation is to be taken seriously, local culture and custom which are not in conflict with the Gospel must be reflected in the liturgy, interacting with the accumulated inculturation of the tradition.[14]

Thus the Anglican Communion is increasingly looking towards the creation of culturally authentic liturgies. However, there is a danger in this process, as in all counter-colonial moves: the essentialist over-reaction to colonialism.

Postcolonial essentialism

We are propelled, understandably, to work towards genuine, authentic forms of Hispanic Anglican liturgy. Some few attempts have been made in this direction. The use of local musical idioms and locally produced vesture and an increasing awareness of specifically Hispanic pastoral rites, for example, have begun to suggest that Anglican liturgy need not always be the aesthetic clone of Canterbury cathedral.

But this well-intentioned and understandable interest has at times created a new set of liturgical anomalies, such as middle class urban Hispanic professionals singing peasant revolutionary songs from Nicaragua while supporting the Contras. Instead of the colonial absolutism of Anglophile liturgy, we sometimes move on to the "ethnic" absolutism of a one-dimensional, caricatured understanding of Hispanic identity. This development mirrors a large scale phenomenon in the history of world colonialism mentioned by Said towards the end of his book: the emergence of separatist, identity-based politics with their (often self-appointed) ayatollahs, in reaction to colonial dominance. When taken to the extreme, this position would require us to develop transprovincial "ethnic" branches of the Episcopal Church and even national "ethnic" Episcopal churches. An example of this extreme cultural essentialism is a question asked by a student recently: "There are so many Hispanic cultures! Like, how can a Guatemalan possibly understand a Salvadorean?"

One possible way to avoid the extremes of separatism and its potential for a balkanization of the Church is to stress the multicultural nature of all good Christian ritual. However, there are two problems with this. First, compared to the Eastern churches, we have a rather weak history of truly indigenous liturgical development in the West, and what we have is lost in the mists of history. Second, and I think more dangerous, multiculturalism sometimes turns out to be a very mixed blessing.

II. Multiculturalism in the Episcopal Church

Is "multiculturalism" an Anglo imperialist plot?
It is understandable that the Episcopal Church might want to pay increasing attention to cultural issues and that it has developed an increasing interest in "multiculturalism." However, old habits die hard, and upon examination, much that passes for "multiculturalism" is colonialism in a new disguise. Our language of inclusion and welcome gives away the colonial presuppositions: "This is *our* (Anglo) church, Juan; you are a *guest* in it."

It turns out, however, that those of us that are being "invited," "hospitably welcomed" and "included" are not guests exactly, but the younger prodigal sons returning to our home. Often we did not leave voluntarily, but through the cunning stratagems of the older (colonizer) brother bent on making the whole creation into his image and likeness. It was not depravity or sinfulness that took us away from home, but systemic abuse and genocide, or at best, alienation and boredom. Yet we have come back to the Table and are sitting at it (and hiring new servants, changing the menu and redecorating) whether or not we are "included" not because we are perversely brazen, but because this is our birthright. Esau is back, no longer so hungry as to live without his birthright or grateful for lentils.

In light of this, "multicultural" situations such as liturgies are suspect because they serve to reinforce the hegemony of the Anglo world by subsuming other cultures *under* the Anglo experience. In such situations, the active players are all Anglo: they design, invite, host, delegate and evaluate what is going on. The presence of culturally different people is at best an honest token of sensitivity to other cultures and at worst a ritualization of "you must play Anglo if you want to play." Truly multicultural liturgies, however, would be those in which Anglo leadership and numbers are one segment among others, not an umbrella encompassing others. Even when they are done conscientiously, such liturgies are an anomaly. We have very, very few truly multicultural congregations in our church. We have some Anglo congregations that include one or more other cultures, but their paid clergy are usually Anglo.

It is baffling, but hardly surprising, to see members of ethnic minorities participating in these cultural anomalies. Hispanics, starved for some token of being taken seriously, often go along with these attempts because something is better than nothing. It is better to be included than to be ignored.

In this light, "multicultural liturgies" designed and/or celebrated by Anglos are profoundly problematic to us members of ethnic minorities in the United States. The reasons for suspicion may be summed up briefly:

> 1. Often conversations about multiculturalism seem an attempt by Anglo Episcopalians to expand markets and secure new clients, at a time when their failure to commend the church to their own people is becoming increasingly evident. Sometimes seminaries develop multicultural curricula to enhance their attractiveness to potential Anglo students or funders. In light of this, multiculturalism runs a

risk of becoming a band-aid solution to the crisis in evangelism in which the Anglo church finds itself. This is not true multiculturalism.

2. Often, "multicultural" programs are run by monocultural Anglos, who are, by definition, incapable of bridging cultures until they have lived for some extended period of time in them. At best, monocultural Anglos can grow in cultural sensitivity, but that alone does not give them the experience of understanding another culture from within, and since they are entirely contained in their own, their cultural assumptions usually seem "objective" to them: true for everyone everywhere. This puts monocultural Anglos at a very real disadvantage when they attempt to administer multicultural programs or design multicultural liturgies. Multicultural situations administered by monocultural Anglos are not true multiculturalism.

3. Multicultural situations in which Hispanics are only the *recipients* of Anglo favors and not historical subjects acting and making decisions are not true multiculturalism.

As suggested above, the rhetoric surrounding multiculturalism gives it away as a project of the colonizing, dominant culture. It is the *monocultural Anglo* version of multiculturalism that wants to host, invite and include us Latinos and others.

True multiculturalism is not about including (or "nesting") others in otherwise Anglo realities and structures. That may be fun and interesting, and at times a necessary if desperate attempt to prevent a church closure due to the attrition of Anglo members, but it is not multiculturalism. Truly multicultural liturgies are *not* otherwise Anglo liturgical scenarios spiced up with a smattering of exotic pizzazz. These are best termed "Anglo liturgies *aware* of the existence of others."

These forms of spurious multiculturalism all manage to keep the Hispanic subsumed under an "inclusive" Anglo situation. However, inclusivity is not the only strategy; spurious multiculturalism also takes the form of loving only the noble savage.

In love with the noble savage

Besides this lame, *noblesse oblige* caricature of multiculturalism which leaves Anglo culture in power, there is a second, more insidious form of colonialism alive in our church today, a form which facilitates and perpetuates the first. It might derive ultimately, I believe, from Rousseau's contention that human beings are intrinsically good and that civilization is at best a mixed blessing. Allow me to refer to this idea as "the noble savage."

Moved by these Enlightenment assumptions, well-meaning liberal Anglo Episcopalians are perpetually on the lookout for a Hispanic caricature. In their view, the true Latino is a native Latin American untainted by either Spanish or Anglo culture. This disqualifies most of the population of Latin America and all Hispanics in this country from being truly Latino! More alarming is the possibility that the Latino noble savage might be a caricature convenient to the Anglo need to supervise, encourage or manipulate dependent others.

The problem, of course, is that Latino culture is an extremely hybrid reality and that Rousseau and the Enlightenment had a different effect on Latin America than on the north Atlantic countries. Latinos do not assume that nature is benign, that everyone is the same (we believe in equality, not sameness) or, for that matter, that less is more (ours is a baroque aesthetic). In our culture, *preparacion* (education) is a value; ignorance, an evil; "he is an ordinary guy" ("*es un tipo ordinario*") is not a nice thing to say about someone. As a colonized people, we daily hone and value our ability to adapt culturally.

Additionally, in contrast to monocultural Anglos in this country, who can and often do live out their lives in cultural isolation, monocultural Latino immigrants to the U.S., by virtue of having to get ahead in a foreign country, must daily learn to bridge cultures. Some of us have been able to develop into fully bicultural people. Others exercise this skill daily for a lifetime without ever becoming fully bicultural. (I have never met a "multicultural" individual, although I once met someone tricultural.)

However, in the search for the noble savage, the adaptable, bicultural person—that is, most of us who have emigrated here—is suspect. Not only are we, like all Latinos, different from Anglos, we are also different from the romantic Anglo notion of what a "real" Latino is. This is extremely convenient for Anglos, for it is precisely our biculturalism that enables us to claim our freedom here and courageously talk back to the Anglo church.

The Anglo romantic attraction to the noble savage has another aspect: the Anglo anti-intellectual assumptions that often accompany it. According to this view, education is a good thing but by no means *necessary* for the well-being of the human being.

The Anglo love of the noble savage reveals the sad, embarrassing anti-intellectualism of Anglo culture. "*Intelectual*" is not a pejorative word in Spanish, nor do we think people are better the less educated they are, for education is the number one element in the economic advancement of Latinos in this country. Thus we Latinos often find ourselves in the strange position of talking well-meaning Anglos into *not* relaxing intellectual standards in special theological programs for Latino seminarians. To design special programs with watered-down pedagogical standards, to make exceptions in the name of evangelism and missiology, usually cheats Latinos of a very real opportunity for advancement, reveals the Anglo church's profound cynicism regarding the value of education itself, and assumes that learning and the intellectual life are an Anglo product.

Much writing about multiculturalism assumes that the church's intellectual standards must be suspended or jettisoned in order to create a space for the culturally other.[15] This tendency among Anglos—and some "ethnics"—to discount intellectual standards when dealing with cross-cultural issues is truly alarming. No Latino of my acquaintance would stand for a liturgical form that, however Latino, would represent a lower standard of liturgical practice than the best liturgies of the Christian tradition. To imply that intellectual probity needs to be suspended as a criterion when engaged in cross-cultural work, on the excuse that the intellectual life is an Anglo phenomenon, is profoundly racist.

Hispanics look around and do not see Anglo programs that are not supposed to be marketable, Anglo learning and teaching that are not directed towards the development of careers; and we watch this knowing that the main ticket out of poverty for us is a marketable education.

The intellectual life is not the sole possession of Anglos. A particular style of intellectual standards (truth, corroboration, critical thought, accountability to a community of discourse) *may* have been generated in the Mediterranean basin (a theory hard to prove), but they certainly are no longer exclusively North-Atlantic phenomena; indeed, in certain segments of Anglo American life, these qualities are disappearing faster than I can type.

Latinos insist upon high educational standards; high intellectual, emotional and volitional criteria; top-notch education, opportunities and advancement. We do not need charity or watered-down expectations. Above all, we do not need to be patronized. God does not have a preferential option for the marginalized because we are cute or exotic, but because we have been exploited.

In light of this, prayer book revision towards a truly Hispanic liturgy must include not only the process of collecting the naive forms of the prayers of our people as they pray them, but the secondary and no less essential task of evaluating and critically examining our prayer life from the point of view not only of our own historical reality but of the development of Anglican liturgy in general. The first alone would cheat our people of the best intellectual resources available; the second alone would hand them the stone of academic research for the bread of living liturgy.

To sum up, liturgical multiculturalism and its concomitant

ingredient, inculturated liturgies, cannot be genuine if they rise from economic expediency or a misguided neocolonial need to "include" the other as an exotic Caliban.

True multiculturalism
We are in need of a critical examination of what we mean by the term "multiculturalism" and of the methods and attitudes involved in its development. Instead of serving a neocolonial expansionist Anglo agenda, true multiculturalism might be living out the Church's catholicity (i.e., universality) through a joint articulation of the call of persons of other cultures to be Anglican in ways appropriate to their own cultural reality.

True multiculturalism in decision-making, for example, is less the "inclusion" of culturally different others in a pre-existing Anglo process than the creation of new processes in which power is shared among several types of culturally different people. To give a further example, a good way to begin is not by inviting Hispanics to an Anglo liturgical planning meeting, but by asking to come to theirs and patiently developing the skills to plan together.

True multiculturalism is not based on fashionable benevolence. The main reason for insisting on liturgical inculturation, for example, is that its opposite, liturgical totalitarianism, is profoundly unjust and a perversion of the Gospel of Jesus Christ; to be true, multicultural institutions, structures and events, from diocesan staffs and commissions to liturgies, must be informed by a much more profound—and less faddish—source: the Gospel.

Multiculturalism and Jesus' good news
> Those people compelled by the system to play subordinate or imprisoning roles within it emerge as conscious antagonists, disrupting it, proposing claims, advancing arguments that dispute the totalitarian compulsions of the world market. Not everything can be bought off.[16]

So Said. The totalitarian compulsions in the Anglican liturgical world market are strong. In part this may be due to our historical affection for liturgical uniformity as a sign of unity, or to the long colonial reality of Anglican liturgy. But it seems to me to be present also as an insidious habit of mind that assumes that the whole gamut of experience must come under Anglo purview. Often our talk about Anglican unity serves to mask this totalitarian impulse.

Thus, liturgical inculturation, seeking cultural authenticity, is sometimes feared as a form of separatism or balkanization of the Church's life, endorsing instead a pluralistic, hybrid "multicultural" liturgy that "includes" everyone. But can human beings in fact be "multicultural"? Aren't all of us, Enlightened Anglos included, living, moving and being within our own cultural envelopes? Who can realistically claim or hope to envelop a multiplicity of cultures? And should we not see this instinct to include everything under our gaze (an *episcopos* is one who oversees, or if you prefer, overlooks!) as the same hubris which organized the erection of a Tower of Babel—now making its appearance not vertically to spite God, but horizontally to spite creation while claiming to "include" within one's cultural mantle the cultural splendor of the world, ignoring that, even if such a feat were possible, one would necessarily have to be standing beyond cultures, that is, nowhere, or at best, in God's place.

Instead of this imperialistic understanding of multiculturalism, we might try a different approach. The emphasis in this approach is less on inclusion and more on the spirituality of acceptance. The otherness of the other, the difference that makes us uncomfortable with the alienness of the alien, is the precise point of entry for our contemplation, in reverence and awe, of a different way of being. The only appropriate attitude, theologically speaking, before this cloud of cultural unknowing, in view of the goodness of creation, is for us to approach the other as a mystery. With this experience we must also be able to accept the fact that our way of being is not the measure of all things, but that other things—or even the same—are being measured otherwise by this wise other. In this process, we might learn something. Over time, we might develop certain skills that facilitate a modicum of cultural tolerance. To accelerate the process, we might move to a foreign country and try to make a living in it.

The importance of liturgical inculturation, however, does not stem from its ability to help Anglos come to a wider, deeper understanding of other cultures. This is a blessed side-effect at best.

Multiculturalism and catholicity

True multiculturalism is not a matter of being politically correct or "inclusive," nor of kindness or generosity, but rather is based in the Gospel news that God has reconciled all. This news in turn creates a duty for the Church not to act as if some folks were beyond the pale. This duty implies a right possessed by the "other": the right to be different. Gospel multiculturalism refers to an attitude that respects the right of Hispanic Episcopalians to speak, be heard and participate fully in the life of the Church as *essential* members of its power structure, precisely in and through our difference.

Respectful listening to the other is essential to the credibility of the Anglican claim to catholicity. Otherwise, Anglicanism would be forever English and colonial, meaning by "catholic" the imposition of Anglophilia throughout the world rather than the ability to see Christ's body incarnate in myriad ways of being. Perhaps becoming truly catholic is our main challenge as a communion.

Colonial liturgies are bad not only because they are unjust; they are unjust in turn because they are profoundly anti-Gospel, for they consist of the presentation of a foreign worldview as God's, confusing, for example, Christian reverence with English "reserve." Additionally, a liturgy (and its concomitant ecclesial life) to which one has to be acculturated as if it were a second culture in order to relate to God enacts a deeply anti-Gospel message: to be acceptable to God, you must be this or that particular cultural way. This is salvation by cultural works, if you will, when in fact both the Gospel and the ensuing early Christian kerygmatic claim were that other than acknowledging the passover of Jesus, there are no requirements for being Christian. Whoever we are, in whatever cultural way that we are, God has reached us in Christ.

Liturgical colonialism is also a perversion because it ascetically trains church members to confuse the romantically exotic with the reign of God. It passes off as spiritual the merely foreign. This is a convenient confusion, loved by the devil. It reassures us that we are getting closer to God the more artificial we are; that foreignness is close to godliness—not as a true Other to be contemplated in awe, but as a costume to don while denying the sanctity of one's own cultural reality. The fact that mammon often lurks around these scenarios (exoticism sells) should give us pause.

The right—and vocation—of other cultures to participate fully—in their own way—in the worship and governance of the Church is not only baptismal but paschal in origin and does not depend on anything else for its existence. It is guaranteed by Christ's tearing down, in his own flesh, our dividing walls. This right does not depend on being invited, hosted, included or patronized; it does not hang upon being "ethnic" in some exotic, *National Geographic* sense; it does not depend on assuaging Anglo charitable egos, avoiding ruffling their feathers or increasing membership in their churches. You cannot host, invite or include—let alone manage—a right; you can only respect, honor and recognize it.

True multiculturalism begins to take place as churches and their leadership grow into a large multicultural array of bicultural persons; when Anglican no longer means English; when it is no longer surprising that our Anglican siblings in Guatemala have Mayan elements in their Anglican liturgy. Eventually this will lead to the revelation of the Anglo church as another ethnic church among many.

Let us be honest. This will entail a certain loss of power on the part of the Anglo church; people do not run cheering towards loss of power. Thus, Anglos who cheer the coming of multiculturalism are either denying their loss, unclear on the concept, or truly holy; for true multiculturalism involves no less than the kenotic self-forgetfulness of the Anglo church.

Nor is true multiculturalism something that the Anglo church is doing or achieving. Rather, multiculturalism is, in the best sense, happening to it. Its doing must be securely in the hands of cultural others, for as Sartre perceptively said, one cannot ask for freedom; one must take it. Anglo Episcopalians should not be surprised if we increasingly do not ask for their permission to speak or to be. This does not mean that the very genuine efforts of well meaning Anglo Episcopalians have passed by unappreciated, but that a portion of the Church which has variously been either invisible, gagged or just plain disregarded is no longer willing to wait for invitations and permissions. We are no longer children or guests, but partners. Permission is not the issue.

Edward Said points out:

> the push or tension [for an emergent non-coercive culture] comes from the surrounding environment—the imperialist power that would otherwise compel you to disappear or to accept some miniature version of yourself as a doctrine to be passed on a course syllabus.[17]

The cultural violence of colonizing attitudes in Anglicanism generates its own reaction. We should not expect this push towards an integrated church to take place without conflict and disagreement. What Ursula LeGuin has written concerning women's words may be said as well of ours; here I am substituting "Latino" for "women":

> many men and even women are afraid and angry when [Latinos] do speak, because in this barbaric society, when [Latinos] speak truly they speak subversively—they can't help it: if you're underneath, if you're kept down you break out, you subvert. We are volcanoes. When we [Latinos] offer our experience as the truth, human truth, all the maps change. There are new mountains.[18]

In the process of seeking a theological foundation for the development of culturally appropriate liturgical forms, the received foundations of Anglican liturgical orthodoxy itself are shaken. Instead of clear national boundaries and orthodox identities, a new paradigm, with the migrant exile as its prototype, emerges:

> Once we accept the actual configuration of literary experiences overlapping with one another and interdependent, despite national boundaries and coercively legislated national [or ecclesiastical?] autonomies, history and geography are transfigured in new maps, in new and far less stable identities, in new types of connections. Exile, far from being the fate of nearly forgotten unfortunates who are dispossessed and expatriated, becomes something closer to a norm and experience of crossing boundaries and charting new territories in defiance of the classic canonic enclosures.[19]

III Liturgiology and Neocolonialism

Said warns that "orthodox, authoritatively national and institutional versions of history tend principally to freeze provisional and highly contestable versions of history into official identities."[20] Liturgists working with the phenomena of Anglicanism and cultures should heed these words carefully. "The identity of Anglican worship" as an orthodox construct may not be anything more than a version of history turned into an official identity for the benefit of the powerful. How else to explain our tendency to relive seventeenth century English liturgical wars in today's Hispanic context? The often-heard claim that these wars involved perennial, ubiquitous issues once for all encapsulating the character of Anglicanism is a bit reminiscent of the preface to the Roman Missal decreed after the Council of Trent, declaring that its liturgy would be celebrated until the second coming of Christ. One has to have an extremely abstract understanding of an historical event in order to make it universally and eternally meaningful.

It may have been crucial to decide in the 1630s whether the altar should be fenced in; the issue is hardly that today in the Hispanic context. And does it matter at all, beyond the scope of local taste, whether office lights are lit for Morning and Evening Prayer? "Ethnic" Anglican liturgists must be wary, lest we dedicate our lives to solving problems set for us by Anglo history while ignoring the much more proximate liturgical questions rising from our own experience, such as the attack on liturgical practice from fundamentalist sects, the infrequency of eucharistic reception, the feminization of Christianity in the Latino context, etc. As Said concludes in the paragraph cited above,

> What matters a great deal more than the stable identity kept current in official discourse is the contestatory force of an interpretive method whose material is the disparate, but intertwined and interdependent, and above all overlapping streams of historical experience.[21]

But this "contestatory force" assumes that the interpreters can avail themselves of the "disparate …intertwined and interdependent… overlapping streams" of [both Hispanic and Anglo] experience.

One of the main problems facing the revision of The Book of Common Prayer is the unavailability of Anglican Hispanic liturgical experience, not because we Hispanics lack it, but because we are taught to repress it in the name of Anglicanism. Therefore one of the first steps towards prayer book revision, if it is going to address the liturgical needs of Hispanics at all, should be the reclamation of our liturgical voice, even at the risk of seeming un-Anglican; for without our liturgical agency we can hardly claim to be developing an authentic Hispanic Anglican liturgy.

Thus a Hispanic liturgiology that ignores the existence of transgressive liturgies—seeking the easily accessed historical official products while ignoring the mass of bootlegged attempts passed along the liturgical black market—is bound to be at best incomplete and at worst myopic. There cannot be a serious Hispanic

Anglican liturgical theology that does not take into account such influences as *Santería* and *Condomblé*, the cult of *Maximón* in Guatemala and our Lady of Guadalupe in Mexico. It is an easy matter to find the essential aspects of Anglican liturgy if by that we mean Roman liturgy of the first four centuries as it has informed recent Books of Common Prayer. But there is beyond this *lex orandi* a much more variegated law of prayer (often *prayed* prayer never written) passed along through "paraliturgical" practitioners and rites and more often communicated through colors, textures and behaviors than through official texts. This will present new problems, as pastors and liturgical theologians begin to compare Anglo and Hispanic liturgical experience and draw new formulations of truly catholic Anglican liturgical practice.

At this point I would hazard to suggest a very few elements of Anglicanism that are, or should be, universal:

> 1. *Hooker's tripod.* In the case of liturgical theology this means that authoritative Anglican liturgy is based on scripture, tradition and reason—including the lived experience of the people it serves. Our *lex orandi* is authoritative because and when (and only when) it is based on these three foundations.
> 2. *Love of vernacular* forms and their multiplicity.
> 3. *Aesthetic excellence.* Anglican worship wants to be excellently crafted, especially in view of its primacy as source of theology.
> 4. *Liturgical unity found in liturgical structure* of action rather than text.
> 5. *Communion with the bishop.* Anglican unity is found primarily in our liturgical communion with each other, symbolized by the bishop. By liturgical communion I do not mean the concurrence of liturgical texts. I mean literally eating bread and drinking wine together. Anglican unity is primarily liturgical before it is dogmatic or canonical, as Massey Shepherd pointed out.[22]

6. The concept of Common Prayer. Though no longer limited to Anglicanism today, the concept of Common Prayer—as opposed to individual devotion and clericalized liturgies—continues to be a formative element of Anglican worship.

Recovering Hispanic praise

Hispanic Anglicans might cooperate with Anglos in the development of truly multicultural liturgies, but before this can happen, an earlier stage must take place: Hispanics must feel secure in their sense of what their worship is like—its flavor, sound, visuals; its rhythm; its sense of sacred space and time. In short, before we can have truly multicultural liturgies, we must develop authentic Latino Anglican liturgy. As Carl Jung said so well about the integration of the Self: before you integrate, you must differentiate.

We should approach the problem of inculturating the liturgy cautiously. Latinos do not want an Anglo colonial liturgy. But neither do we want a neoromantic "ethnic" liturgy worthy of the noble savage and *National Geographic.* Instead, our liturgy must be authentic, developed from our own cultural resources while being also orthodox Anglican liturgy, the equal of the best Canterbury has to offer and informed by the same theological and creative standards, passing the tests of orthodoxy, cultural authenticity and intellectual probity. It is defeatist, however, to begin with orthodoxy. The first step must be towards authentic expression, and in this area, the role of liturgical creativity in the life of our congregations must be examined.

We must encourage parishes and missions of cultures other than Anglo to develop their liturgical life from their own inner resources, relying on their ethnic and cultural instincts. Towards this end, some practical suggestions for liturgical scholars and worship commissions of the Church may be useful.

Nathan Mitchell has recently suggested that we are desperately in need of liturgical renewal, particularly renewal brought about through a rediscovery of the poetic aspects of worship:

> In a poem we do not "grasp" meaning; we surren-
> der to it. That is also the way of Christian conver-
> sion and faith, the way of worship. And it is, I sus-
> pect, the way of that renewal which still awaits
> us.[23]

In the same manner, liberation theologians like Juan Luis Segundo
have pointed out the role of the imagination in liberation, while
noting that officialdom tends to work against it:

> [Liberation in history] ...clearly depends on the
> active work of creative imagination which is linked
> up with the relative value of any and all historical
> constructions.... The essential values of man [sic]
> both as an individual and as a social group, call for
> an ongoing process of creation in the face of new
> situations and problems.... Yet there is a tendency
> in ecclesiastical authorities and academic theology
> to fix dogmatically things that are part and parcel
> of the realm of means, which are relative by their
> very definition.[24]

Said, in turn, pleads for a culturally contrapuntal reading of literature, oscillating between center and periphery.[25] But this assumes
that the periphery is creative, producing cultural artifacts such as
liturgies. Our peripheral Hispanic congregations rarely do this,
either because their leadership see no reason to try, or because they
fear standing out in a homogeneous Anglophile liturgical land-
scape (cultural adaptation is a survival skill for us), or because they
honestly do not think congregations should be liturgically creative.
Several suggestions present themselves as attempts to remedy this
situation. I list them from the most locally based to the broadest in
scope, while reminding the reader that local initiative should not
be counted upon unless there are diocesan and national expectations of—and rewards for—it:

> 1. Recognize and reward the *imaginative* life of the
> congregation. Try new things and recover long-lost

ones from our cultural treasure-house. Recognize
that this creative process is messy, dangerous and
often involves conflict; address it pastorally.

2. Pay attention to paraliturgical forms of worship
and integrate them within the liturgy if possible.
(For example, Good Friday pageant/processions
may be integrated with the reading of the Passion.)

3. Exploit the high degree of freedom already present in the 1979 Book of Common Prayer.
Dioceses may band together to offer workshops for
clergy and lay leaders on the creative use of the
prayer book.

4. At the diocesan, provincial and national levels,
develop ways of encouraging and gathering the
liturgical creativity of our Hispanic congregations
so as to share it with other congregations in the
diocese and in the wider church.

5. At the national level, and with the active support
of the Standing Liturgical Commission, officially
recognize the creativity of Episcopal congregations.
Their creativity should not rest on the personal
decision of the priest or the benevolence of bishops.

6. The Standing Liturgical Commission might also
collect, evaluate and further disseminate the creative work of these congregations.

7. Through periodic forums, some of them ecumenical and others such as the International
Anglican Liturgical Consultation, develop Hispanic
standards for Hispanic Anglican liturgy, discovering
and naming, when appropriate, the relation of
Hispanic Anglican liturgy to the wider history of
liturgy, both Anglican and throughout other
denominations.

In order to implement these suggestions, I suggest that, supported by General Convention, the Standing Liturgical Commission:

1. Recognize episcopal authority to authorize forms of worship not contained in the prayer book. Although this authority is not granted by the Standing Liturgical Commission but by the prayer book itself, it is important for the authority structures of the Church to endorse it again, in the wake of recent attempts at using episcopal collegiality to freeze creative organic liturgical growth.

2. Bishops might authorize interdiocesan Hispanic liturgy subcommissions—perhaps at a provincial level—to develop and facilitate congregational creativity.

3. Within a diocese, a bishop, consulting with the diocesan liturgy commission, might designate one or more Hispanic congregations, or develop new missions, as experimental communities.

4. The Standing Liturgical Commission might make available to diocesan/provincial Hispanic liturgical subcommissions a protocol for encouraging, assisting and reporting creative liturgical developments.

5. The Standing Liturgical Commission might then gather results, catalog them and select liturgical materials to make available to other liturgical communities.

6. From time to time the Standing Liturgical Commission might suggest to General Convention the addition (or removal) of specific liturgical forms to or from the corpus of The Book of Common Prayer, *The Book of Occasional Services, Lesser Feasts and Fasts,* and hymnal(s).

7. Finally, this effort should be part of a church-wide effort to support congregations in their effort

> towards the development of grassroots liturgical,
> exegetical, theological/critical and diaconal skills.

The prospect of all this creative activity may daunt some. For others it will be energizing, perhaps life-giving. For both, it will mean suspending monolithic culture-bound definitions of "Anglicanism" and striving in an ongoing manner towards complexity and nuance, no longer as secure as we were in the old definitions but trusting the worthiness of the journey and the travellers. As Ali Shariati has said,

> Man [sic], this dialectical phenomenon, is compelled to be always in motion.... Man, then, can never attain a final resting place and take up residence in God.... How disgraceful, then, are all the fixed standards. Who can ever fix a standard? Man is a "choice," a struggle, a constant becoming. He is an infinite migration within himself, from clay to God; he is a migrant within his own soul.[26]

Notes

1. Edward Said, *Culture and Imperialism* (New York: Random House, 1994), p. 314.
2. John Kater, "Ministry and the Reign of God: Learning from Latin American Christians," *Sewanee Theological Review* 36 (1993): 322.
3. Ibid.
4. For a fuller treatment of these insights into the relation between the liturgy and the Church, see my "Language Shaped and Shaping," in Ruth A. Meyers, ed., *How Shall We Pray? Expanding Our Language about God,* Liturgical Studies 2 (New York: Church Hymnal Corporation, 1994), pp. 140-1.
5. Clifford Geertz, *The Interpretation of Cultures* (New York: Basic Books, 1973), pp. 126-41.
6. See, for example, Jon Sobrino, "La Centralidad del 'Reino de

Dios' en la teología de la liberación," *Revista Latinoamericana de teología* 9 (1986).

7. Geoffrey Wainwright, *Liturgy and Eschatology* (New York: Oxford University Press, 1981).

8. Said, p. 316 and *passim*.

9. Justo González, *Mañana: Christian Theology from a Hispanic Perspective* (Nashville: Abingdon, 1990), p. 85.

10. For a broader review of recent theory of liturgical incultura-tion, see my "Language Shaped and Shaping," pp. 138ff.

11. "Resolution 22: Christ and culture," in Roger Coleman, ed., *Resolutions of the twelve Lambeth Conferences 1867-1988* (Toronto: Anglican Book Centre, 1992), p. 210.

12. "Resolution 47: Liturgical freedom," ibid., p. 222.

13. "Down to Earth Worship: Findings of the Third International Anglican Liturgical Consultation, York, England, 1989," in David Holeton, ed., *Liturgical Inculturation in the Anglican Communion*, Alcuin/GROW Liturgical Study 15 (Bramcote, Nottingham: Grove Books, 1990), p. 9.

14. David R. Holeton, ed., *Renewing the Anglican Eucharist: Findings of the Fifth International Anglican Liturgical Consultation, Dublin, Eire, 1995*, Grove Worship Series 135 (Bramcote, Nottingham: Grove Books, 1996), p. 7.

15. For a mild form of this, see, for example, Hartshorn Murphy, "Reflecting on the Queries," *The Witness,* Jan/Feb 1995, p. 25.

16. Said, p. 335.

17. Ibid., p. 334.

18. Ursula LeGuin, cited in Gabe Hauck, ed., *A Sourcebook about Liturgy* (Chicago: Liturgy Training Publications, 1994), p. 57.

19. Said, p. 317.

20. Ibid., p. 312.

21. Ibid.

22. Massey H. Shepherd, Jr., "The Berakah Award: Response," *Worship* 52 (1978): 312-13.

23. Nathan Mitchell, "The Amen Corner: The Renewal That Awaits Us," *Worship* 70 (1996): 172.

24. Juan Luis Segundo, *Liberación de la Teología* (Buenos Aires: Carlos Lohlé, 1975), pp. 207-8; English translation: *The Liberation of Theology*, trans. John Drury (Maryknoll, NY: Orbis Books, 1985), pp. 183-4.

25. Said, p. 318.

26. Ali Shariati, *On the Sociology of Islam: Lectures by Ali Shariati*, trans. Hamid Algar (Berkeley: Mizan Press, 1979), pp. 92-3, quoted in Said, p. 334.

Appendix:
Some Recent Prayer Books in the
Anglican Communion

The Anglican Church in Aotearoa, New Zealand and Polynesia: *A New Zealand Prayer Book*. Auckland: William Collins Publishers, 1989.

The Anglican Church of Australia: *A Prayer Book for Australia*. Alexandria, NSW: Broughton Books, 1995.

The Anglican Church of Canada: *The Book of Alternative Services*. Toronto: Anglican Book Centre, 1985.

The Church of England. *The Alternative Service Book 1980*.

The Church of Ireland. *Alternative Prayer Book*. London: Collins Liturgical Publications, 1984.

Church of the Province of Southern Africa: *An Anglican Prayer Book 1989*. London: Collins Liturgical Publications, 1989.